Sakharov Remembered

"*Like a gleam in the darkness, we have appeared for an instant from the black nothingness of the ever-unconscious matter, in order to make good the demands of Reason and create a life worthy of ourselves and of the Goal we only dimly perceive.*"

Andrei D. Sakharov
1921-1989

Sakharov Remembered

A Tribute by Friends and Colleagues

Edited by

Sidney D. Drell

Sergei P. Kapitza

Published in cooperation with the
Physical Society of the USSR
and *Priroda* magazine

American Institute of Physics
New York

Published by the American Institute of Physics in cooperation with the Physical
Society of the USSR and *Priroda* magazine, published by Nauka Publishers.

American Institute of Physics
335 East 45th Street
New York, New York 10017-3483

Physical Society of the USSR
Kursovoi per. 17
119034 Moscow, USSR

Nauka Publishers
Profsoyuznaya ul. 90
117864 Moscow, USSR

Copyright and permission notices for use of previously published material are
provided in the Acknowledgments section at the back of this volume.

Library of Congress Cataloging-in-Publication Data

Sakharov remembered / edited by Sidney D. Drell, Sergei P. Kapitza.
p.   cm.
Includes bibliographical references and index.
ISBN 0-88318-853-8 (case) — ISBN 0-88318-852-X (paper)   1. Sakharov,
Andrei, 1921-1989 Congresses.   2. Physicists — Soviet Union — Biography —
Congresses.   I. Sakharov, Andrei, 1921-1989.   II. Drell, S. D. (Sidney
David), 1926-   .   III. Kapitsa, Sergei Petrovich.   IV. American Institute
of Physics.
QC16.S255S25   1991
530'.092 — dc20
[B]   91-11396
                                                                      CIP

Contents

Preface

THE WORLD WAS SADDENED to learn on December 14, 1989, of the death of one of its greatest and most widely admired heroes, Andrei Dmitrievich Sakharov. In the days and months that followed, there was an overwhelming outpouring of testimonials to this scientist and humanitarian, a man viewed by many as a living saint, a leader whose voice made him recognized as a spokesman for the conscience of mankind. This volume includes essays by many of Sakharov's close friends and professional colleagues as a tribute to his memory.

The main reason to publish this collection is to fill gaps in our knowledge of his life, so much of which was hidden behind the veil of secrecy while he worked to develop the Soviet hydrogen bomb. Indeed, it wasn't until the publication of his seminal 1968 essay, "Reflections on Progress, Peaceful Coexistence, and Intellectual Freedom," that the name of Andrei Sakharov became known to the world at large.

From the testimonials gathered here of those who worked with and knew this remarkable scientist and humanist, we may build up an image of the man and gain some insight into his personality and the motives that guided his lone and independent mind. These comments and explanations help to place in perspective Sakharov's important scientific contributions to some of the most fundamental problems of theoretical physics and his inventive ingenuity in applied science, as well as his emergence as a world-wide leader in man's quest for peace and his struggle for human rights.

In the belief that there is great interest in learning Sakharov's background, his development from a scientist to a humanitarian leader, his way of thinking, his role in the Soviet H-bomb project, and his emergence as a political figure and citizen of the world, we have included all the essays prepared for special issues of two magazines, both of which appeared originally in August 1990: *Priroda* in the Soviet Union and *Physics Today* in the United States. Also included are several other appropriate essays that did not appear in either publication.

Some of the comments may seem too personal, some casual, some very biased. The reader will find repetitions in this collection, as well as, on occasion, the conflicting recollections that are inevitably present in human memories. However, we did not find it proper to streamline these presentations and remove redundancies, as they tend to enhance, rather than merely lengthen, the message. They add to the human side of the story.

This volume is divided into three parts. While recollections of Sakharov's life and scientific work are spread throughout the volume, the first section (which we call "Personal Reminiscences") focuses more on his life, character, and work on behalf of human rights, while the second section ("Scientific Perspectives") examines in more detail his contributions to science and technology. The third section presents a lengthy and revealing panel discussion organized by *Priroda* about Sakharov's involvement in the moral and intellectual issues he faced as a scientist living through dramatic and occasionally tragic events in Soviet history. In addition, there are two sections of photographs drawn from across Sakharov's life, but focusing in particular on his remarkable final years following his December 23, 1986 return to Moscow from his exile in Gorki.

This volume is being published by the American Institute of Physics, in cooperation with the Physical Society of the USSR, on the seventieth anniversary of Sakharov's birth on May 21, 1921. It can be read as a complement alongside Sakharov's two autobiographical volumes, *Memoirs* and *Moscow and Beyond: 1986 to 1989*. It also serves as a companion to a similar volume of reminiscences being published in English and Russian on the same date by Nauka, the publishing arm of the Soviet Academy of Sciences.

Many people helped make this volume possible. On the Soviet side, special thanks are due to Elena Bonner for her help with corrections and to Irene Arutunian and Natalia Morosova of the *Priroda* staff, without whose persistent efforts we would not have the present volume. The staff of Nauka Publishers also assisted with preparing many of the photographs. In the United States, Gloria Lubkin of *Physics Today* helped initiate this undertaking, and Kenneth W. Ford, Executive Director of the American Institute of Physics, has been a supporter from the beginning. Also at AIP,

thanks go to Maya Flikop and her translators—including Michael Alferi-
eff, Steven Amoretty, Clark Robinson, Irina Nelson, and Dave Parsons—
as well as to John T. Scott, Alla Novoselskaya, Larry Feinberg, Christa
Turley, Irene Aranovich, Ezra Sitea, and Graham P. Collins. Finally, our
particular thanks to AIP Books Division Manager Tim Taylor for his
orchestration of the project.

We hope this volume may help in understanding the complexities of some
events in recent history and the dilemmas facing humanity in general, and
especially scientists, in their efforts to resolve global problems of our own
making. Here we see them through the events of the life of one of the most
sensitive, courageous, and outspoken figures of our times. Andrei
Sakharov is one of those very rare figures in history of whom it may be
said, as did Anatole France in his eulogy at Emil Zola's funeral, noting his
persistent and effective pursuit of justice in the Dreyfus case:

> His destiny and his courage combine to endow him with the greatest of fates.
> He was a moment in the conscience of humanity.

Sidney D. Drell
Sergei P. Kapitza

Personal
Reminiscences

Overleaf: Sakharov in Moscow, 1979.

A Biographical Sketch

E. L. Feinberg

Lebedev Physical Institute, Moscow

ANDREI DMITRIEVICH SAKHAROV was born on May 21, 1921, in Moscow, into "a cultured and close family," as he wrote in the introduction to the collection of his articles issued in the West in 1974. He added: "Since my childhood, I lived in an atmosphere of decency, mutual help, and tact, a liking for work, and respect for the mastery of one's chosen profession."[1] These few but precise words deserve comment. Sakharov cannot be understood apart from his roots, from the spirit of his family and the features of the Russian intelligentsia at the beginning of the twentieth century—an amazing phenomenon in itself, which is still to be studied.

Sakharov's family did not belong to that wing of the intelligentsia represented, for example, by successful and talented engineers, or to the revolutionary wing, for which everything was determined by the merciless principle "my life belongs to the revolution." His family was typical of the average working intelligentsia, which established by itself its moral norms and life values, its high principles concerning how one should live, when one is to be tolerant, and when to be inflexible.

His personality was formed to a great extent under the influence of his parents—his father, Dmitri Ivanovich (a physics teacher and the son of a lawyer) and his mother, Ekaterina Alekseyevna (neé Sofiano, the family name of a Greek forefather)—and his paternal grandmother, Maria Petrovna, with her kindness and calm, optimistic nature. Although Sakharov's great-grandfather was a priest and his mother was religiously inclined, his father was an atheist and religion did not play a major role in the family. Dmitri Ivanovich played the piano well and admired Scriabin and this musical taste left an impression on the son.

To the basic principles of the family transmitted to Sakharov one should add personal modesty and the absence of vanity (its evidence in others evoked a smile and even compassion). The material side of life was not of great interest within this environment—spirituality dominated. Equally fundamental was the sense of social duty and responsibility toward other people.[2] The family was closely bound by relatives and friends to the Moscow intelligentsia, still vast and preserving its traditions.

Sakharov's father was at that time teaching at the so-called Second Moscow State University (now the V. I. Lenin Pedagogic Institute). Scientific institutions of that type grew like mushrooms, and the rude meddling of the official ideologists was at that time not as brutal as among the humanitarians and the performing artists.

Sakharov entered school directly in the seventh grade. Up until that time, he was taught at home with a group of children of the same age under the supervision of private teachers, and had only to pass the school examinations at the end of the year. (Such practices were not uncommon in those years.) In 1938, he started his studies in the physics department of Moscow State University.

At home, Sakharov's parents avoided focusing attention on political events. The horrible times of collectivization and terror largely passed him by. He, like many others at that time, was not aware of the tremendous scale of the lawlessness. His political views formed in accordance with official ideology, although he was neither a Pioneer (a mass communist organization of young scouts) or a member of the *Komsomol*, the youth organization of the Communist Party. He accepted Marxist ideas as being totally natural.

During the fall of 1941, Moscow State University was evacuated to Ashkhabad in Middle Asia. Sakharov lived there in a dormitory, became seriously ill of dysentery, and survived only through the care of his classmates. In 1942, after completing his degree in four years rather than the usual five, he was sent first to a small munitions factory in Kovrov, worked in the forest as a woodcutter, and later the same year was transferred to a laboratory in a cartridge factory in Ulyanovsk on the Volga. There he met Klavdia Alekseyevna Vikhireva, a chemist who, because of the war, could not finish her coursework at the Technological Institute in Leningrad. They married in 1943 and upon Klavdia fell the burden of caring for Sakharov's health.

At this time Sakharov began his scientific work. He made four inventions in production quality control (one of which was granted a patent), and wrote four papers on theoretical physics. These papers were not published, but as he wrote later, they gave him confidence in his own capabilities. In one of these papers he considered the chain reaction in uranium mixed with a moderator, and understood that one of the main difficulties in achieving this reaction—the resonant capture of neutrons in uranium—could be overcome: uranium should not be mixed uniformly with the moderator, but be placed in the shape of blocks. This important principle was already known in several countries, but was classified.

Sakharov sent his work to Igor Evgenievich Tamm, head of the theoretical department of the Lebedev Physical Institute of the Soviet Academy of Sciences (FIAN), and in January 1945 he was accepted by Tamm as a postgraduate student. He was liked immediately by everyone because of his gentle nature, his culture, his kindness and goodwill. His charm was quite natural and his talent was immediately evident.

Soon afterwards, he was joined in Moscow by Klavdia and their newly born daughter Tatyana. They did not have a permanent place to live (his parents' apartment had been bombed during the war), and although his student allowance was meager, he devoted himself vigorously to science. For two years he published papers on various subjects, including pion generation in high-energy nucleon collisions, optical determination of the temperature of gas discharges, and nuclear theory. These were serious studies showing sparks of an outstanding mind. One of the publications was based on the results of his doctoral thesis, which he submitted in the spring of 1947. The defense of his thesis, however, was postponed until the fall, since Sakharov could not pass the ideological examination. One should not see in this any hidden political motives: at that time Sakharov used to express his thoughts in such a laconic manner that he often could not be understood. The trend of his arguments was unusual and he simply omitted what he considered obvious. This delay troubled him only because it postponed the improvement of his living conditions which would follow receipt of his scientific degree.

Soon, however, the Institute provided a room in the rather shabby Academy of Science hotel and his living conditions improved somewhat. For additional income he began teaching physics at the Moscow Energetics Institute.

In 1948, Tamm included him in a group of young collaborators from the theoretical department who were organized to study the possibility of constructing a hydrogen bomb. He also began working at the secret weapons laboratory outside of Moscow and in 1950 moved to "the Installation."

In addition to the many years and much effort he devoted to the main task of developing a thermonuclear bomb, Sakharov also worked on a variety of related fundamental problems. He offered basic ideas for three methods of controlled thermonuclear fusion: the magnetic thermonuclear reactor, now known as a tokamak (proposed in 1950 and theoretically investigated together with Tamm); muon-catalyzed nuclear fusion (1948); and the use of pulsed laser radiation for heating of deuterium (proposed in 1960–61, according to his *Memoirs*). In the same period, he proposed the magnetic cumulator, a method of producing superstrong magnetic fields by using the energy of explosions.

Sakharov worked with enthusiasm. Like his colleagues, he was convinced that only a balance of arms could save the world from thermonuclear war. In July 1953, he was granted a second doctoral degree corresponding to a professorship in the West. After the successful test of the first hydrogen bomb, he was in October elected to full membership in the Soviet Academy of Sciences.

SAKHAROV'S LIFE throughout this period was limited to work in a small, isolated town and to socializing with his family, colleagues, and friends. Among them were personalities outstanding in intellect and talent, including Tamm, Ya. B. Zel'dovich, Yu. B. Khariton, and other less prominent scientists. He spent his vacation together with his wife and children, to whom he was greatly attached. A second daughter Lyubov was born in 1949 and his son Dima, short for Dmitri, in 1957.

Gradually, however, a new outlook on social and political problems was maturing in him. The disclosure of Stalin's crimes at the Twentieth Party Congress no doubt had a significant effect upon him. He began to realize that the politicians and the military, having obtained nuclear arms from the scientists, had no intention of taking into consideration their opinions concerning how they should be used. Feeling responsible for the radioactive fallout from nuclear tests, Sakharov started the struggle to ban tests that were not essential for weapons development. He calculated and demonstrated the danger these tests posed to the life and health of tens of thousands of people. He played an essential role in achieving the Limited Test Ban Treaty prohibiting atmospheric tests. But his concerns increased and his relationship with the political authorities deteriorated. The catastrophic state of the economy and the populace's lack of rights became more and more evident, both incomprehensible in such a period of peace.

Sakharov began to visit Moscow more often, always attending the weekly seminars of the theoretical department of the Lebedev Institute and devoting more attention to the problems of elementary particles, cosmology, and gravity, which always interested him.

In 1965, he published his first important work on cosmology, in which the formation of inhomogeneities such as stars and galaxies was explained in terms of quantum fluctuations. This was followed by one of his most important papers: an explanation of the baryon asymmetry of the universe. Shortly after this, he wrote a paper that laid the basis for a new branch in the theory of gravitation called in the West "induced gravity." There were also other works containing completely new ideas in the field of cosmology.[3]

At the same time, Sakharov's political views continued to evolve. I remember that in 1965, he came to my home in a state of great excitement with the manuscript of a book by Roy Medvedev about Stalin titled *Let History Judge*. Most of the facts it contained had already been published during the period of Khrushchev's "thaw," but collected together and supplemented with new material, they made a powerful impression on Sakharov.

This continuing evolution led in 1968 to "Reflections on Progress, Peaceful Coexistence, and Intellectual Freedom." Published abroad and made known to us through the Voice of America and *samizdat*, it produced a shattering effect. As a result, Sakharov was dismissed from his classified work.

This crisis coincided with a personal tragedy in Sakharov's life. In 1969, Klavdia Alekseyevna died of cancer diagnosed too late.

The quiet, brave, uninhibited expression of his political ideas placed Sakharov in a very special position. Expressed by any other man, they could have resulted in the loss of personal freedom, but his great service to his country, recognized by the highest possible awards, protected him from direct repression to a large extent. In the climate of that time, many feared to have any association with him.

In 1969 Tamm, confined to his bed by an incurable illness, asked Sakharov to return to the Lebedev Institute. He accepted this invitation and soon, after overcoming the opposition of the authorities at various levels, he again became a member of the staff in the theoretical department, with which he remained associated to the end of his life.

Sakharov's militant position attracted to him almost everyone involved in human rights activity. As a result, his (so to speak) theoretical political activity, which found its direction in developing and expressing ideas, became closely linked with his personal involvement in the human rights movement. He threw himself into the defense of people who were persecuted in any way, but nevertheless managed to find time and energy for work on new scientific problems.

IN 1970, SAKHAROV met Elena Georgievna Bonner and in January 1972 they were married. Bonner was the daughter of G. S. Alikhanov, a prominent Komintern worker arrested and shot in 1937. She studied philology before the war, and after the fighting began, volunteered for the front as a nurse. There she was wounded and received a concussion, but later returned to her duties. After the war, she graduated from medical school and worked as a pediatrician. At the time she and Sakharov met, Bonner already had a long history of dissident activity. This union brought to Sakharov a much longed for feeling of personal happiness.

Sakharov was by this time a legendary figure. He had enormous moral and political influence in both the Soviet Union and the world. He showed others what he had known for a long time: that only a just and open society can ensure mutual confidence between countries. In 1975 he was awarded the Nobel Peace Prize. At that time our mass media began to harass him. Waves of odious attacks and slander were directed against both him and Bonner. Finally, after protesting the invasion of Afghanistan, he was deported to Gorki in 1980 without due process of law or any formal charges. In August 1984, his wife was also sentenced to internal exile.

The staff of the theoretical department managed to prevent his dismissal from the Lebedev Institute and won permission from the authorities for his colleagues to visit him regularly for scientific consultations. Those who were selected to visit Sakharov had scientific interests closest to his own, and each visit took place on a voluntary basis.[4]

Sakharov went on hunger strikes three times in Gorki (in 1981, 1984, and 1985) in defending the rights of members of his new family (in particular, requesting permission for Bonner to travel abroad for medical treatment).[5] He suffered the most inhuman torture of forced feeding. Aside from his openly expressed goals, the hunger strikes were an expression of the rebellious soul of an indomitable person.[6]

The storm of indignation and the actions that occurred in his defense abroad were an important moral support for Sakharov. Unfortunately, they did not have a great influence on the leaders of the Soviet Union. In spite of the general indignation throughout the world and the condemnation by the United Nations, the war in Afghanistan continued crippling and taking the lives of many thousands of Soviet soldiers and killing hundreds of thousands of Afghans. The promise given by Sakharov before his last hunger strike, that he would concentrate only on scientific work if his requirement was met, had no effect. However, a week later, the famous April 1985 Plenum of the Central Committee of the Soviet Communist Party took place and, on May 31, Sakharov was visited by a high official of the KGB. From the conversation with this man, Bonner concluded that "Gorbachev gave the KGB orders to look this matter over. But the KGB carried on its policies. Thus they were involved in a conflict in which it was not clear who was stronger—Gorbachev or the KGB."[7] This became clear five months later when, after repeated promises by Sakharov to abstain from open political activities, Bonner was allowed to travel to the United States, where she underwent heart surgery which saved her life. In December 1986, Gorbachev, ignoring Sakharov's promise to cut off his political activity, invited him to return to Moscow and "to carry on his patriotic activity."

The following three years of Sakharov's stormy life were open to the public. I cannot refrain from mentioning that on the very first day of his return to Moscow, he went to the Lebedev Institute, his other home, and spent about six hours there in a seminar and just talking with his old colleagues.

His subsequent political activity considerably limited his time to do scientific work but, in spite of this, he participated in the weekly seminars and in scientific conferences.

The life of this great man ended on December 14, 1989.

Notes and References

1. Andrei Sakharov, *Sakharov Speaks*, New York: Knopf, 1974, p. 30.

2. This dedication to common people was personified, in a particularly touching form, by the multitude of rural doctors and teachers. In my younger days, it was my good fortune to meet these crystal clear souls, sincere to the point of naiveté, indifferent to material things.

3. In particular, a series of four articles published by Sakharov. One of them (written jointly with Zel'dovich) includes a derivation of a semiempirical formula for the hadron mass, based on the quark model. Sakharov always liked to "tidy up his work," and here he succeeded in finding agreement with the experimentally determined values.

4. A total of seventeen colleagues traveled to Gorki, some of them many times.

5. His acute sense of responsibility toward others was evident even earlier. For example, in his Nobel lecture, as well as at other times, he produced long lists of prisoners of conscience in the Soviet Union and campaigned for them. Once, at the beginning of the 1970s, I told him, "In my opinion, you play a game that cannot be lost: If your ideas are accepted, then it would mean victory. If instead you are imprisoned, you will be satisfied that you are suffering just like your fellow brothers." He laughed and agreed.

6. During my first visit to Gorki in June 1980, I quoted to Sakharov (I thought in consolation) the verse of, if I am not mistaken, Kaysin Kuliev: "Patience is the weapon of the hero if he has no other weapon." He became indignant: "Patience? The struggle continues!"

7. E. G. Bonner, Post-scriptum, *On the Deportation to Gorki* (in Russian), 1988, p. 129.

Precursor of *Perestroika*

VLADIMIR YA. FAINBERG

Lebedev Physical Institute, Moscow

A LITTLE TIME has now passed since the death of Andrei Dmitrievich Sakharov. Many articles and papers have been published reflecting on this tragic event from various points of view, but time alone will reveal the depth of the loss suffered by our country and humanity and the grief felt by all people of discernment. It will be some time before we cease to feel our bereavement at the crumbling of the foothold that supported us in hard times, in our hour of need.

My image of this man took shape gradually over a period of forty years. I accumulated many impressions from my discussions, sometimes even disputes, with him on a wide variety of topics ranging from the scientific to the sociopolitical, as well as from the contradictory, sometimes even diametrically opposed, opinions of our mutual acquaintances and friends concerning his personality. Without claiming completeness, I shall try to reproduce the most vivid of my impressions.

Busy Inner Workings

I first met Sakharov in the theoretical department of the Lebedev Physical Institute of the Soviet Academy of Sciences, just after I had graduated from the Moscow Physical Engineering Institute. The year was 1949, and the theoretical department was headed by our mutual teacher, the well-known Nobel Prize winner Igor E. Tamm. Sakharov was already an old-timer in the department, having taken the postgraduate course in 1945 and defended his dissertation in 1947. Our first, brief scientific conversation did not leave any appreciably clear impression on me; he spoke slowly, as if it were difficult for him to choose words and phrases. This characteristic remained with him throughout his life, and only after several years did it become evident to me that it was a consequence of the busy inner workings of his innumerable thoughts and of his desire to think each one through before voicing it. This was an obstacle in his teaching: He complained to Tamm that his students did not understand him fully. It was for this reason that Sakharov had to leave the Moscow Energetics Institute, where he had taught in the first difficult postwar years.

Then, literally within several months, I completely revised my opinion of Sakharov. Whenever anyone mentioned his name, it would be to relate what Sakharov said or how he had solved a problem, and always the anecdote would be accompanied by epithets such as "brilliant" and "superb." When, in the early 1950s, I was engaged in classified work, I found that Sakharov had great authority among the leading scientists in atomic research, although he had not yet reached thirty. His brain was probably of some special construction, for he solved all problems in unorthodox ways. Andrei A. Kolomensky, a Lenin Prize winner and one of the oldest professors at the Lebedev Institute, who studied with Sakharov at Moscow State University, has particularly mentioned this aspect of Sakharov's thinking to me.

Sakharov's ability to explain complicated physical phenomena from general principles and by using qualitative scaling estimates was surprising. I remember Yuri A. Romanov, a physicist in the theoretical department at the Lebedev Institute from 1949 to 1951, telling me with admiration in 1950 that after he had discussed with Sakharov his idea for calculating the magnetic moments of nuclei, "everything fell into place!" (Romanov went on to become a collaborator at the All-Union Scientific Research Institute of Experimental Physics, to earn a doctorate in physics, and to be named a Hero of Socialist Labor.)

There is a wealth of legendary stories about Sakharov in those days (and later), most of them based on his postgraduate exams and on his famous report on a classified subject. On the exams, he found the correct solution to a problem but was unable to explain it convincingly to his examiners — Tamm, Evgeny L. Feinberg and Serge M. Rytov — who gave him a grade of 4, the top being 5. In his classified report he derived the equation-of-state in a mere seven pages. Researchers at the Institute of Applied Mathematics were using their most powerful computer at that time, the *Strela* (meaning "arrow"), to solve the same problem. Their findings confirmed

Sakharov's estimates with a high degree of accuracy. Another story involves the time Victor P. Silin (now director of solid-state physics at the Lebedev Institute) and I took a postgraduate exam in German. At the end the teacher told us nostalgically that she would of course give us the highest grade of E and that we were obviously capable young men, but that our translations in no way compared with the magnificent translations of Einstein's papers done by Sakharov!

A Hero of Socialist Labor

Sakharov and Tamm's 1950 report on controlled thermonuclear fusion made an especially indelible impression. Tamm told me how everyone in their group was working on the project with tunnel vision, fully absorbed in the atomic problem, and had not a single minute to spare. One evening, in walked Sakharov and produced the idea that one could try to keep (that is, thermally insulate) hot plasma in a closed toroidal volume and, in principle, heat it up to the temperature of a thermonuclear reaction. The joint development of this idea by these two outstanding physicists resulted in the debut of a new area of research: the theory and construction of "magnetic thermonuclear reactors" (Tamm proposed the term).

From the very beginning Tamm and Sakharov, the teacher and the disciple, were on very friendly terms. Their relationship was imbued with mutual affection and trust, which lasted till the final days of Tamm's life (he died in 1971). Tamm always spoke of Sakharov very warmly, with high praise for his outstanding talent as a scientist and inventor and for his high moral qualities. In the last years of his life Tamm often returned to "the phenomenon of Sakharov"; he said that Sakharov's tragedy was that he had to sacrifice his great passion—elementary-particle physics—first to create an atomic and hydrogen bomb and then, after he comprehended the troubles of our civilization, to lead the struggle for the survival of mankind, to which he gave almost all his strength.

From 1950 to 1969, except for rather frequent stays in Moscow and participation in seminars and scientific discussions at the theoretical department of the Lebedev Institute, Sakharov devoted the major part of his time and strength to his work at the All-Union Scientific Research Institute of Experimental Physics, where he made great contributions to devising and creating nuclear weapons, an effort that ensured nuclear parity between the United States and our country. Simultaneously he started new trends in science. In 1952 he put forward the idea of exploding magnetic generators— devices that would convert energy from chemical or nuclear explosions

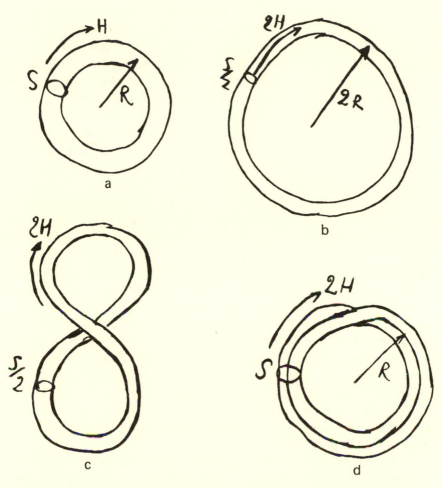

Magnetohydrodynamic dynamo, one of Sakharov's "pastime problems."
Sakharov's sketches show a closed torus (a) of large radius R and cross sec-
tion S containing a "frozen" magnetic field H in an incompressible con-
ducting medium. The sequence of stretching (b), twisting (c), and folding
(d) doubles the magnetic field. The process can be repeated any number
of times. (From A. D. Sakharov, Collected Scientific Works, *New York:*
Marcel Dekker, 1982. Used by permission.)

into magnetic field energy. In 1964 such generators produced record magnetic fields of 25×10^6 gauss. In 1967 he published a paper on the possible
instability of the proton—the principal particle of the universe—in which
he predicted its lifetime. This bold hypothesis was later developed in the
so-called unified models of elementary particles—the grand unified theories. Experimental searches for this unique phenomenon are now under

way, and new ones are planned in many countries throughout the world, including the USSR.

In the 1950s and early 1960s a steady stream of well-deserved rewards and official accolades was showered upon Sakharov. He was elected to the Soviet Academy of Sciences in 1953, was awarded the title Hero of Socialist Labor three times (in 1953, 1956 and 1962), and won a Lenin Prize and a USSR State Prize. Yet all this affected neither his outward behavior nor his moral and ethical principles; he remained the same man to the end and, so to speak, stood the test of glory and wealth. (In 1969 Sakharov gave all his savings and prizes, totaling 143,000 rubles, to the building of the Oncological Center in Moscow.)

Speaks His Mind

From the late 1950s on, Sakharov came to realize ever more acutely the danger inherent in the accumulation of nuclear weapons by the two opposing superpowers—the USSR and the U.S.—and in particular the increasing ecological threat posed by the testing of these weapons. He was the only expert who openly voiced objection to Nikita Khrushchev, at that time the head of the party and the state, when in 1961 a sixty-megaton hydrogen bomb was tested on an island named Novaya Zemlya ("New Land"). His voice was not heard. It was obviously then that it was borne in on him that the probability of a nuclear conflict increases immeasurably when crucial political solutions depend on the uncontrolled will of one leader or a group of leaders heading the party and the state.

The next turning point in Sakharov's life was in 1968, when in his memorandum "Reflections on Progress, Peaceful Coexistence, and Intellectual Freedom" he drew attention to the three main problems faced by humanity: the nuclear and ecological problems and the danger of incompetent, authoritative power. Many people read the manuscript, but it was not accepted for publication in the USSR. (Twenty million copies, however, were printed abroad.) Our country was becoming increasingly stagnant. After almost twenty years, Sakharov had to leave the All-Union Scientific Research Institute of Experimental Physics, and in 1969 he returned to the Lebedev Institute's theoretical department as a senior research worker.

From 1969 to 1980 Sakharov's life was full of drama. The basic tenets of his principles manifested themselves to the full during this period: in his consistent and uncompromising defense of dissidents; in his fight for radical democratization and fundamental change in our entire economic, social, and political system; and in his fight against the nuclear threat and for the survival of mankind. (His book *My Country and the World* has been widely published abroad.) In 1975 he was deservedly awarded the Nobel Prize for his outstanding contribution to the struggle for peace. Andrei Sakharov can justly be called the precursor of *perestroika* in our country.

Sakharov was unshakable in matters of principle but at the same time lent an attentive ear to critical remarks. He always showed respect and tolerance for the opinions of others. I can attest personally to the thoughtfulness he showed toward the staff of the theoretical department at the Lebedev Institute. He never tried to involve anyone there in activities that would at that time have been called "dissident." Moreover, so as not to jeopardize his coworkers, Sakharov promised the head of the department that he would not involve people from the department or from the institute in his political activities.

In the end, however, he was unable to keep this promise, through no fault of his own. On the one hand, the party organization and the head of the department were constantly under pressure from the party committee and from some of the directors of the institute to create around Sakharov an atmosphere of intolerance and isolation within the department and the institute. A campaign was organized to collect signatures on a document libelously protesting his activities. To the credit of the head of the department and the department staff, none of them signed. On the other hand, Sakharov's vigorous political activities outside the Lebedev Institute were reflected inside the institute. I remember his struggle to have the biologist and author Zhores A. Medvedev liberated from an asylum, and his attempt to organize a public discussion on this matter in the institute. Sakharov, as well as representatives from the procurator's office and the Ministry of Health, were to participate. However, there was a peremptory shout from on high: No discussion of nonscientific problems with Sakharov; he should not be given a rostrum for propagating his views.

From the Seminar Audience

Sakharov devoted much of his mental and physical strength to his patriotic activity. But he also found time for scientific work and attended the Tuesday all-Moscow seminars held in the theoretical department. Between 1969 and 1979 he published six scientific papers. His participation in the seminars was almost always useful. I'll give two typical examples.

The speaker at one 1974 seminar spoke on the state of research on laser-induced thermonuclear reactions. At the end of the talk Sakharov asked a very unusual question: "What do you think one neutron in your installation will cost?"

"I haven't thought about it," answered the speaker.

"About half a kopeck," said Sakharov. "If we bear in mind that for a nuclear reaction, the neutron density must be greater than $10^{15}/cm^3$, it is easy to estimate how much the installation will cost!" The discussion ceased immediately.

Another time the seminar speaker was Victor M. Galitsky, a corresponding member of the Soviet Academy of Sciences, who spoke on the hydrodynamic theory of nuclear collisions. I was sitting near Sakharov and saw him draw some intersecting circles on a scrap of paper. He seemed not to be listening very attentively to the speaker. Unexpectedly he asked, "Is your adiabatic exponent equal to one-quarter?"

"How did you know?" countered Galitsky in astonishment. "I was just about to address that." Sakharov answered that he had calculated it for himself.

Exiled for Opposing a War

By the end of 1979 the international situation had worsened. That December our troops advanced into Afghanistan and a senseless nine-year war began. A few days after the invasion began, Sakharov issued a statement, for the benefit of the foreign press, in which he severely condemned our military action, calling it a tragic mistake. Sakharov's reaction followed logically from his belief that when a totalitarian government possesses nuclear weapons, involvement in military conflicts poses a strong danger, since it brings with it a threat of nuclear war and all its catastrophic consequences. ("Recall the Caribbean crisis in 1963," he said, "when the world hung by a thread and everything depended on the will of one man—N.S. Khrushchev!") He emphasized that our foreign policy at that time was based on the belief that after the outbreak of a nuclear war it would be capitalism that would be annihilated.

The authorities reacted swiftly to Sakharov's statement. On January 22, 1980, when Sakharov went out to go to the Lebedev Institute, where he was planning to attend a seminar, two KGB officers got into his car with him and escorted him to the office of the deputy procurator—General A. Rekunkov. The general read to Sakharov the decision to deport him to Gorki and to strip him of all his government awards. He was then taken to the airport, and from there, accompanied by KGB vice-chairman S. Tsvigun, he was flown to Gorki. His wife and friend, Elena Bonner, went to Gorki on the same plane. This was the beginning of Sakharov's unlawful seven-year exile in Gorki—unlawful because it was imposed without a trial and by no court of law. He and his wife were placed in three rooms of a four-room apartment at 214 Gagarin Avenue in the district of

Shcherbinka—in a "golden cage," as it was christened with bitter humor by foreign correspondents. (The fourth room was at first occupied by a housemaid, but Sakharov had to decline her services, as she was a KGB agent. Her room was then sealed up.)

Reaction to Exile

Sakharov's deportation gave rise to a great international wave of protests. Many international scientific (and nonscientific) conferences and meetings in the USSR were boycotted; a number of international organizations protested to the leaders of our country; some Soviet scientists were not admitted as participants in conferences in other countries; and the activity of many of our missions abroad was boycotted. All this did a great deal of damage to the economy and moral prestige of our country and our academy of sciences, which was unable to defend its member Sakharov.

Leading statesmen and public figures in many countries asked the leadership of the USSR generally, and General Secretary Leonid Brezhnev personally, to reconsider Sakharov's exile. There was no response. Sakharov's prestige as an unbending fighter for freedom and civil rights for democracy, peace and disarmament, which was already very high, soared.

Initially, a general atmosphere of shock pervaded our department. Nobody believed that it would be possible to free Sakharov from exile. It was even difficult to prevent his dismissal from the Lebedev Institute. However, after long deliberations we decided to ask Academician Vitaly L. Ginzburg to go to the Communist Party of the Soviet Union and convince the authorities of the Central Committee's department of science of the necessity to initiate scientific contacts with Sakharov. Ginzburg not only complied with our request but also obviously managed to convince them, for reason prevailed and research workers from our department were permitted to make scientific visits to Sakharov in Gorki.

Visits to Gorki

The first official visitors were the head of our department, Ginzburg, and the party secretary of our institute, Alexander Golovashkin. Following this, employees of our department paid visits to Sakharov on a more or less regular basis. In the course of seven years, a total of seventeen employees visited him in Gorki. These trips gave Sakharov not only scientific support but also a moral boost (as he himself admitted).

During his exile Sakharov published six original articles in the Soviet scientific journals *JETP* and *JETP Letters*. In my opinion the most significant of these were "Cosmological Models of the Universe with Reversal of Time's Arrow" (1980) and "Multisheet Cosmological Models of the Universe" (1982). These articles reflected Sakharov's deep interest in general questions about cosmology and gravity, whose close interrelationship has been revealed in the last ten to fifteen years in the form of connections between the quark-lepton structure of elementary particles and the processes by which the early stages of the universe evolved.

It is difficult to comprehend fully the moral and physical suffering Sakharov endured in exile. His scientific work in this context was truly an act of heroism. At the same time he never ceased his struggle on behalf of human rights, progress and intellectual freedom.

I will mention only briefly my own personal impressions gained during meetings with Sakharov in Gorki. On my first trip, in May 1980, I was accompanied by a young collaborator, Andrei Linde. We stayed in the guest house of the Chemical Institute of the Academy of Sciences in Gorki, near Sakharov's house. I remember telling Linde about Sakharov's capabilities as a man and as a scientist, calling him a genius. Then we went to see Sakharov. We passed through the passport control station in the corridor in front of Sakharov's apartment, where a militiaman (a KGB agent) sat, and then entered the apartment. Sakharov and Bonner greeted us in a very friendly manner. They were upset that we had already eaten breakfast because they had prepared some for us. Then for about four hours we conversed with Sakharov about many scientific matters and news items. At dinner that evening Sakharov and Bonner told us of some of the problems connected with their life in Gorki. We returned to Moscow late that evening.

Looking back on the visit now, it seems to me that we barely touched on political matters. Yet, as became clear, the KGB had listened in on our conversations—not only in Sakharov's apartment but in the guesthouse, too—for on our return to Moscow, the reaction of the KGB was disappointment. The deputy director of the KGB at the Lebedev Institute informed me that the "General" was dissatisfied with my conduct because I had overstepped my authority: I had promised, without sufficient grounds, to resolve many of Sakharov's problems and had overly complimented his human qualities, even to the extent of calling him a genius. Moreover, I had discussed political matters with him, too. In response to this I suggested that we invite the "General" to join us one day and that together we all listen to the recordings. "What recordings?" exploded the deputy director. "What do you mean?" To my next question—"Where did you get all this information?" —his reply was a *non sequitur*. As I took my leave of him, he told me that there was some unpleasantness in store for me: In the first place, I was now refused permission to go abroad at least until 1988.

I made my last trip to Gorki with Arkady Tseitlin, a research collaborator, on the day of Sakharov's sixty-fifth birthday, May 21, 1986. *Perestroika* was in its second year. A new wave of letters and appeals for Sakharov's release was inundating Mikhail Gorbachev's mailbox. This time there were no official checks outside Sakharov's apartment, but the memory of those who had been there before still lingered in the minds of both of us. Nevertheless, I did not refuse to take a letter from Sakharov to Gorbachev. From my conversations with Sakharov it became evident that he keenly sensed the approach of decisive changes in our country and was in an optimistic mood, even though he himself had undergone three hunger strikes, followed by violent bouts of eating, and three thefts by KGB agents of the manuscripts of his memoirs. (He laboriously reconstructed them each time they were stolen and finished them literally on the day of his death.) He had also suffered through the conviction and exile of Bonner, whom the authorities graciously permitted to live with her husband in Gorki, as well as through innumerable other "small" unpleasantnesses.

Bonner's support for her husband throughout those years of hardship was the decisive factor that kept him alive, ensuring that he did not become physically or morally broken. His best human qualities were made manifest in Gorki: his genuine lack of superficiality, his joy in the companionship of those close to him, the simplicity of his behavior at home, his hospitality, his ability to listen without interrupting to opinions that contradicted his own, and the absence of any bitterness despite almost unbearable suffering and injustice. All this created around him an aura of kindness and integrity. On the other hand, he was hard-nosed, sticking to his convictions while engaged in conversation with opinionated people. Scientific discussions with him were not easy—at each step tricky questions needed to be answered—but relations with him inspired an additional belief in life, even in those bitter days in Gorki.

On December 16, 1986, the telephone rang in Sakharov's flat. Gorbachev was on the line. The following day, the president of the Soviet Academy of Sciences, Guri Marchuk, arrived in Gorki and spent two hours negotiating scientific plans with Sakharov. Then followed the triumphal return to Moscow.

To conclude, I would like to elaborate on one of Sakharov's last remarks to me—that the ongoing influence of *perestroika* in our country and the rest of the world demands deep and broad analysis. It is clear to me that the influence of Sakharov himself is likewise gigantic, and that it is only with great difficulty that we lesser mortals can analyze it and give some quantitative estimate of it. There exist in the depths of the soul of every single one of us the capacities for both good and evil, and through Sakharov's influence most sensible people in our land now opt for kindness. This influence has necessarily embittered many of the opponents of *perestroika*, but it has undoubtedly given rise to more kindness in the world, and this has benefited the whole of humanity. Let us hope that this additional reserve of compassion, together with his belief that there will be no reversal of *perestroika*, which he also bequeathed to us, will compensate in some small degree for the loss of this man, this scientist, this citizen.

Scientist, Thinker, Humanist

Vitalii I. Goldanskii

Semenov Institute of Chemical Physics, Moscow

I CANNOT SAY that I knew Andrei Dmitrievich Sakharov well, so this will be a view of him from off to the side, so to speak.

It was 1950, in Dubna, when I first saw Sakharov. I was working at the first of the Dubna accelerators at the time. One day, while a management team headed by Igor Kurchatov was visiting the place to get a look at the experimental results, a very quiet and shy young man caught my attention. When I asked some acquaintances who he was, I was told, "Sakharov, candidate in sciences from the Lebedev Physical Institute." I was advised to remember his name, since even at the time a very bright future was seen for him.

At a seminar, the leaders of the various groups working at the accelerator spoke about what they were doing. I was one of these speakers, representing my colleagues in the Institute of Chemical Physics. After the seminar, Sakharov walked over and said some kind words about our work, but I sensed that he was saying much the same thing to almost all the speakers. That was the style of his generosity: Very polite and attentive, Andrei Dmitrievich strived to emphasize the positive aspects of his impressions.

In 1953 I heard that Sakharov had defended his doctoral dissertation. The defense had been specially organized on short notice. The reason for the hurry was that elections to the Academy of Sciences were to be held that same year, and Sakharov was to be promoted to the rank of full member of the Academy. Although no one doubted that eventually he would go far above the doctoral level, it was important to observe the formality: It would have been a bit awkward to elect a person without a doctorate to the top rank of academician. To the best of my memory he received twenty-three of the twenty-three votes from his own department.

In 1961 our paths crossed at a Crimean resort, where Andrei Dmitrievich was taking a vacation with his children. Beyond the very ordinary conversations that all the guests had, I did not talk with him. I was not alone in this regard: I do not recall that my father-in-law, the physicist Nikolai Nikolaevich Semenov, who was also there, spent much time with Sakharov. It may have been that contact with him was discouraged by the thick air of secrecy about him—I had been hearing since 1953 that he was the creator of the hydrogen bomb.

Speaking Against Nuclear Testing

It was also in 1961 that I learned of an action by Sakharov that attracted publicity. Since 1958 our country had been observing a moratorium on nuclear testing, as had the U.S. In 1961 we were the first to resume testing, offering the obviously contrived excuse that France was said to have been carrying out tests. In fact, this was a raw show of force. By that time Sakharov had developed a most powerful hydrogen bomb, whose explosive power—about sixty megatons—has not since been surpassed. When he learned of the decision to explode the bomb on Novaya Zemlya, Sakharov launched a very vigorous protest against the test.

Sakharov had spoken out against nuclear testing before, but never had his protests been so categorical. He probably felt that these tests imposed a particular responsibility on him. In addition he understood the absurdity of such a nuclear explosion. Such a gigantic explosion was meaningless, even from a military standpoint, since its energy would not have a corresponding destructive effect. The energy would go mostly into the atmosphere, which would then become severely contaminated with radioactive products. From an ecological standpoint, such a powerful explosion would be exceedingly harmful. Sakharov fought to prevent the explosion, arguing his case all the way to the top.

Sakharov was unable to prevent the explosion, but he apparently succeeded in causing the military to start looking at him with suspicion: Here was a man doing some overly independent thinking. His job was viewed as that of simply creating the weapon; beyond that, his advice was not needed—or wanted.

I saw Sakharov engaged in verbal combat in 1964, at a general meeting of the Soviet Academy of Sciences. At this meeting nominees for academician and corresponding member chosen by the various departments were to be confirmed. The department of general biology had selected Nikolai I. Nuzhdin—one of the closest colleagues of Trofim D. Lysenko—for promotion to academician. The debate over Nuzhdin's candidacy, which drew in Sakharov, Igor E. Tamm, Vladimir A. Engelgardt and Vladimir N. Sukachev, among others, began with some seemingly innocent questions: How many papers had he published? Why had these papers been published for the most part in popular magazines? And so forth. However innocent they may have seemed, these questions and the members' speeches exposed the antiscientific essence of Lysenko's "theories." Particularly sharp and uncompromising was the speech by Sakharov, who directly attacked not only Nuzhdin but also Lysenko. The results of the vote humiliated the Lysenkoites: Nuzhdin received only 23 of 137 votes.

This was the first time a general meeting of the Academy had ever failed to confirm a candidate selected by a department. Because Lysenko was at that time back in good standing with Premier Nikita S. Khrushchev after a brief fall from grace, these election results provoked intense anger among the authorities. In a report of the meeting that appeared in one newspaper, for example, Sakharov was labeled an "engineer," and it was asked just what an engineer could know about matters of biology.

In 1966 I attended a discussion on "Science of the Future" held by the State Committee on Science and Technology. A Rand Corporation prediction of the future of the U.S. through the year 2025 had been circulated for internal use in the Soviet scientific community, and Vladimir A. Kirillin, chairman of the committee at the time, decided to conduct a discussion of corresponding problems and predictions under the conditions of our own society. He gathered a few scientists, including Sakharov, Nikolai G. Basov, Vitaly L. Ginzburg, Yakov B. Zel'dovich, Bruno M. Pontecorvo, Alexander M. Prokhorov, and me. Each participant offered his own predictions regarding the development of the particular scientific fields in which he was working. Sakharov was very interested in the possible use of nuclear explosions for scientific and economic purposes, in particular, to produce immensely strong magnetic fields. Later, in the 1980s, he was to suggest that low-yield underground nuclear explosions be used to prevent earthquakes or to trigger them at a set time.

1968: Final Suppression of "Khrushchev Thaw"

The next vivid event linked with Sakharov's name came in 1968. This was a difficult year for all of us. It marked the irrevocable end of the "Khrushchev thaw." In March, student uprisings in Poland were sternly suppressed. On August 21, armed forces of the Warsaw Pact countries marched into Czechoslovakia to put an end to the democratic movement known as the "Prague Spring." That day is remembered by many of us as one of the tragic days of our lives.

That same year Sakharov wrote his famous essay "Reflections on Progress, Peaceful Coexistence, and Intellectual Freedom." The treatise was distributed to all the members of the Presidium of the Soviet Academy of Sciences. I had an opportunity to read Semenov's personal copy. This essay was a cry of the heart, quite appropriate for the period but coming at absolutely the wrong time in the opinion of the authorities. They fired Sakharov from his job at Yuli B. Khariton's "Installation," a secret atomic research facility. Soon after, Sakharov showed up in Moscow.

Actually, there was a short period in my life during which I *did* see Andrei Dmitrievich fairly frequently. In late 1973, an infarction put me in the academic hospital. Recuperating there at the time were Andrei Dmitrievich; his wife, Elena Georgievna Bonner; and the eminent astrophysicist Iosif Samuilovich Shklovskii. Shklovskii had known Sakharov for a long time, and through him Sakharov and I became better acquainted. Since I was bedridden, they came to visit me, and we had some long conversations. Aleksandr Solzhenitsyn's *Gulag Archipelago* appeared at about that time, and we discussed it.

This account would be quite incomplete without a few kind words about Elena Georgievna. When I first saw her in the hospital with Andrei Dmitrievich, it seemed to me that they complemented each other in a surprisingly harmonious way. When the times were tough, she always supported him, and he her. (When Sakharov and his wife were banished to Gorki in 1980, the corner of 67th Street and 3rd Avenue in New York, by the building housing the Soviet UN mission, was named "Sakharov-Bonner Corner" in protest. Now they will remain there together forever.)

An event that draws a clear picture of Sakharov occurred on February 13, 1974. By that time he had checked out of the hospital, but I was still there. I was sitting with two colleagues in the lobby, reading a plan for a joint paper, when Andrei Dmitrievich appeared. We greeted each other. He said he had come for his mail, which was still arriving in packets for him at the hospital, several weeks after he had checked out. He said he was happy to see that I was up and around, and then he slipped immediately into what was really on his mind: "You know, an outrageous act has been committed. They have exiled Solzhenitsyn. They have simply thrown him out of the country by force!" Sakharov had come straight to the hospital from the airport; his excited words could be heard by everyone in that overcrowded lobby.

Although I understood and indeed shared Sakharov's feelings, at that particular moment I was somewhat uncomfortable with the idea that his words would drown out the other conversations and would attract everyone's curiosity, which by no means would be benevolent in all cases. I attempted to steer the conversation to another topic, asking him about his health and that of Elena Georgievna. He answered briefly and then lapsed back into the Solzhenitsyn affair; Solzhenitsyn's fate was blocking all other thoughts from Sakharov's mind at that moment. Having blurted out his indignation, Andrei Dmitrievich walked out quickly. My colleagues were curious to know just who this strange man was. Hearing the answer, they forgot about the unread paper and ran out of the hospital to watch Sakharov leave, if only from a distance.

Humanist

I cannot say that Sakharov was the greatest scientist of all time and all places. To say so would be an exaggeration, and Sakharov needs none of that. However, on the basis of an "all-around score" — computed from his personality and his scientific, social, and humanitarian activity — Sakharov can legitimately be ranked among the greatest sons of humankind.

We saw Sakharov in three roles: a scientist who created the most destructive weapon ever, a humanist who invested his soul in the effort to see humanity live without weapons in a democratic and free society, and a remarkable thinker, not only in the realm of the natural sciences but also in the realm of the social sciences. We do not know of another such person — at any rate, I do not intend to waste time searching for another example or even for a reasonable approximation.

Looking at Sakharov in his later years, you would see a weak and stooped man, his physical strength apparently on the decline. The poet Yevgeny Yevtushenko has drawn a surprisingly accurate picture by comparing Sakharov's head with a dandelion. Inside this by no means Herculean body, however, thrived an inflexible strength of spirit. Sakharov's strength of spirit was seen particularly clearly during his exile to Gorki, where he went on several hunger strikes, and where his life was in danger (since there are a fair number of active hatemongers in our society).

His inflexible strength of spirit also emerged in words and deeds that at times looked like mistakes to me. I was present at his many speeches at the First and Second Congresses of People's Deputies of the USSR. It sometimes seemed to me that in deliberately stirring up trouble and drawing fire to himself he was making it difficult to reach a compromise solution that might have been a step forward. However, I and many other deputies were apparently not always given to understanding his internal logic or just where his thoughts were leading, so it is difficult for me now, in retrospect, to judge whether one or another of his steps was tactically correct. Indeed, the matter is unimportant. The only important point now is that Sakharov lived and acted among us. I hope that in doing so he succeeded, to some extent, in changing all of us—the entire world—for the better.

My Schoolmate

A. M. YAGLOM

Institute of Atmospheric Physics, Moscow

I HAVE NEVER written memoirs, but I see now that I must make an exception to that rule. It appears that I knew A. D. Sakharov longer than anyone whom he continued to see until the end of his life. Add my conviction that everything concerning Sakharov should be preserved, and I have taken up a pen.

I met Andrei Sakharov in the eighth grade in late 1935 or early 1936. Before then I had been a pupil in a seven-year school (along with my twin brother, Isaak, who has now, unfortunately, passed away). After completing that school, those of us who wished to study further were obliged to move on to another school. On the advice of friends, my brother and I applied to School No. 114 on Bolshoi Gruzinskii Street. Some of the other pupils in our class chose School No. 113 on Second Brestskoi Street.

In seventh grade, my brother and I had been regarded as good mathematicians. One day, a friend from School No. 113 told us that there was also a good mathematician in his new class: Andryusha Sakharov. We thus met Andrei (we never called him by the diminutive "Andryusha"). The first time we met, we talked primarily about mathematics (my brother and I did most of the talking by far; Andrei was never very talkative). We seemed to like each other; at any rate, we exchanged telephone numbers and agreed to meet again. We immediately told our new friend about the mathematics circle at Moscow State University, which we visited, and about the lectures at the university for pre-college students on Sundays. Andrei listened with interest but expressed no desire to join us.

Nevertheless, we met fairly often. We told Andrei what we learned at the sessions of the mathematics circle and in the journals *Mathematics in School* and *Mathematics Education*, which we read regularly. He was interested in this, and he often came up with unexpected comments which led us to look at a mathematics problem from a new perspective. On several occasions he tried to suggest physics problems to us, but they didn't arouse any enthusiasm in us: In those days, the physics course in school had no problems except those which had become totally trivial exercises, so we had no taste for solving physics problems. It was in the spring of 1936, I think, that we persuaded Andrei to accompany us to the Sunday mathematics lecture at Moscow State University. Just what happened at the lecture, and just what impression it made on Andrei, I could not tell you. Nor do I remember anything beyond mathematics and physics that we discussed in our meetings. All that I do remember is that before the next school year we agreed to go together to the sessions of a section of the mathematics circle at Moscow State University.

And that is what indeed happened. When we entered ninth grade, Andrei accompanied us to a section of the mathematics circle at the university. The classes were held one evening a week in one of the lecture rooms of the mechanics and mathematics department in an old university building on Mokhovoy Street. The classes usually lasted about two hours. They included a brief report by the leader of the section, who was an upper-level undergraduate student or a graduate student. In the process, several problems were proposed, and a discussion of solutions began. On occasion, the participants found solutions on the spot, but more often at home. The descriptions of the solutions frequently became rather long reports, but Andrei rarely talked for long. He clearly preferred geometrical construction problems or the combinatorial problems popular in school, in which it was necessary to find an answer, rather than exercises in proving theorems. He was often the first to find a correct solution, but the other students were often unable to understand his explanations without some additional commentary from the leader of the circle. On occasion, even the leader had difficulty. I could not help recall this situation many years later (probably in the early 1970s), in the course of a conversation with Sakharov. I was complaining that writing papers was a very slow and difficult process for me. In response, I heard that he was totally unable to write long papers, since over a matter of years he had become accustomed to limiting himself to brief formulas and predictions of results; detailed explanations were not required of him.

My brother and I were very enthusiastic about the school mathematics circle, but when, at the beginning of tenth grade, we called Andrei and suggested going back to the university, we heard that he had decided not to attend the classes of the mathematics circle this year. He added, "If there were a high-school physics circle at the university, I would attend without fail." Such a circle was indeed set up at the university only two years later, but I think that in 1937–38 mathematics was generally far more popular than physics among high-school students in Moscow. For that reason, the conversation with Andrei was a bit surprising to us; we even had the thought that he was unhappy that so much time was spent on rigorous proofs of theorems in the classes.

IN THE SUMMER of 1938, Andrei Sakharov, my brother, and I finished school and entered Moscow State University. There was no fierce competition in those days, and getting in was easy. Andrei, of course, chose the department of physics, and I did the same. My brother went into the mechanics and mathematics department. (We agreed to carry out parallel studies in both departments.) A fairly large number of Sakharov's university classmates still survive, fortunately, but I think that, at least during the first few years, Andrei and I were closer than the others (we had of course been friends even back before college). On the other hand, I cannot say that I was his *close* friend: It seemed to me that in those days he had no close friends at all. It may be that an intense inner life fenced him off from other people for a long time. He was always good-natured; no one in our class disliked him, but he never let anyone get really close to him.

He was a good student, but not brilliant. I think his teachers sometimes did not understand him completely. Furthermore, in taking exams he usually spoke slowly and as if he were unsure of himself. There were thus a fair number of 4's along with the 5's beside his name in the grade book. He had particular difficulty with the social disciplines. I guess they were a world apart from him at the time, and he was totally incapable of shooting the breeze. Accordingly, he sometimes received even 3s in the social disciplines; in fact, he was obliged to repeat one of these exams. When, in the late 1960s, I read his excellently written "Reflections on Progress, Peaceful Coexistence, and Intellectual Freedom," the effect was striking: It looked as though this essay had been written by someone else—not by my good acquaintance Andrei, aloof from everything outside physics. Later, at the end of his life, the entire country would be glued to its television sets and would follow Sakharov's speeches in parliament with great excitement. He was still not a brilliant orator, but he spoke extremely precisely and clearly, demonstrating a striking ability to compress the essence of the matter into a few words. I think he was developing internally throughout his life, slowly but in an extremely fundamental way, always thinking things through thoroughly, in contrast with the people who mature quickly but soon come to a standstill and develop no further.

However, I'd like to go back to our university days. Sakharov was not a brilliant student. At a purely formal level, M. L. Levin, for example, or I myself was regarded as a better student than Sakharov in our class. Observing the custom of our pre-college days, however, we frequently talked "about science," and I became convinced that he was stronger than me — that he understood things beyond me. Here is a case I remember clearly. In the third year, at lectures on the equations of mathematical physics, we learned about Bessel functions and the relationship between the zeros of the Bessel function and the natural vibrational frequencies of a circular membrane. Soon thereafter, Andrei told me about a method he had devised for evaluating the zeros of the Bessel function of index zero. As had happened before, it was difficult to understand his entire reasoning (it often seemed to me that Andrei was passing over some logical steps which were not very simple but seemed obvious to him; this habit might be likened to his dislike for long, logically flawless proofs of theorems), but I was left with the impression that "there was something there." As a test, I suggested that he take a sheet of paper and calculate the first few zeros. He consented, and in a few moments he presented me the results of his calculations. We went over to the university library and tracked down a handbook. It turned out that the values which he had calculated for the first three or four zeros were nearly identical to those given in the table. I perceived this as miraculous (it seemed to me that his theory could not help being awfully crude), and I have remembered it ever since. Andrei, in contrast, didn't take any particular satisfaction from this success; he was completely confident of his results.

Unfortunately, the third year in the physics faculty turned out to be the last one that I spent studying with Sakharov. War began in the summer of 1941. During the first days of the war, many of us tried without success to volunteer for the army (of those who succeeded, not one was to return from the war). In July and August of 1941 we were assigned to the construction of defensive positions in the Smolensk Oblast (for some reason that I don't recall, Andrei was not with us). In September, all the students in our class were summoned to an air force academy, but Andrei and I failed the physical. Moscow State University was to be evacuated to Tashkent on October 16. The last time I saw Sakharov in the fall of 1941 was two days before the scheduled evacuation, when he helped my brother and me move our things to the department of physics, from which they were to be transported to Tashkent. The evacuation did not occur on October 16, however. Early in the morning, a terrible news bulletin from Sovinformburo came over the radio. Panic had struck Moscow, and the students were told that the university was closing. It was recommended that all students move eastward on foot along railroad tracks. Many did just that; I myself remained with my parents in Moscow. On October 20, our family was transported in metro cars to Sverdovsk along with the remaining staff of the People's Comissariat of Ferrous Metallurgy, where my father worked. The university, on the other hand, had begun to function again on the twentieth, and a few days later Andrei, along with a large group of undergraduates, graduate students, and professors, was evacuated, but to Ashkhabad, not Tashkent.

My next meeting with Sakharov took place in Moscow in 1945. He had returned from Ulyanovsk, where he had worked at a munitions factory after completing studies at the university, and where he had married. I also graduated from the university. After working a year and a half in a scientific institute in Sverdlovsk, I went to Moscow as a graduate student in the Mathematics Institute of the Soviet Academy of Sciences. I was very interested in theoretical physics, and I regularly attended I. E. Tamm's seminar in the theoretical department of the Lebedev Physical Institute. Andrei dreamed of becoming a graduate student at the Lebedev Institute. At his request, our classmate P. E. Kunin (one of Tamm's graduate students at the time) and I brought him over to the institute and introduced him to Tamm. (I learned later that, when his son came to Moscow, Dmitri Ivanovich Sakharov, Andrei's father, sent some sort of scientific manuscript that he had written to Tamm through A. M. Lopshits, who worked at the Pedagogical Institute and who had known Tamm for a long time.) Tamm told Andrei that in order to become a graduate student he would have to take an entrance exam in the form of a report in the seminar of the theoretical department. He could choose the topic himself, or he could request to have one assigned. Andrei selected his topic himself (it was something about the diffraction of electromagnetic waves by solids). Kunin and I were in attendance, and we both decided that he had not done very well. Tamm, on the other hand, found the report remarkable and announced on the spot that he was taking Andrei on as a graduate student.

During the years as a graduate student and for the first few years thereafter, I frequently ran into Andrei, and we talked a lot. The discussions of physical topics were always interesting, but quite often I was later forced to rethink what I had heard during these conversations. One summer he rented a *dacha* on the Moscow-Volga canal, not far from the station Vodniki, where the laboratory at which I was working was carrying out measurements of the characteristics of atmospheric turbulence that year. At that time I became better acquainted with his first wife, Klavdia Alekseyevna, and I introduced him to the director of my laboratory, A. M. Obukhov, and his wife. Andrei and Klavdia quickly became friends with the Obukhovs.

At that point Andrei disappeared from sight, and he remained out of sight for a long time. He was involved in intense work outside Moscow and was essentially inaccessible.

AFTER ANDREI RETURNED to Moscow, I did not see much of him. I think it was in the summer of 1971 (two years after Klavdia's death) that my wife and I were walking in Peredelkino and met Andrei and his second wife, Elena Georgievna Bonner (Lusia), whom I had not met previously. At the time, Sakharov was collecting signatures for a letter seeking abolition of the death penalty. I said that in my own opinion the abolition of the death penalty was not the most important thing to strive for in the USSR those days, and that furthermore the death penalty should be retained for terrorist acts, to discourage people from taking hostages in order to liberate terrorists who had already been arrested.

Andrei objected, quietly, but sounding quite sure of himself. "No, there can be no law requiring the killing of people. Have you ever thought about just who would carry out the death penalty?" (I was convinced that everything he was saying had been thought out much earlier—in contrast with his scientific reports, which frequently gave the impression that he was thinking the stuff up as he went along.) We did not return to this question after that incident. At the time, of course, he was right, not I. I also remember that while walking one day, all of us taking pleasure from the forest, the grass, and the sun, Elena said that this excursion was remarkable, since Andrei had never walked in the woods before he met her.

In the fall of the following year, my wife and I met Andrei and Elena in a snack bar in a hotel in Tbilisi, which we were visiting for a few days. Two of my Georgian graduate students suggested driving us over to Mtskheta on the following day. We would also visit Ateni and Kintsvissi temples, with their fascinating twelfth-century frescoes. I invited Andrei and Elena to come along. The trip was wonderful. Also with us were my wife's sister and her husband at the time, Yuri Tuvin, who fell in love with Andrei Dmitrievich on the spot. Later, Tuvin was to look after him and Elena in a very moving way in Moscow, helping them in any way possible.

Because of the friendship with Tuvin, I unexpectedly witnessed Andrei's hearing the news that he had been awarded the Nobel Peace Prize in 1975. That fall, when Elena traveled to the West to recuperate, Andrei Dmitrievich agreed to visit Tuvin some evening. When the date of this visit was fixed, Tuvin called me and suggested spending an evening in pleasant

company (but he did not say who would be there; at the time, people preferred not to speak Sakharov's name over the telephone). Unexpectedly,
this was the day that the awarding of the Nobel Prize to Sakharov was
announced in Oslo. Many journalists attempted to make contact with this
new laureate, but there was no answer at his telephone, and no one knew
where to find him. Finally, one of Sakharov's friends (apparently Lydia
Korneevna Chukovskaya) said, in response to one of the calls from a foreign country, that Sakharov might be at Tuvin's place. She provided
Tuvin's telephone number and address. Suspecting nothing, I arrived at
Tuvin's place at precisely the moment that a crowd of foreign journalists
and human rights advocates associated with Sakharov burst into the apartment. I remember that evening quite well: It was a very happy one (it
seemed to me that Andrei himself enjoyed it least), but Tuvin's plan for a
cozy evening with a few friends of course didn't work out at all.

The next day, Tuvin and I took another walk to celebrate the awarding of
the prize to Andrei, on Chkalov Street, where we ran into many acquaintances. The telephone never stopped ringing. All the calls from foreign
countries were answered by Lev Kopelev, who was quite familiar with several foreign languages. When he left, however, and the calls from foreign
countries kept coming, Tuvin appealed to me: "Take the phone; you can
speak English!"

I don't know whether Sakharov noticed my embarrassment or simply
guessed that this might not be a good idea for me, but he said: "No, it's not
up to you to speak for me over the telephone." (Indeed, I did not want to
talk with someone in a foreign country, on that telephone, which was
undoubtedly tapped. I was certain that such a conversation could not fail to
bring me to the attention of the KGB.)

BETWEEN 1975 and Sakharov's exile to Gorki in early 1980, I saw Andrei
only twice. On one of these encounters (and I think even before 1975), I
asked him whether he was disturbed by the fact that his scientific work
involved the development of a superbomb intended for annihilating
people. (I was particularly interested in this question, since I myself, upon
completing graduate work in late 1946, and despite being very caught up in
theoretical physics, declined to work at the Lebedev Physical Institute
because I would have been obliged to spend part of my time on an application associated with work on the atomic bomb.) Andrei listened carefully
to what I had to say. After thinking for a moment, he answered, "No. You
know, at the time I did not think about this. I was *very* interested in learning
whether everything we had imagined would in fact work."

I am aware that Andrei sometimes answered that question differently; he regarded the presence of the bomb in the arsenals of both sides as the best guarantee that it would never be used. Nevertheless, it seems that the answer he gave me was interesting. I believe that both answers were truthful (not that anything untruthful could have escaped Sakharov's lips), and probably both considerations had operated. The first answer possibly reflected his feelings at the beginning of his work, while the second applied to a later stage. Remember that Sakharov was always in a process of development, and his views underwent many changes.

After Sakharov returned from his exile in Gorki, I immediately called him up to congratulate him on his arrival. I wanted very much to get together with him, but he kept postponing a meeting because he was too busy. Nevertheless, I frequently called him, and I always heard, "It's good that you're calling; call again." I don't know whether this was a manifestation of his unusual tact and gentleness or whether calls from such an old friend were indeed enjoyable for him, despite his incredible pace of activity.

In the summer of 1988 we met at a conference in Leningrad marking the one-hundredth anniversary of the birthday of A. A. Friedmann. Sakharov gave a very interesting scientific report (apparently the last in his life). He took a childlike delight in the opportunity to speak with physicists about physics. In particular, he told me with a sense of deep pity and rapture about his conversation with Stephen Hawking—the eminent British scientist who has been left almost completely paralyzed by a rare disease. In discussing Friedmann—specifically, in response to my comment that Friedmann had perceived the exact solution of Einstein's equations, which he had found as a purely mathematical exercise—Andrei objected that he didn't believe that: "Any physicist who has found a new and elegant solution will immediately begin to look around for something in nature to which the solution should correspond." (Later, Friedmann's solution turned out to be in excellent agreement with observational data, but Friedmann himself did not live to see this.)

I also met Andrei several times at sessions of the "Moscow Tribune" and, alas, at funerals. In the spring of 1988 he attended the funeral of my brother. In early December of 1989, not long before his death, he attended the funeral of A. M. Obukhov, the director of our Institute of Atmospheric Physics.

Some explanation is in order here. Obukhov, whose friendship with Andrei had been at a level such that they visited each other at their homes, had signed the infamous letter of forty academicians in condemnation of Sakharov. After this event, our director attempted for some time to justify his deed, citing the disgusting things that had been said about Sakharov in certain high academic circles. Soon, however, he fell silent. In conversations with me he expressed pity for Sakharov, and he referred to his signing the letter as "getting into a scrape." It turns out that he had not been on the original list of people who were supposed to sign the letter; he had been drafted at the last moment to replace someone who could not be found.

I mentioned Obukhov in a conversation, and Sakharov immediately said, "I understand. Keldysh pressured him, and he couldn't refuse. I bear no resentment toward him." (It seems that he never bore any resentment toward those who had done harm to him personally.) I was thus not surprised to see him at Obukhov's funeral. I later learned that he had told the daughter of the deceased, "Tell your mom that I owe her a long letter." Unfortunately, he was not able to pay this debt.

The funeral of S. V. Kalistratova, a lawyer, was held the next day. She had for many years defended all the people who were being persecuted unjustly. She was an old friend of our family. Seeing Andrei there, I said to him, "How I would like to chat with you, even for just half an hour, somewhere other than at a funeral."

Very seriously, he responded, "You know, I absolutely do not have time, but you must call." Possibly as a result of this conversation, after the funeral service he walked up to me in the church: "A car is waiting for Elena and us; let us give you a ride home." I answered that I could not fail to go to the cemetary. We chatted for a couple of minutes. Andrei said that he liked the church funeral service ("It's so human"). He then recalled the funeral of my brother, where my brother's son and his friends had read Jewish prayers over the coffin. We kissed each other good-bye, and a week later came the terrible news: Sakharov was gone.

Facets of a Talent

D. A. KIRZHNITS

Lebedev Physical Institute, Moscow

THESE REMARKS, which are rather subjective and fragmentary, are based on impressions accumulated during twenty years of working with Andrei Dmitrievich Sakharov at the Lebedev Physical Institute. Their purpose is to add several strokes to the portrait of Sakharov the physicist, without the pretension of attempting to disclose the true depths of his creative personality. This task would be too difficult: it is hard to penetrate into the image of Sakharov the scientist without analyzing his social activity. In both cases, we see the same features of his inimitable personality. In addition, the greater the image, the more deceptive are the external impressions. (For example, who could suppose, not knowing Sakharov, that behind his soft, intelligent external manner there is the iron character of an inflexible fighter?) I think of all this when I look at a gift obtained from the Sakharovs—two balls, absolutely indistinguishable externally, one of which bounces elastically from the floor, while the other sticks to it.

Everyone who came into contact with Sakharov in science felt to one degree or another the distinguishing features of his creative personality. These include first of all the unusual breadth of his scientific interests. If anything related to the extremely varied problems with which he was occupied (from engineering problems up to the most fundamental questions), it was their global nature. We have in mind things which are global in essence (the theory of the formation and evolution of the universe as a whole) or things which are global in their significance to all mankind (the problem of utilizing the energy of nuclear fusion, or recent projects on nuclear power engineering safety and the prevention of earthquakes). People frequently ask "What attracted Sakharov more: fundamental or applied problems?" Primarily the latter, it is thought. In any case, when Andrei Dmitrievich was cut off from applied research and was able to concentrate on fundamental activities, he strove to be included in work on laser-induced thermonuclear fusion which promised in time a new source of energy. We have to think that this was a manifestation not only of the immensity of his creative personality, but also of a social position—the desire to bring to people direct and visible advantage.

It is important to mention that in his occupation with global problems, Sakharov did not limit himself to expressing general ideas while leaving it to others to bring them to a concrete form. In this sense, he did not suffer from either farsightedness or nearsightedness—the trees did not prevent him from seeing the forest, and the forest did not prevent him from seeing the trees. According to the testimony of his colleagues in applied work, he had the ability to reach quantitative results at least as well as others, and found satisfaction in this work. However, do we not perhaps see the same unbiased thinking in Sakharov's social activity, in which he not only produced such epochal documents as the memorandum "Reflections on Progress, Peaceful Coexistence, and Intellectual Freedom" or the plan of a new Soviet constitution, but also personally cut through the closed dissident's court or the tribune of parliament?

Sakharov the scientist was distinguished by an astonishing independence and originality of his physical thinking. I. E. Tamm, his teacher, recalled that already on entering graduate school Sakharov struck his examiners with his nonstandard approach to very simple and apparently obvious things. In listening to Sakharov's reports or in a discussion with him, one had to think that he knew some more direct path of his own from premise to conclusion—so rapidly did he perceive the remote consequences of the statement under discussion. Sakharov's ideas were frequently surprising in their unexpected simplicity and obviousness (which became clear, of course, only after they were stated)—as if he picked a mushroom growing in the road which all others, following the usual trend, passed by. We can only think that Sakharov's independence of thought originated in the inner freedom and organic nonconformism which appeared so clearly in his social activity.

Another characteristic feature of Sakharov's creative personality was his physical intuition.[1] Being very well versed in the technique of theoretical physics, he was distinguished to a high degree by the ability to foresee a result before doing any calculations (colleagues in his applied work confirm that he frequently predicted even the value of numerical coefficients).

Sometimes, when struck with the ability of Sakharov to represent with extreme clarity the details of the behavior of an electron or a nucleon, it was hard to avoid the feeling that he could mentally transform himself into these particles, as if his very skin could feel what fell to their lot. Was it not a similar ability to transform himself that created the compassion which led Andrei Dmitrievich both to the defense of persecuted fighters for human rights and to the struggle for a better lot for our unfortunate people?

Closely connected with his physical intuition was the graphic nature of his thinking. We do not take it upon ourselves to state that Sakharov was characterized by symmetry between left-handed and right-handed brain activity, although we joked on just this subject, observing, spellbound, that during his lectures, having written a line, he transferred the chalk to his left hand and continued to write with the same ease. In any case, during our visits to Gorki, Sakharov, listening carefully to the news, continuously drew on sheets of paper (later stolen by me) various figures: moustached faces, sphinxes, and so forth. (See figure.) Perhaps these facts will mean something to psychologists.

Another distinctive feature of Sakharov, the scientist, was his scientific boldness. In fact, how else can we characterize his prophetic idea of proton decay which conflicted with the former picture of the microworld, or the hypothesis that during the evolution of the universe, the direction of time

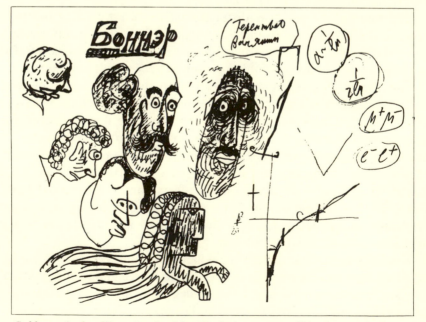

Sakharov's doodlings "stolen" by Kirzhnits on one of his visits to Gorki.

changed and a stage existed in which there was no motion (the Parmenides Universe in Sakharov's terminology)? Nevertheless, we will now surprise no one by associating the words *Sakharov* and *fearlessness*.

In conclusion, here are several anecdotes which I hope will give additional strokes to the portrait of Sakharov, the scientist. After hearing one of Sakharov's papers, a self-confident young theoretician approached him, clearly wishing to instruct him, and announced that one of the results could be obtained by a more rigorous method, that another one had already been obtained by Julian Schwinger, and so forth. Expecting that Sakharov would simply brush aside this critic, we were not a little surprised when, after the seminar, Andrei Dmitrievich went up to this not-too-tactful opponent and, sitting down with him, discussed the details of the paper for a long time. Apparently Sakharov felt that the young man was a specialist, and nothing else mattered.

Another episode occurred during my visit to Gorki, together with a colleague who was much younger and smaller than Sakharov. When we sat down at a table and began to work, Sakharov said "I seem to be cold; I will put on a jacket." On his return, I noticed that the jacket fitted Sakharov rather poorly. After several hours of concentrated work, as we were getting ready to leave, my colleague asked, "Andrei Dmitrievich, will you please return my jacket." During the discussion Sakharov had not felt any physical discomfort.

One more fact, which characterizes Sakharov as punctilious about crediting the work of others. It must be said that moral standards in this area are not too high: many people do not cite a work carried out independently and at nearly the same time, and almost no one does so if, in addition, the work contains errors. Here is an excerpt from Sakharov's letter sent from Gorki to A. D. Linde and me: "I read Vilenkin's article only the other day. I was not in a hurry, since Andrei [Linde] said that the article was erroneous. It turned out that the main idea of the author is the same as my main idea. . . . Even if the author makes a mistake in something later, this is not important. I therefore cited Vilenkin very seriously. . . ."

There is a legend that Sakharov's path in science was determined by an accidental meeting of Tamm with Sakharov's father—physicist D. I. Sakharov, who is supposed to have said: "Igor Evgenievich, I have a son Andrusha. Of course he is not 'N. N.' but nevertheless talk with him—he will make a passable physicist." Whether this is true or not, eventually Sakharov became a pupil of Tamm, and consequently as a theoretical physicist he belonged to the school of Mandelshtam and Tamm. Surprisingly (and perhaps not just surprisingly), Sakharov's personality corresponded somewhat to the scientific, human, and civil principles of this school, although in many respects he stepped far beyond its limits, putting these principles into practice.

Notes and References

1. Perhaps the best way to understand Sakharov's physical intuition is by analogy with the feat of the World War I Russian pilot K. K. Artseulov (A. D. agreed with the comparison after I told him this story). Artseulov risked his life checking his intuitive imagination about the mechanisms by which airplanes go into "spin" and emerge from it. He felt that he should do something absolutely opposite to that which follows from life-saving instinct and pilots' experience up to that time—that is, he should not resist the plane's deviations from the initial course (which usually lead to a spin) but, on the contrary, should increase them. Only in this way could one keep control of the plane during maneuvers that usually lead to the pilot's death. Artseulov was the first in the history of aviation who deliberately went into a spin and safely came out of it, creating the method which saved many pilots' lives later. Only after ten years did aerodynamicists prove the method to be scientifically based.

"Nothing Will Come of This, Andrei!"

I. S. Shklovskii

Fall of 1941: Evacuation to Ashkhabad[1]

Lying to my left on a wooden bed in the railway car was a twenty-year-old lad of a completely different cast of mind, who was taking almost no part in our fun and games. He was tall and thin, with deeply set eyes. His clothing suggested that he had been bounced around somewhat and had let himself slide a bit. You seldom heard a peep out of him. He did his rough and dirty work—of which there was quite a bit—quite diligently. It was clear from everything that a whirlwind had torn this boy from a family of the intelligentsia but hadn't managed to harm him. People like this were not rare in the train carrying us away from the war.

One day this boy came to me with a totally wild request: "Do you have anything about physics I could read?" He asked this deferentially of his "old comrade," that is, me. I have to explain that most of these lads used the familiar form of the word "you" in addressing me, so this request from my next-door neighbor phrased with the formal "you" made me smile.

My first instinct was to send this mama's boy with his absurd request on his way. "Get lost, you fool," I thought, but just before I spoke, a malicious thought came to my mind. I recalled that in fact my backpack contained a copy of Heitler's *The Quantum Theory of Radiation*, brought along in the course of a not altogether leisurely evacuation from Moscow on October 26, 1941.

I clearly remember buying, in April 1940, a copy of Heitler's monograph, which had just been translated into Russian, at a bookstore on Mokhovyi Street, near the entrance to an old building of Moscow State University. The book had tempted me with the possibility that I could immediately plunge into profound theory and thus be "in the know." Alas, I quickly realized I had bitten off more than I could chew: I could not get beyond the preface and the very beginning of the first paragraph (which discussed first-order processes). I recall the wind spilling from my sails: It was not for me to be a theoretical physicist after all! How was I to know at the time that the book was simply very difficult and furthermore was written in a very opaque style? And then why, after all that, had I stuffed it in my backpack?

I thought I was pulling a fast one on this boy in handing him a copy of Heitler. Almost at once I forgot about this strange youth, whom I unconsciously saw out of the corner of my eye from time to time. In the faint, flickering light from an oil lamp, amidst the wild songs and jolly story-telling, this lad lay quietly on his wooden bed and read.

It was just after arriving at Ashkhabad that I learned he had read my Heitler. "Thank you," he said, returning my book to me in its very loose black binding.

"Do you mean to say you're read it?" I asked hesitantly.

"Yes, and why do you ask?" I felt defeated and didn't answer. "This is a difficult book, but very profound and pithy. I am very grateful to you," he finished.

I was very upset. There I was, a graduate student, unable, try as I might, to wade through even the first paragraph of this cursed Heitler, while this *child*, in his third year of college, had not merely read it but had even worked through it. (I recall that while he had been reading it he had also been writing something.) And that's not all: He had accomplished this under (to put it mildly) extreme conditions![2]

However, the bitterness faded away quickly, and surprise took its place, because an absolutely fantastic, hungry but happy life, unlike anything else in the world, started to unfold for us in Ashkhabad. . . .

From time to time, I saw this lad who had struck my fancy, as ragged and hungry as the rest of us. I think he sometimes worked overtime as general help in the mess hall or, as we called it, the "soup-station" (by logical extension, Ashkhabad became the "soup-tropics," the guy standing in front of you in the soup line became a "soup-versive," and so on).[3]

In April of 1943 I returned from evacuation to Moscow (I was an early bird) and found the place totally empty. In late 1944, Nikolai Nikolaevich Piriiskii, an extremely kind man and my adviser in my graduate studies, also came back. We were happy to see each other: It had been three years, and such years! There were questions, big news, and small news. "And where is X? And where did the family of Y end up?" We must have talked about everybody.

However, everything has its end, and eventually (but not quickly) the list of our common friends and acquaintances was essentially exhausted. The conversation drifted to perhaps less urgent matters. Among other things, Piriiskii reported that Igor Evgenievich Tamm, an old friend of his, ". . . has acquired a totally unusual graduate student. There has been no one like him before. Not even V. L. [Ginzburg] could hold a candle to him!"

"What's his name?"

"Give me a second; let me think. The main thing . . . such a simple name, running around my head. . . . Damn! I've gone completely senile." That was vintage Nikolai Nikolaevich, famous in the world of astronomy for his legendary absent-mindedness.

I started thinking. The entire output of the Moscow State University physics faculty had spent the war years right in front of my eyes in the Ashkhabad echelon. Just where had this remarkable graduate student been hiding? Then it came to me in a flash: It had to be my next-door neighbor on the wooden beds in the shelter—the one who had shocked me by reading Heitler. "Is it Andrei Sakharov?" I asked Nikolai Nikolaevich.

"Oh, yes, yes; such a simple name, and it escapes me completely!"

I did not see Sakharov for twenty-four years after Ashkhabad. In 1966, on my fiftieth birthday as it happened, I was elected (on the fifth try) a corresponding member of the Soviet Academy of Sciences. At the first fall meeting of the Academy, Yakov Borisovich Zel'dovich asked me, "Would you like me to introduce you to Sakharov?"

Barely managing to elbow our way through the thickly packed hall, formerly the foyer of the House of Scientists, Zel'dovich presented me to Andrei. Andrei said, "We have known each other for a long time." I recognized him immediately; the only change was that the eyes were now set even deeper. Strangely, his bald spot did not detract at all from his aristocratic appearance.

In late May of 1971, on Andrei Dmitrievich's fiftieth birthday, I made him a gift of that copy of Heitler's *The Quantum Theory of Radiation*, which had somehow, miraculously, survived intact.

January of 1967 in the U.S.

It was already five after six when I entered the brightly lit and luxurious house of the eminent physicist known as the "father of the American hydrogen bomb." The elite of American science was present at this reception at Edward Teller's place. There were at least six Nobel laureates. To my great confusion, Teller pounced on me the instant I entered the place and tried to wring out of me what I thought about these mysterious quasars. He thus thrust me into the limelight, while all I wanted was to step into the wallpaper. This torture continued for at least a quarter of an hour.

I finally decided I had to somehow "unexpectedly" disengage myself from him. Steering the conversation completely away from the problem of quasars, I said, "And do you know, Dr. Teller, that a few years back your name was extremely popular in our country?" Teller was very interested. What I had in mind was the famous "special report" provocatively titled "The cannibal Teller" in the newspaper *Literaturnaya gazeta*. In attempting to recount the contents of this article for my host, I was mortified to discover that I had forgotten how to translate the Russian word for "cannibal" into English. The seconds ticked off as I tried to recall. Then I recalled that Teller was a Hungarian Jew, so his native language was German. I said "*Menschenfreser*."

"Oh!" moaned Teller with delight. "A cannibal! But how do you say it in Russian?"

"*Lyu-do-yed*," I said, syllable by syllable.

Teller pulled out a notebook and wrote down the easily pronounced Russian word. "Tomorrow I'm giving a lecture to some students in Berkeley, and I'll tell them that I am a *lyu-do-yed*!"

At that point I "castled myself" into a corner of the veranda, where I had time to think over Teller's reaction to this accusation of cannibalism.

Six years after this conversation with Teller, as I was lying in a bed in the hospital of the Academy of Sciences, I asked Andrei Dmitrievich Sakharov, who frequently visited my ward, whether he suffered from an "Eatherly complex."[4]

"Of course not," was the quiet answer from one of the most eminent humanitarians on our planet.

November of 1973 in the Hospital of the Soviet Academy of Sciences

Lying there in my private ward, I began to establish progressively better contact with the external world, thanks to my little Sony radio. For several hours a day, I listened to the various "enemy voices." At the time these voices were giving a lot of play to this person Andrei Dmitrievich Sakharov and his wife, whom I had known for a long time as "Lusia," although the first name on her passport was Elena. She was constantly being picked up for questioning by a certain comrade Malyarov, the public prosecutor. Each day, this academic couple reported all the difficulties of their complicated relations with the authorities to foreign journalists, so I was kept up-to-date.

One day, after hearing the latest installment of this news, I halfway dozed off. When some noise woke me up, I realized the lighting was different. I saw something I never would have expected. Standing beside my bed in the empty ward were this person himself, Academician Sakharov, and his wife! When it finally dawned on me that this was not a delusion, I was very happy indeed, to see this familiar couple whom I had known for so long. I immediately learned the reason for their appearance in the Academy hospital, and it was not a bad idea: to move into the hospital to escape from comrade Malyarov. So the evening before (Friday), they had dropped in on the doctor on duty in the reception room. One could, of course, feel sorry for this poor doctor; he had a *problem*. Ultimately, a consultation with the hospital management produced a Solomonic decision: The academician was to go into a private luxury ward (there would be no scrimping on cost—the law is the law!), while his wife would go into a common ward! Upset by this arbitrariness, the couple came to me, an "old timer" in the place (somehow they knew I was in the hospital), for advice on how to fight this mess.

"It's not necessary to hold a press conference," I said. "None of the directors will be around here except on regular working days. Be patient for two more days, and you'll be back together on Monday." And that's how it turned out.

My hospital life thus entered a new and very lively stage. In their rush to escape from comrade Malyarov, this couple, like the ancient Judeans fleeing from Egyptian captivity, forgot one vital thing. While those ancient Jews had forgotten yeast, the academic couple had forgotten a transistor radio. Accordingly, every evening after supper Andrei Dmitrievich, either alone or with his wife, visited me in the ward to listen to one of the "voices." It was touching to see them there, sitting beside my bed and listening to the radio, constantly holding hands. Not even newlyweds would sit like that.

As you can imagine, it was amusing to be there with them as they heard, courtesy of the BBC, that rumor had it that Academician Sakharov had been forced into the hospital, and that the progressive community in Moscow was seriously upset by this turn of events.

My hospital life became considerably more complicated because of these regular visits by Andrei and Lusia. All of a sudden, the number of visits to my ward by various guests increased dramatically. Many of these people I had not seen in years. Most of the visits were in the evening; the visitors had somehow learned at what time this famous wedded couple visited my ward. Often, as we were listening to the radio in the evening, the door would open unexpectedly, and in would walk some total stranger with an extremely unsympathetic physiognomy. My visitors told me that the outpatients—the main contingent in the Academy hospital—would sit along the entire corridor, waiting for Sakharov to visit me. Long before the academician and his wife proceeded through the corridor of my section to visit my ward, this contingent took the best seats (they were obliged to bring their own chairs) and waited patiently (everybody had plenty of time to spare) for the "phenomenon." As a result of this type of life, my mind filled with vivid impressions, and my blood pressure would jump twenty points during the evening rounds.

Despite all these complications, the nightly conversations with one of the most remarkable people of our time were immensely delightful. They were very rewarding for me, and they gave me a better understanding of this astonishing man. We talked a lot about science, about the ethics of a scientist, and about the climate in scientific research. I remember a remarkable sentence by Sakharov: "You astronomers are lucky people: A poetry of facts has been preserved for you!"

How true this was! and how profoundly he would have to understand the very heart of this field of knowledge, far from his own interests, in order to make such an appraisal of the situation!

I was struck by his scrupulous objectivity and his limitless good will in his comments about the eminent physicists who were his colleagues. These qualities and his kindness emerged particularly clearly during our conversations.

These conversations of course ran beyond the field of science. One day I asked him, "Do you believe that you can accomplish anything by your social activism in this country?"

Without pausing to think, he answered, "No."

"Then why do you go on this way?"

"I cannot do otherwise!" he answered. In general, he was a combination of an inflexible strength with a somewhat childlike spontaneity, kindness, and even naivete.

1972 in Moscow

My mind was on upcoming events. Another period of serious political trials was beginning. Two months earlier, in early February, I had happened by chance to catch Andrei Dmitrievich Sakharov, a day before my regular trip to Maleevka. He asked me to join him in signing a paper addressed to the public prosecutor of the USSR. This paper contained a request to learn the status of a certain Cronid Lubarsky, so that a study could be made of the possibility of getting him out on bail before his trial, because of his poor health. "Wait a minute—that will be my own fate!" I immediately said.

Andrei proved to me that we would be acting in strict adherence with the criminal-proceedings code. For some reason, there had to be two signatures "in the way that the spin of an electron can assume two orientations," the academician joked (not very pertinently). "One signature is mine, and the second will of course be yours; he is, after all, an astrophysicist—your own colleague!"

Just as they say, Andrei was a real expert on the law. I didn't know this Lyubarskii very well; he was involved at a semi-amateur level with the planets in G.A. Tikhov's Martian astrobotany sector in Alma-Ata. However, I would not be able to face myself in the mirror for the rest of my life if I did not add my signature to that of this highly respected man. Clearly understanding that I was putting myself in danger, I signed. (I simply could not do otherwise.)

"Nothing will come of this, Andrei!" I said.

"I think the same," he answered rather quietly. Neither before nor after this event did Andrei Dmitrievich ever come to me with a similar request.

Notes and References

1. Excerpts from *Éshelon* (evacuation train), an unpublished collection of family history.

2. Sakharov notes this story in his *Memoirs*, but writes that he recalls reading Heitler a year or so later (editor's note).

3. The Russian word for "soup" sounds nearly the same as the Russian version of the prefix "sub-" (translator's note).

4. Claude Eatherly, an American army major, was the pilot of the *Straight Flush*, a weather plane that escorted the *Enola Gay* in dropping the first atomic bomb on Hiroshima. Shortly after, this nervous major, consumed by guilt, went into a deep depression. He ended his days in a mental hospital.

"A Criminal Matter"

B. M. Bolotovskii

Institute of Atmospheric Physics, Moscow

In 1948, a few months after Andrei Dmitrievich Sakharov had joined a team of scientists (headed by Igor Evgenievich Tamm) working on the development of thermonuclear weapons, the infamous August session of the Academy of Agricultural Sciences was held in Moscow. Although Sakharov and Tamm were separated from the external world by their intense and supersecret work, events in biology which threatened a total devastation of the study of genetics could not have escaped their attention. One can say with complete confidence that Tamm's opinion on this matter was a decisive influence on the young Sakharov.

A few decades later, Andrei Dmitrievich recalled his years of working at the Installation as follows:

> After the working day, I would walk over to Igor Evgenievich's house, and we would have a heart-to-heart conversation. We spent three years with him in this fashion, and then he was allowed to return to science. That was the correct decision, since he was best fitted for the purpose. I remained at the Installation and the most dramatic developments lay ahead. I did not get to Moscow frequently, but whenever I did I visited Igor Evgenievich. We remained close, although I did evolve somewhat further as time elapsed.[1]

Sakharov was to go far further than Tamm as a social activist, but at the time Tamm was Sakharov's teacher in many ways.

For Tamm, biology was a familiar subject. He had been interested in science since his student days and possibly even from his years in secondary school. In 1918–20, he became a close friend of A. G. Gurevich, a famous researcher in the physiology of cell division, and became intensely interested in his work. Tamm was also interested in the problem of life from the standpoint of a physicist. In his recollections of Ya. I. Frenkel he mentions that during the years of joint work at Tavricheski (now Simferopol) University they had several discussions of the thermodynamics of living systems, with which Frenkel was involved at the time.

Learning of the session of the Academy of Agricultural Sciences, Tamm evaluated its results unambiguously. Since for Tamm it was a routine matter, in fact a need, to discuss all the more or less important news, there can be no doubt that in his conversations with Sakharov he went on at length about "Weissmann-Morganism" and "Michurinist biology."

This suggestion fits easily into Sakharov's account:

> In my opinion, one has every right to say that it was a very good fortune for all of us that Igor Evgenievich was there with us. Without him, much would have turned out differently; in our work, in the scientific arena, and at the psychological level. During the evening walk, Igor Evgenievich was our old comrade, a bit tired and on the quiet side, inhaling the moist forest smells, as we all were. Over a cup of tea, on the other hand, anything might be discussed. Igor Evgenievich told us a lot about his life and simply about what he knew and had heard (and he knew a great deal). At a blackboard in an office at work we would receive a lesson in methods of theoretical work. In a meeting with the management we obtained a lesson in ethical behavior in work matters, personal relations, and scientific ethics. In any setting, we received a lesson in conscientiousness, diligence, and thoughtfulness.[2]

History of a Legend

Recalling the first hydrogen bomb tests (in August of 1953), Sakharov related that no one foresaw precisely how all this would look. There were reasons to fear radioactive fallout, but the scientists didn't have much credibility. It required much courage and much work on the part of Tamm and Kurchatov to succeed in their effort to achieve an expensive evacuation of the population from the adjacent regions. As it later turned out, this evacuation was necessary.

After the successful tests, Tamm and Sakharov were decorated, and in the next election they became academicians. Tamm had been nominated earlier, but the matter had not reached the voting stage: His candidacy had been sidetracked by the all-powerful authorities, since he was regarded as politically unreliable. On this occasion he was elected, along with his former student.

In the shaping of Sakharov, however, a change was coming. "I once confided in Igor Evgenievich," recalled Sakharov, "how it was difficult, even torturous, for me to realize what an awesome affair we were involved with. He was very receptive to my words, although he did not expect to hear them. We were struck by the huge scale of the business we had been involved in."[3]

Great human and material resources were brought into the effort at the Installation. The understanding that the work was of colossal importance gave strength to the people carrying it out. Sakharov, however, developed some new concerns.

Many stories circulated about Sakharov at the Lebedev Physical Institute. Perceived as legends, it was later learned that most of them had some basis in reality. In the late 1950s I heard that two weeks before each test explosion Sakharov would allegedly lock himself in his office and calculate how many people on the earth would be crippled and disfigured as a result of the upcoming radioactive pollution of the atmosphere. (The explosions in question were set off fairly high above the ground.)

The details of this legend are unimportant. What is important is that it echoed real developments. In the second half of the 1950s, Sakharov made the transition from recognizing the danger which nuclear weapons posed to the human race, to attempting to evaluate this danger quantitatively. By that time, he was thus already fairly well acquainted with genetics.

He later wrote,

Starting in 1957 (and not without being influenced by opinions which were being expressed throughout the world on this matter by such people as Albert Schweitzer, Linus Pauling, and several others), I felt responsible for the problem of the radioactive fallout resulting from nuclear testing. We know that the absorption of radioactive products of nuclear explosions by the Earth's billions of inhabitants increases the frequency of several diseases and birth defects (because of so-called nonthreshold biological effects, e.g., effects resulting from damage to DNA molecules—the carriers of heredity). When radioactive explosion products enter the atmosphere, each megaton of explosive power means thousands of unknown victims. And each series of nuclear weapons tests (whether by the U.S., the USSR, Great Britain, China, or France is irrelevant) involves tens of megatons, i.e., tens of thousands of victims.[4]

After Stalin's death, the strict prohibition against genetics studies began to show cracks. This transition can be credited to both some liberalization of society and (in particular) an expansion of work on radioactive substances and the need to determine their effect on human heredity. Radiation genetics began to develop. Genetic laboratories opened up in several physics institutes. A biology seminar guided by Tamm was started at the Lebedev Institute. However, Lysenko and his adherents still held the high ground.

I recall Tamm saying in those days, "Geneticists now have the opportunity to work. They will not be persecuted any further. They will be accepted in jobs. They may themselves determine the topics of their research. Their results will be published. Many of them, however, cannot work today at full steam. They see as their primary task that of finally carrying out an appraisal based on scientific principles of all the messes that Lysenko and his followers have made."

And thus it turned out that Andrei Dmitrievich Sakharov was one of the first to offer an honest and merciless appraisal of the results of that infamous session of the Academy of Agricultural Sciences.

Elections to the Academy of Science were conducted in 1964. Lysenko nominated N. I. Nuzhdin, an extremely close colleague, for membership in the Academy. During the voting in the department of biology, Lysenko's majority swung into action. Nuzhdin survived this stage (there were four votes "for" and two "against"). Lying ahead was a confirmation vote at the general assembly of the Academy. It was there the battle took place. Actually, the attack went against Lysenko, rather than Nuzhdin. Andrei Dmitrievich took an active part in the "battle." Tamm also spoke. Based on his later comments about the incident, I wrote down the following account.

Tamm's Account

Vladimir Aleksandrovich Engelgardt came to me and said that Nuzhdin's candidacy had been put forward by the department of biology and that he had survived an election in that department in the Academy. Nuzhdin was against the science of genetics. The worst aspect of this was not a matter of scientific convictions but considerations of quite a different nature. I knew about this even before my conversation with Engelgardt. A biologist had told me about a meeting he had had with Nuzhdin shortly before the session of the Academy of Agricultural Sciences in August of 1948. Nuzhdin asked what this biologist (whose name I did not write down and have now forgotten) was presently working on. The biologist began to discuss his research on mutations in some living organism. Nuzhdin listened and listened, and then he put his hand on the other person's shoulder and said, "You bet on the wrong horse!" Do you see? He did not understand everything, but he knew that there was a prohibition against genetics.

I asked Engelgardt what could be done. He answered that it was necessary to speak out against Nuzhdin at the general assembly. I said that I could do that, but it would be a bit awkward for me if the biologists remained silent. If even one of them would speak up, then I also would be ready.

Engelgardt thought for a moment, but he did not yet reach a decision. Shortly before the meeting, Vladimir Aleksandrovich told me that he would speak out. I made my preparations, too.

I arrived at the hall. We came to the matter of seconding the candidates. The first to speak was the president of the Party group of the general assembly. He declared that the Party group had examined the results of the elections by the individual department and had decided to vote for all who had been selected. Oh dear, I thought, things are bad; Nuzhdin is going to get through. Nevertheless, I decided to speak my piece.

When, after a while, they came to Nuzhdin's name, Engelgardt spoke out. Then Andrei Dmitrievich did the same. I also said something. My words were very brief, and none of them were sharp. I said that it was in the interest of the state that the stage be set for the unrestricted development of biological science. In particular, it was necessary to support in every possible way those people who would develop biology, and to combat those who would obstruct that development. On the basis of both goals, I would vote against Nuzhdin. The discussion warmed up. The end result was that Nuzhdin was rejected by an overwhelming majority of the votes.

After the voting, participants of the meeting walked over, squeezed my hand, and thanked me for speaking. I said to one of them, "You are a member of the Party group. How could you have decided beforehand to vote for every candidate who was selected by his department?"

The answer was "We did not know then what we know now. I thank you for your speech."

Excerpts From Syrovatskii's Words

I heard more details about the same confrontation from Sergei Ivanovich Syrovatskii, who has now passed away. At the time he was working in the theoretical department of the Lebedev Institute. He was also present at this meeting, and he has described it very colorfully.

Engelgardt spoke first. His words ran roughly as follows: In recent years, not a single paper by Nuzhdin has been published in a journal. There have been no references to his work in papers by other authors. No one has thanked him for his advice or for discussions. The meaning here is that he himself has not been working, he has had no students; and he has had no influence on the development of science. In addition, he defended a doctoral dissertation on formal genetics, but he was selected as a corresponding member of the Academy for work on Michurinist biology. He is apparently being promoted into the Academy on the basis of these mutually exclusive works. Engelgardt announced that on the basis of these considerations, he was going to vote against Nuzhdin.

It was then Sakharov's turn to speak. Syrovatskii related the contents of his speech fairly accurately. We will use the text reproduced from the stenographer's notes.

> I will be very brief [said Andrei Dmitrievich]. We all recognize—we all know—that the scientific reputation of an academician of the Soviet Academy of Sciences must be irreproachable. In discussing Nuzhdin's candidacy, we must therefore take a very careful look at this question. In the document which has been furnished us there are the following words:
>
> "N.I. Nuzhdin devotes much attention to such questions as the struggle against anti-Michurinist perversions in biological science, constantly criticizing various idealistic theories in the field of heredity and variability. His general philosophical works associated with the further development of the materialistic studies of I. V. Michurin and other leading figures in biological science are widely known not only in our own country but also in other countries."
>
> The matter of scientific concern of each of those academicians who will vote, as you can see, is what actual content is concealed behind this struggle with anti-Michurinist perversions, the philosophical works of other leading figures in biological science, and so forth. I will not read this quotation a second time.
>
> As far as I am concerned, I call upon all the academicians present here to vote in such a way that the only ballots marked "for" are the ballots of those people who, along with Nuzhdin, and along with Lysenko, bear the responsibility for those shameful and difficult pages in the development of Soviet science which are now, fortunately, coming to an end. [Applause.]

Interestingly, Syrovatskii's account is slightly at odds with the stenographer's notes. In particular, he said—I remember this quite well—that Sakharov mentioned in his speech the thousands of geneticists who were dismissed after the infamous 1948 session of the Academy of Agricultural Sciences and that many of them had been persecuted. According to Syrovatskii, Sakharov ended his speech by saying, "Let those who vote for Nuzhdin be those whose hands are dripping with the blood of Soviet biology."

These words are not in the stenographer's notes. One might suspect that the notes have been toned down. Sakharov's sharpest words are not there. There is also indirect evidence for this conclusion in Tamm's account, which stressed several times that he (Tamm) "was speaking properly." At the time I did not understand why Tamm made a point of stressing this. Further confirmation is a direct quote from Sakharov himself, from a meeting on June 8, 1988, with B. L. Altshuler: "The stenographer's notes of my speech do not contain the sentences which decode the substance of the shameful, difficult pages in the development of Soviet science, namely, the disintegration of Soviet genetics and the physical extermination of scientists."

Andrei Dmitrievich has also said that he did not know about Tamm's understanding with Engelgardt and that he spoke independently, on his own initiative.

When Sakharov finished, Lysenko requested the opportunity to speak from where he sat. The person presiding over the meeting (M. V. Keldysh, president of the Soviet Academy of Sciences) responded that Tamm was next on the list, and then Lysenko would speak.

We know what Tamm had to say. However, Syrovatskii mentions a curious detail in his account. When Sakharov returned to his seat he noted that he was sitting not far from Lysenko. Up to that point, he did not know the latter's face. While Tamm was speaking, and Lysenko was waiting his turn, the latter uttered the words "a criminal matter" several times, while nervously rubbing his hands.

Mounting the rostrum, Lysenko called Sakharov's words slander and then repeated this accusation several times, in a variety of ways. He demanded that the president and the presidium spell out their attitude toward Sakharov's speech. Keldysh first stated that the presidium was not responsible for Sakharov's opinion. Lysenko, however, was not satisfied with that answer. Keldysh then said that he did not share Sakharov's opinion and that he furthermore thought that Sakharov's opinion was not shared by the presidium. It was plain that Keldysh was afraid of Lysenko and also that Lysenko remained unsatisfied with Keldysh.

Next to speak was Ya. B. Zel'dovich. For this occasion he was wearing all three of his Hero stars. He was wearing a simple-minded, foolish look on his face (managing that could not have been easy). He said that he, no expert in biology, was obliged to reach conclusions on the basis of the debate that had occurred. Three people had spoken against confirming Nuzhdin's candidacy: Engelgardt, Sakharov, and Tamm. They had expressed several objections which led them to plan to vote against the confirmation. Lysenko had spoken in Nuzhdin's defense. His actual words, however, were primarily a criticism of Sakharov, and they did not answer the objections which had been raised against Nuzhdin. Zel'dovich emphasized that all these objections remained unanswered. He announced that he would therefore vote against Nuzhdin.

Zel'dovich's speech was accompanied by cries from the audience: "All is clear!", "There is no need for further discussion!", and so on.

Nuzhdin was rejected. The results of the vote were as follows: Of the 137 academicians participating, twenty-three voted "for," and the rest voted "against." Since the Party group of the general assembly contained some eighty to ninety people, that group must have voted against its own decision.

It is the general opinion that Sakharov's speech played a decisive role. This was the first time he had spoken out on a matter of civic responsibility. That speech can be labeled the beginning of the open struggle against the trampling of truth, honor, and conscience. The speech was remarkable in another way, also. "That was the first occasion," he recalled, "on which my name appeared in the Soviet press, in a paper by the president of the Academy of Agricultural Sciences, which contained totally shameless attacks on me."[5] However, Andrei Dmitrievich was to see that those were in fact not the most shameless attacks. I conclude with two letters by Sakharov:

To the Editor of *Izvestiya*:

Being a regular reader of *Izvestiya*, I'll mention a paper by Olshanskii which was published in the newspaper *Selskaya zhizn* ("Country Life") on August 29, 1964. Olshanskii's paper contained some intolerable distortions of the truth, not only regarding me personally but also regarding fundamental questions of the development of Soviet science. The latter circumstance requires the publication in the Soviet press of information which clarifies the matter. I recommend the publication of a paper by the well-known geneticist and scientist V. P. Efroimson, who is also mentioned in the paper by Olshanskii.

A few words are in order about my own attitude toward biological science. By education I am a theoretical physicist, a student of Academician I. E. Tamm. I was Tamm's student in more than matters of science. For sixteen years I worked in a large group of people who devoted themselves in a vital way to technological questions of importance to our country. We were all deeply convinced that for a scientist there is nothing more important than absolute scientific and professional objectivity. Personal interests, the scientific environment, and the work on problems concerning the effect of nuclear explosions on the health of people (two papers were published) brought me to know the situation in biological science well. The situation there differs tragically from that in the physicotechnical and mathematical sciences.

In the 1930s a pseudo-scientific group arose, and in 1948 took its final form. By means of demagoguery, falsification of facts, false promises, political provocation, intimidation, and repression, that group captured key posts in Soviet biology. Unfortunately, we must recognize that that group, which arose during the years of the cult of personality, sank its roots so deep into all the most important party and state organizations that its existence, although based on fraud, continued for many years after the Twentieth Party

Congress, causing a huge amount of damage to our agriculture, to our medical care, and to our international standing.

This group works under the fraudulent banner of Michurinist biology, but it is actually an unprincipled alliance, based on career ambitions and various forms of pressure, around Lysenko, and for this reason it is known as "Lysenkoism."

Here are the characteristics of Lysenkoism:

1. Scientific bankruptcy. In the century of the successes of chemical genetics, which promise unprecedented mastery of living nature, Lysenkoism is steering Soviet science away from Darwinism toward the idealistic views of de Lamarck. There are innumerable anecdotal comments in the "works" of Lysenko and his followers. Dozens of them have obtained lifelong financial support from the highest certification commission, e.g., for work on the spontaneous transformation of species under the influence of the environment.

2. Political provocation and false information at all levels, including the Central Committee of the Communist Party of the Soviet Union. . . .

3. Economic adventurism (discussed in detail in the paper by Efroimson), which has cost us billions.

4. Destruction of the system for training scientific cadre, scientific traditions, and scientific propaganda. Even the ninth grade textbook is permeated with Lysenkoism.

5. The absence of an opportunity for people with unorthodox views to perform fruitful labor. Incidentally, this situation has the consequence that many people who are less courageous but still capable (some of them were named Olshanskii) serve as false advertising for the group, without sharing its methods. *However, the primary consequence of this circumstance is that Soviet science is lagging intolerably far behind, with a huge economic loss and a huge loss in morale.*

All these points can be verified in the voluminous documentary and scientific record.

Knowing all these facts, I do not believe I have the right to remain silent. I add my voice to the voices of those honest Soviet biological scientists who are struggling for the triumph of scientific truth in the interests of our native land.

A. Sakharov

Dear Nikita Sergeevich [Khrushchev]:

The mention of my name at the plenum of the Central Committee of the Communist Party of the Soviet Union gives me the courage to write you with some explanation.

I have recently been accused of slander (by an "offended" Lysenko) and incompetence.

First, the "incompetence": The most advanced ideas of the exact sciences are now increasingly making their presence felt in biology, and a physicist who follows the Soviet and foreign popular-science literature in the field of biology is perhaps in a better position than a specialist with narrower interests. The author of this letter has been forced to deal with the problem of radiation genetics at a higher than purely speculative level. I am quite familiar with the tragically abnormal situation in Soviet biology, and I cannot remain quiet about it. It does not require any great expertise—simply general skills of scientific practice—to distinguish between a creative scientific theory (the chromosomal biochemical theory of heredity) and a futile babbling about the effect of the environment, interspecies mutual assistance, the spontaneous transformation of oats into wild oats, etc. . . . There is even less need for specialized knowledge in order to distinguish honest scientists from falsifiers and demagogues.

Now the "slander": All I said was that Lysenko bears the responsibility for the darkest and most disgraceful period in the history of Soviet science (that is only a tiny bit of what I *might* say about him). The fact that 114 academicians (out of 137) voted against the candidacy of Lysenko's "faithful companion" N. I. Nuzhdin showed that this accusation did not shock anyone. The speeches by academicians Engelgardt and Tamm and my own were met with applause. For 114 academicians, the question is thus clear.

On the whole, however, the legs of our science are still hobbled by Lysenkoism. . . .

We are aware of the huge practical successes of genetics—the raising of new strains of animals and plants in the realm of hybrid varieties and strains, the raising of new and productive microorganisms for industrial microbiology by methods of radiogenetics, etc.—in other countries. There can be no doubt that we would have had similar successes except for Lysenkoism.

1. The volume of the work being carried out in the field of molecular biology, i.e., the most important theoretical research, is shamefully low. Lacking staff, equipment, reagents, and money, we are braided up in the tail of world science, and this creates the threat of lagging behind by a catastrophic distance. The situation is even worse in those fields of science which are generating practical results even today.

2. All the key positions which bring the opportunity to carry out expensive experiments or to convert experimental results to practical use, all the agricultural experimental stations, and most of the scientific institutions pertinent to practical matters are under the control of the Lysenkoites.

I accordingly ask for your attention to the interesting manuscript by comrade Zh. Medvedev, which is based on a study of a large amount of documentary evidence. . . .

In their day, Ioffe, Kurchatov, Mandelshtam, and S. I. Vavilov assumed personal responsibility for entire branches of physics. A leader of this rank in the biological sciences is N. I. Vavilov, a great scientist and a patriot of our native land. . . . His death, the death of dozens of other leading scientists, and the dismissal of thousands of honest scientists constitute an indelible blot on Lysenkoism. Over nearly thirty years, our youth have been educated in a disorganized way, and this damage is not going to be undone in a flash. . . . The economic adventurism of the irresponsible phony scientists has caused a huge amount of harm to our country (vernalization, sowing seeds in stubble, dogmatic grassland agriculture on a country-wide scale, the cluster planting of forests, and much else). All these "great discoveries" were achieved on the basis of falsified experiments and demagoguery and failures have been forgiven: Lysenko was quite at home in the leadership. Many important undertakings were held up if they ran contrary to dogma (hybrid corn based on self-pollinating lines, studies of the artificial multiple propagation of oats, studies of mutagenic substances, studies in medical genetics, and much more). Lysenko and his adherents, who have made their way into many key posts in the party and state organs, constitute a group from which no scientific objectivity can be expected, since scientific objectivity works against the self-preservation of that group. The demagoguery of Lysenkoism does not fool anyone who knows its shameful history. Unfortunately, in the press we are still running into barriers to an open discussion of questions concerning the history of biological science in the USSR. Even many leading party workers do not know this history. However, I am convinced that the general improvement of the political health of our country means the certain and early end to Lysenkoism.

A. Sakharov

Notes and References

1. An interview with A. D. Sakharov by the newspaper *Molodezh' Estonii* on October 11, 1988.

2. From A. D. Sakharov's manuscript entitled "Memories of I. E. Tamm." E. G. Bonner has the original.

3. An interview with A. D. Sakharov by the newspaper *Molodezh' Estonii* on October 11, 1988.

4. A. D. Sakharov, *Peace, Progress, and Human Rights: Articles and Speeches* [in Russian], Leningrad 1990, p. 5.

5. *Ibid.* page 7. Andrei Dmitrievitch had in mind M. Olshanskii's article "Against Disinformation and Slander" in the newspaper *Country Life*, August 29, 1964. In this article, among other things, is the following passage: "At one of the meetings of the Soviet Academy of Sciences, Academician Sakharov, engineer by profession, made an abusive, nonscientific attack against scientist-Michurinists in the style of anonymous, slanderous letters."

Three Episodes

Lev B. Okun

Institute of Theoretical and Experimental Physics, Moscow

November 1974

An international seminar titled "Partons and Quarks" was being held at the Moscow House of Scientists. During a break between reports, I talked with Andrei Dmitrievich Sakharov about a paper which M. B. Voloshin, I. Yu. Kobzarev, and I had submitted to a journal. The basic idea of the paper was that a vacuum can be unstable. For example, in our world a vacuum is capable of converting spontaneously into another, stabler state through a quantum-mechanical tunneling in which a microscopic bubble is formed. Inside this bubble there is a new vacuum; the old one is outside it. Once born, this bubble will begin to expand rapidly; its envelope, of super nuclear density, will acquire a velocity approaching the velocity of light, and then our entire universe will be destroyed completely.

When I first had the thought that such a bubble might be produced at a particle accelerator in which a particle beam was colliding with a target or another beam, shivers ran up my spine.

At this point Andrei Dmitrievich interrupted me: "Such theoretical studies must be forbidden."

I objected that accelerators would go on working regardless of such theoretical work. Furthermore, I said that if the universe had indeed an unstable vacuum at some time then it would have been replaced long ago by a stable one, because all possible collisions occurred in the universe in its infancy.

"But at the time no one was slamming lead nuclei into each other," retorted Sakharov. This conversation occurred in the White Room of the House of Scientists, under the portrait of its first director, N. F. Andreeva.

July 21, 1976

A ceremonial dinner was being held in the Aragvi restaurant in Tbilisi for participants of the International Conference on High-Energy Physics (this was Conference XVIII in the series of so-called Rochester Conferences). There were many long tables. At one of them, I found myself close to Andrei Dmitrievich. The general conversation was switching direction in a random fashion. At one point it turned to problems of quick-wittedness. It was then that I suggested to Andrei Dmitrievich the problem of a beetle on an ideal rubber band.

One end of a rubber band one kilometer long is attached to a wall, and you are holding the other end in your hand. A beetle begins to crawl along this rubber band from the wall toward you, at a velocity of one centimeter per second. While it is crawling the first centimeter, you stretch out the rubber band by one kilometer; while it is crawling the second centimeter, you stretch the rubber band out another kilometer; and so on, each second. The question is, does the beetle manage to crawl all the way to you, and if so, then how long does it take?

I have posed the same problem to various people both before and after that evening. It took one person about an hour to solve it, it took another person a day, and a third remained firmly convinced that the beetle would not manage to creep all the way and claimed that the question about the time was simply a red herring.

Andrei Dmitrievich asked for a repetition of the problem and requested a piece of paper. I gave him my written invitation to the banquet, and he wrote out the solution of the problem on the back of the envelope, then and there, without comment. The total elapsed time was about a minute.

May 23, 1978

An International Seminar on Gauge Field Theories was being held in the conference room of the Institute of Control Problems, Soviet Academy of Sciences, on Profsoyuznaya Street in Moscow. Only two or three foreign participants had shown up. Most of the people who had been invited declined to come because of the prosecution of dissidents and, especially,

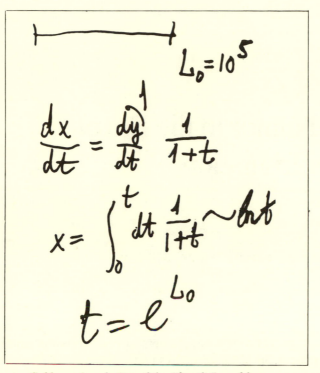

$$\vdash\!\!-\!\!-\!\!-\!\!-\!\!-\!\!\dashv \quad L_0 = 10^5$$

$$\frac{dx}{dt} = \frac{dy}{dt}^1 \frac{1}{1+t}$$

$$x = \int_0^t dt \frac{1}{1+t} \sim \ell n t$$

$$t = e^{L_0}$$

Sakharov's solution of the "beetle" problem.

to protest the arrest of Yu. F. Orlov in February 1977. A boycott had begun and was to continue for many years; it eventually became nearly global after our armed forces invaded Afghanistan, and A. D. Sakharov was banished to Gorki.

About ten minutes before the beginning of the session, Andrei Dmitrievich walked up to a blackboard at the rostrum. Forming the letters very carefully, he wrote approximately the following words: We thank all those people who, by virtue of their absence from this seminar, have expressed solidarity with and support of our struggle for freedom. (I remember the meaning well, but I cannot guarantee an exact quote.)

This inscription lasted about five minutes. Someone I did not know walked up to the blackboard and erased everything thoroughly. Glistening moist streaks remained on the blackboard.

Sad Humor in the Era of "Confrontation"

G. A. ASKARYAN

Institute of General Physics, Moscow

To MY DEEP REGRET I had few direct scientific contacts with Andrei Dmitriev-ich (or, as I am more accustomed to saying, "A. D."). There were only two or three brief discussions (back in the 1970s) of using explosions to cause an extreme compression of magnetic fields for application to laser bursts for controlled fusion. There was also a preliminary attempt to discuss with him the ecologically harmful consequences of discharges in the strato-sphere (1988). I remember being struck by how quickly he would immerse himself in the subject and how critical his reasoning was. I came to believe that A. D. was keen for a well-reasoned confrontation in a scientific dis-pute. At any rate, I sensed at once the nontriviality and strength of his logic.

Working at the time at the Lebedev Physical Institute in Moscow, I had the opportunity to observe A. D.'s behavior over many difficult years, how the people around him regarded him, and his indulgence for the frailties of human nature. In the sketches below I attempt to reproduce the atmosphere of well-meant but sad humor with which A. D. and my colleagues attempted to reduce or relieve the tension of our situation.

Birthday Congratulations

This was the period during which Sakharov's confrontation began: his words had been broadcast throughout the country by the western radio networks. A frenzied criticism took place in our press, with accusations of anti-Soviet propaganda.

At a seminar of the theoretical department organized to celebrate his birthday, we congratulated him and gave him a radio receiver as a gift. A. D. thanked us with some embarrassment and added, "Admittedly, many people think a radio *transmitter* would be more fitting."

A Most Grateful Audience

We are standing near the entrance to the courtyard of the Lebedev Institute. A taxi drives up with A. D., but he does not climb out; he sits there explaining something to the driver, with the meter running. We time him: forty minutes. Finally, A. D. completes his lecture. The driver turns the meter off and his green light turns on. A. D., having noticed the meter in horror, pays the driver off and climbs out. We greet each other. Some deep thinker points out that the meter might have been turned off.

"I now understand why he showed so much interest in my theory of convergence," A. D. answers with a smile.

In a World of His Own

At a seminar celebrating the birthday of V. L. Ginzburg, D. A. Kirzhnits gives a humorous speech in which he points out to the audience that tens of kilotons of paper had been expended on the papers and books of the prolific V. L. Ginzburg. This expenditure required the annihilation of thousands of hectares of forests.

Thinking about something of his own, A. D. objects, "That much forest could not perish as a result of ten kilotons."

Nothing Should Be Lost in the Economy

After the seminar, A. D. leaves the Lebedev Institute, accompanied by a crowd of Institute people. A Volga belonging to the Academy drives up to the gate. Behind it is a second car. (An escort? Someone tailing him? A bodyguard? At that time, contacts with A. D. were being monitored and severed.) A. D. gets into the first car and offers a lift. "If there's not enough room for everybody, the rest can get in the second car," he adds, gesturing at the "escort" car. Inside the second car, a Tweedledum and a Tweedledee are sullenly looking back out. A silent scene.

A few more sketches will illuminate the behavior of the others on the staff of the Institute regarding A.D.

B. M. Bolotovskii, the Party organizer in the theoretical department, and the man whom the Party committee had assigned to "oppose" A. D., explained the ineffectiveness of his mission to the committee in the following way: "A. D. talks to me all the time; everything sounds logical, and I cannot muster equally weighty arguments to throw back at him. After all, he's a full academician, and I'm a simple professor. But if you were to make me a member of the Academy, my voice would have vastly more authority."

I'd like to point out that even in the most difficult years the scientific references to papers by A. D. were not cut out, at least from my own papers.

In the years of a "sharpening opposition," when A. D. announced a hunger strike in protest, a birthday party was held for P. L. Kapitza. I took part in a skit and read an alleged letter from the director of the Tretyakovka gallery, proposing the organization of an exhibition of pictures with an admission fee. In Tretyakovka, Academician Kapitza will display Kustodiev's picture "Young Kapitza and Young Semenov beside Home Still" from his personal collection, while in the presidium of the Academy of Sciences Tretyakovka will exhibit Shishkin's picture "Oak Trees in the Sun" and Surikov's "Boyarina Morozova."[1] Understanding the subtle allusion, the listeners lost all interest in me, but after the next sentence — "The earnings will go into a fund to assist the families of academicians on hunger strikes" — the storm of applause in the overcrowded room of the Institute of Physical Problems merged with the happy remarks of P. L. Kapitza himself.

At the V. L. Ginzburg birthday seminar I read what was supposedly an encyclical from the Pope in Rome which had been broadcast over Western radio. The encyclical spoke of the immense importance of Ginzburg and his seminar in bringing the faithful peasants together. The encyclical ended with the following sentence about this Great Physicist: "And Andrei the First strikes with his sword the multiple-warhead missiles of the evil Serpent and saves the Russian land from its foes."

I will not forget how considerate A. D. was of the people around him. When the persecution reached full swing, and access to him was restricted and monitored, A. D. stopped greeting many people in order to avoid tainting them with "political corruption." Actually, I was offended when he began ignoring me. When he returned from Gorki, however, he again acknowledged all his old acquaintances.

All these fragments of a large mirror of memory, broken by time, do not relieve our growing sense of guilt: We were not able to help this eminent man in any meaningful way, since we were tangled up in the threads of apparent material well-being and our duty to our families and relatives— threads which could easily have been ripped off. We thus tried to convince ourselves that A. D. was a Don Quixote, that he was not a politician, that he believed in castles in the air and the unity of mankind, and that it was easy for him to behave that way because of his special position and major services. And then he turns out to have been a prophet, a messiah, a strategist for humanitarianism; and he passed through our life nearly in solitude, with a sad smile, awkward, tongue-tied, but with head unbowed. That was the way heroes went to the scaffold.

And I am beginning to understand that our jokes were for us merely a simulation of support, in a nearly safe (for us) form. He understood this game and in fact sometimes participated in it, but also (or only) for us. He did this so that we would not be as bitter and ashamed of our own noninvolvement in his great enterprise.

Notes and References

1. The picture of Kapitza and Semenov is well known, and shows a chemical apparatus in the background. The title here humorously suggests the two are operating an illicit still. The allusion to oak trees suggests Sakharov's own strength, like a mighty oak. Morosova, a Boyar or member of the upper Russian nobility, was sent into exile by the tzar for her religious opposition. The analogy is to Sakharov's own exile to Gorki.

From the Contributions to the Sakharov Readings: Gorki, January 27, 1990

A. V. Gaponov-Grekhov

Institute of Applied Physics, Gorki

M. L. Levin

Moscow Radiotechnical Institute

THE OPENING of the Sakharov Readings in Gorki brought mixed feelings to me, and possibly many of us.

There was a sense of shame for the role which was assigned to our city in the life of this great person and for the fact that our city indeed played this role. Then there was a sense of guilt for the alienation and rejection to which Andrei Dmitrievich was subjected for many agonizing years. There was also a sense of limitless surprise and delight in his entire life, which was rich with creativity, successes, and struggle, while at the same time clear, pure, and to the very end devoted to humanity. Finally, we cannot help making a comparison with the sad fate of many talented Russians who went without recognition and were persecuted in their own strange Native Land in a troubled, dangerous time.

I did not know Andrei Dmitrievich well at all; we probably crossed paths no more than ten times over two decades. Each meeting left in my memory those features of this remarkable personality which (as we later recognized) turn out to be completely nontrivial. Even our first conversation revealed his tolerance and benevolence, with the strictest sense of ethical behavior. This was, I recall, in 1972, when he prepared two letters of appeal to the government: one requesting amnesty for political prisoners and another requesting abolition of the death penalty. When we met, he asked me to sign these appeals. I signed the one about amnesty, but not the one for the abolition of the death penalty. Today, I probably would sign both—not because of my increased respect for Sakharov but simply because my views have changed. It seemed to me at the time that the abolition of the death penalty was premature. Andrei Dmitrievich did not try to discuss the matter with me and change my mind; he instead listened to my opinion with respect and tolerance. Far later, I would see the true merits of his behavior.

I am convinced that it is difficult or, more likely, simply impossible to pigeonhole him in one of the usual human categories. People—I am thinking primarily of strong and talented people—usually show their worth in one of three arenas: their creative work, their practical work, or their organizational and community life (politics). It is possible that this definition is not totally correct, and the idea might be expressed more precisely and more correctly. However, in a nutshell, all people can be put in one of the three categories: creators, builders, or fighters. These fundamentally different qualities are never combined in a single person: Some people wage revolutions, others build, and yet others sit in ivory towers and create. It is rare to find, even among the greatest people, individuals who have managed to achieve equal or comparable successes in even two of these three areas of human activity.

The absolutely exceptional nature of Andrei Dmitrievich lies in his equal greatness in all fields: as scientist, engineer, and public figure. His importance is so much greater than the capabilities of a single person that one involuntarily thinks of the analogy with Pushkin—who "stood on good and evil," in the words of Sinyavskii—with his uncompromising nature but also with his infinite patience and kindness.

However, Andrei Dmitrievich's premature death evoked deep feelings throughout the country. He held close to his heart the fate of our people, the fate of all mankind, and the fate of each individual person.

We will not waste time weighing each aspect of his activity. Perhaps the main thing is that we, having known him and having lived beside him, will always remember the following: In a difficult time for our people—a time of the triumph of mediocrity, conformity, and stagnation—he set for us the standard of a person who combined absolute honesty, supreme intellect, and complete fearlessness. These are the qualities which provide true spiritual freedom.

A. V. Gaponov-Grekhov

THE ONLY JUSTIFICATION for putting my speech at the beginning of these readings is that I am the only person sitting in this room who knew Andrei Dmitrievich from his youth.

There's more. Among those present here, I seem to be the only physicist who visited him not on a matter of work, and not on an errand for an institute, but simply on my own, over the seven years he spent in Gorki. Perhaps I thus saw him in, so to speak, a free state, unencumbered by formal restrictions.

Great people are not born often. When Mayakovskii died, some mistakes were made at the funeral, and a militiaman soothed the writers: Don't be upset; next time, everything will be done right. He did not know that great poets are not born and do not die all that frequently.

I'll begin with the young years of Andrei Dmitrievich, but I would like to say at the outset that there is the danger of mythmaking here. In fact, this mythmaking began while he was alive, and it continues after his death. I do not want to be part of it. It is of course a very simple matter to create a myth about a young genius who was recognized as such by everybody from the outset. There is also the possibility of going to the other extreme and saying that he was a total dunce as a youth who at some later time suddenly became a remarkable scientist.

He was neither a dunce nor the most brilliant student in our class. Both teachers and students quickly came to recognize his unusual strength, but they did not understand him and his way of reasoning. They also did not understand that his "logical steps" were much broader than those of ordinary people. Later, when (as a grown man) I was reading about the outstanding mathematicians Galois and Ramunujan, who were not understood by their contemporaries, I compared them with Andrei Dmitrievich in a way. His position with respect to us—and we had a strong class—was roughly the same as yours and mine with respect to that of a philosopher who is accustomed to reasoning in accordance with the laws of formal logic. For example, the sentence "Peter is mortal" is obvious for us, while a philosopher needs "steps": Peter is a human. Humans are mortal. Peter is thus mortal.

There's another myth I wouldn't like to see created: that Sakharov regarded me as a close friend. I was not that, and it is my impression that in neither his young years nor his middle years did he have any other close friends. He had his comrades at work, and, in his later years, his comrades in his great pursuit, but I know of only a single genuinely close friend that he had: his wife.

I was to him his "old university pal" (this very precise definition is that of Sakharov himself, who stated it to a KGB representative whom we bumped into during our first meeting on the streets of Gorki). Actually, this is not a trifle, because each loves his youth. University friends bear the imprint of this. I do not wish to compare him with the *lycée* students of the previous century, but there is some similarity. I think it was this relationship which explains the happiness which I had the good fortune to bring him by means of my visits: We met four times in Gorki, and there was some sensation of a restored youth on those occasions.

Let me go back to where I began. Andrei Dmitrievich was indeed difficult to understand, and he remained so for a very long time during his university years. His results and conclusions were always correct. He solved the problems correctly, and he gave the correct answers to questions, but he was difficult to understand. Things went on this way for a long time. However, when we met again after a long time apart (we studied together three years before World War II and then met after the Twentieth Party Congress), I immediately noted that he was expressing his thoughts clearly. He explained: "Yes, I have learned. I have been obliged to deal with bosses in generals' uniforms and to explain things to them. I have learned to speak their language."

They sometimes write in the newspapers that he was inarticulate. That is not correct. He did seem "inarticulate" in his youth, but that was not an actual inarticulateness. It was a consequence of the overly long leaps that he made in his arguments, while other people could not keep up the pace.

I can cite another example: When we met and I was introduced to his first wife, Klavdia Alekseyevna, she told me with some pride that they had met during the war and that she was perhaps the only woman in the country who had been proposed to in writing. He wrote not because he was shy but simply because otherwise she wouldn't have known what he was talking about.

Later on, he learned to speak, and I don't think one could ask for much more in terms of clarity of exposition.

Now about Gorki. For me the entire history of Andrei's stay in this city is an open wound. When he was sent to Gorki ten years ago, everyone was upset. In my own case, however, it was something of a relief to hear that it would be specifically Gorki: I love this city very much. I spent six years of my life here, and my initial situation was also complicated. I arrived in Gorki with the right to teach in a university and to live in a village on the opposite bank of the Volga. Although times were hard and rough, things were very good for me in Gorki. I had a sense of freedom after Butyrka prison. Friends and students appeared, and I am left with very bright impressions of life in Gorki, with the external distress put aside. I therefore thought that specifically in Gorki, where so many outstanding physicists and so many genuine people live, that things would be quite good for him.

I do not know just how this happened, but on the day he was exiled, January 22, 1980, by a surprising coincidence (I think this was pure chance), a note about the ninety-fifth anniversary of the beginning of Korolenko's exile in Gorki[1] appeared in the newspaper *Gorkovskii rabochii*.[2] The article related how Korolenko had been brought here in 1885, after a long exile in Yakutia, and how he had been greeted by Gorki.

When Korolenko turned up in Gorki the intelligentsia immediately began to group around him. Here there was no university, there was no polytechnical institute, and there were no academic institutes. There were college-preparatory high schools, a religious seminary, clerks, physicians, and lawyers. A small group of intellectuals immediately formed around Korolenko. This story is told best by the writer Maksim Gorki, who obtained Korolenko's blessings specifically in the city of Gorki. His words are in the note. Their meaning is that one can speak of a "Korolenko epoch" in Gorki. I cannot swear that the quote is exact; it may have instead been a "Korolenko era" in the history of Gorki. I do, however, wish to make the following point: The year was 1885, four years after the assassination of Aleksandr II and three years before the last failed attempt on Aleksandr III's life, so you can get an idea of what the atmosphere in the country was. In the midst of all that it was the "Korolenko epoch" in Nizhni Novgorod.

There was, in contrast, no "Sakharov epoch" in Gorki. Instead, there were the "Gorki years" in Sakharov's life.

At the time I subconsciously hoped that something similar would occur a hundred years later: Gorki intelligentsia, primarily physicists. Here was a rare—unique—opportunity to have such an eminent physicist in their midst. This man was both a theoretician and an incomparable expert in applied physics. That hope stayed with me for a while, until it finally became clear that it was not to be.

To recall this is bitter, even more bitter than to recall how the "best representatives of the academy" signed "letters of censure." That was of course disgusting, but it did not affect me personally.

During the first hunger strike, when Liza Alekseyeva was the topic, there was much agitation in the corridors of the presidium of the Academy of Sciences. Various people ranted and raved there, but the predominant thought was that if Andrei Dmitrievich dies no one outside the country will shake hands with us. There will be no place for us in the West. Only that really upset them.

However, in Gorki it was not like this: Here were genuine people, whom I love and respect. What forced them to accept boundary conditions laid down by the authorities? I still do not understand that. I understand that when at Rome, do as the Romans do, that "we should mind our own business," and that "you can't fight city hall." But really now, wasn't it worth a try?

In the middle of Sakharov's Gorki period I regained hope, when the president of the Academy of Sciences declared to the entire world that our government had proceeded in a very humanitarian way in sending Andrei Dmitrievich to Gorki, where conditions were outstanding, there were many academic institutes, and the academicians who lived there did not want to leave.

All this was said in an interview with the magazine *Newsweek*—that famous interview in which it was asserted that Andrei Dmitrievich had had a serious psychic shift. The statement of the Academy's president about the paradise in Gorki was repeated over and over by the scientists "traveling on professional business" when, outside the country, they were asked what was going on over here with Sakharov.

That was the time to make an effort: to invite Andrei Dmitrievich to conferences and to go see him for counsel on science. What they should have done was not take the hint regarding the wishes of the authorities but instead, with the wise bluntness of a seamstress, behave in accordance with the published assertion of the president.

Unfortunately, nothing of the sort occurred. That fact still causes me pain.

Today I attended the opening of a memorial session, and I listened carefully to all the speeches. I am afraid that an incorrect picture was drawn and that that picture justified the puzzling behavior of Gorki residents. They say that Andrei Dmitrievich was under such a tight siege here and that it was so difficult to get in to see him that there was nothing we could do.

I do not believe that that was the case. I believe the "full-court press" was intended primarily for the Moscow dissidents. They were the ones whom the authorities actually intended to prevent from seeing Andrei Dmitrievich, and they were the ones who found it difficult to get through. Admittedly, some role may have been played by the fact that when they set out to see him their trip was known in Moscow. It was difficult to refrain from telling at least close friends. Even I would know when so-and-so was planning a trip. The first three times I went to Gorki my trips were all prearranged, but I did not tell anyone about them beforehand.

Incidentally, on the first trip I made a mistake: I did not consider what I might be inflicting on my Gorki hosts. I was invited to a conference, and toward its end I met Andrei Dmitrievich. This happened two months after he had been sent into exile. The organizers of the conference said that they were then reprimanded and warned that if anything like this happened again—I do not remember the exact words—then no one from Moscow would be allowed in, or there would be no further conferences. After that event, I never went to see Andrei Dmitrievich at the expense of the organization employing me. I went only on my days off, and I never let anyone down.

In my opinion, the worst thing that might have happened to most of the people who visited (or tried to visit) Andrei Dmitrievich would have been to be shipped off to Moscow, sometimes even free of charge. Such a measure of suppression could hardly have intimidated the residents of Gorki.

With me, things were simpler. Once they were convinced that I was not an emissary of some group or other and was instead actually the old university pal that Andrei Dmitrievich said I was, they did not send me away, and I traveled myself. No one ever interfered with my visiting him after that. It is true, though, that they used up film in still and motion-picture cameras at a lavish pace.

I will conclude with a surprising intersection of two events, separated in time, about which I had no time to ask Sakharov.

The last time I talked with Andrei Dmitrievich was on December 8, six days before his death. We talked at the funeral of the lawyer S. V. Kalistratova.[3] A civil funeral service was held at the bar office (i.e., lawyers' association) on Pushkinski Street. They held a service for her on Obydenski Lane, near the Kropotkinski metro station. We rode over together in a car, passing through the area where both of us had spent our youth. It was in the car that memories of these places came back. In particular, the conversation ran to School No. 110. Andrei said that some mythmaking was beginning. He did not study for long at that school, and it was plain to see that he recognized and remembered little. However, pupils were already popping up who "recalled" what a genial person Andrei Sakharov was, how all the teachers exalted him, how the girls admired him, and how the boys envied him.

In a way, he thus asked me beforehand not to take part in this mythmaking, and I have not done so, in my opinion.

Before the war, we university students took a very serious interest in astronomy. Today, astronomy is not taught at all in the physics faculty, while we took a course, participated in seminars, and carried out practical work in the Shternberg Institute. The practical work was led by a remarkable observer, who later went to Pulkovo: M. S. Zverev.

We sat in the observatory for a fairly long time, waiting for the sky to clear up. At one point, one of the girls lamented that she would never be able to memorize the order of Draper's spectral classes by temperature (they go in the order O, B, A, F, G, K, M, N). That's difficult to memorize, but you have to know it for the tests. Zverev said that when he was studying in the university in the 1920s they had a mnemonic rule. Although it didn't make a whole lot of sense, one of the words in it contained three of the letters needed: *O, Bozhe, AFGanistan! Kuda My Nesemsya?* ("Oh, God, Afghanistan! Where are we off to in such a rush?", equivalent to the English "O Be A Fine Girl: Kiss Me Now!").

And then on the evening of December 8, on my way home, I suddenly recalled that phrase. Forty years later it had taken on a despairingly clear meaning, which was closely related to Andrei Dmitrievich's exile to Gorki.

M. L. Levin

Notes and References

1. V. I. Korolenko (1853–1921) was a novelist, journalist, and editor. The old Russian town Nizhni Novgorod in 1932 was renamed Gorki. The old name has recently been restored.

2. The meaning of the name is "The Gorki worker."

3. Five days earlier, Aleksandr Mikhailovich Obukhov, director of the Institute of Atmospheric Physics, had died. At one time, he had been a friend of Andrei Dmitrievich. He later signed the famous "letter of forty." Andrei Dmitrievich was naturally disappointed and pained. However, he attended Obukhov's funeral. During Kalistratova's funeral, there had been conversation about the betrayal by friends, and I asked, "How was it for you at Obukhov's funeral?"

    He told me, "You know, Obukhov's name is associated in my mind today with only one person: a physician from Gorki. When they tied me down and force-fed me there, I came to understand for the first time what the slaves in ancient Rome went through when they were crucified."

An American's Glimpses of Sakharov

KIP S. THORNE

California Institute of Technology, Pasadena

Tbilisi, USSR, Early September 1968

IN JULY 1968, *The New York Times* published Sakharov's essay "Reflections on Progress, Peaceful Coexistence, and Intellectual Freedom," creating a sensation in the Western world and condemnation of Sakharov in the USSR. In August, Soviet Troops invaded Czechoslovakia. In September, against this backdrop, physicists from around the world congregated in Tbilisi, deep in the south of the USSR, for the Fifth International Conference on General Relativity and Gravitation. Among the physicists were Sakharov; his close friend and colleague in the design of Soviet nuclear weapons, Yakov Borisovich Zel'dovich; a former leader of the American hydrogen bomb design effort, John Archibald Wheeler; and me. Sakharov, Zel'dovich, and Wheeler, though formerly nuclear adversaries, had become members of the same team in recent years: the world's team of scientists who try to understand the nature of space, time, and gravitation, and the origin and evolution of the universe. As an apprentice of Wheeler's, I had recently joined the team. Wheeler and I had read with enthusiasm the cosmological and astrophysical ideas of Sakharov and Zel'dovich, and they had read ours. Tbilisi, September 1968 was our first chance to meet and exchange ideas face-to-face.

On a hot, dry afternoon, shortly after the conference began, Zel'dovich and Sakharov invited Wheeler and me to share a lunch of bread, cheese, sausage, fruit juice, wine, and cognac in Zel'dovich's spacious hotel room. For two hours or so we munched and talked intensely about the cosmos.

What a contrast there was between our two hosts! Zel'dovich was a short, muscular, bulldozer of a man, vibrant and impatient in conversation, extroverted and demanding — and exciting to listen to. Sakharov, of whom I had read so much in Western newspapers in recent weeks, was tall and shy; he seemed painfully shy. But his hesitant conversation was ladened with fascinating, original ideas. He showed no outward signs of the stress that he must have been under; no indication that he was about to be, or had just been fired from his elite position at the "Installation" in the Yural Mountains, where Soviet nuclear weapons are designed. It was hard to imagine this mild, unassuming man challenging the Soviet government in the way he had just done, and embarking on the life of dissidence that he was just entering.

Suddenly in midafternoon, in the midst of our intense conversation, Zel'dovich announced that it was time to take a nap. (This was how he managed to keep up his vigorous pace: total interaction intermixed with total relaxation.) Zel'dovich then laid down and slept soundly for a half hour while, in deference to his needs, Sakharov, Wheeler, and I sat quietly and read or wrote, awaiting nap's end.

Moscow Through The 1970s

Through the next decade I frequently visited Moscow to carry out joint research with an outstanding group of physicists that Zel'dovich collected around himself. During each visit, I gave a lecture at an astrophysical seminar that Zel'dovich ran with a benevolent iron hand.

Though most of Sakharov's energies were directed toward humanitarian and political goals, he nevertheless came to my seminars, thirsty for the latest news about American astrophysical research. He sat always in the same seat, beside the window on my left, halfway to the back of the room. I soon learned to expect from him at the end of the lecture one or two questions, meekly offered but filled with piercing insight. As in 1968, he showed no outward signs of the pressure the Soviet government and KGB were putting on him in response to his increasingly vigorous "anti-Soviet activities."

However, I glimpsed the pressure briefly in 1971 when Wheeler, then an adviser to Richard Nixon on nuclear arms control negotiations with the

USSR, visited Moscow with me. Sakharov, uncharacteristically, failed to show up for our lectures at the Zel'dovich seminar, so in the parking lot afterward, presumably far from the KGB's prying bugs, Wheeler handed Zel'dovich a book and asked that he give it to Sakharov. Taking the gift, Zel'dovich said, in a hushed voice: "Notice my hands. They do not shake."

Jena, East Germany, July 1980

In December 1979, Soviet troops invaded Afghanistan. In January 1980, the Presidium of the Supreme Soviet stripped Sakharov of all his state awards and banished him to Gorki. Six months later, physicists from throughout the world congregated in Jena, East Germany for the Ninth International Conference on General Relativity and Gravitation.

At the end of the conference, at 7:15 the morning of my departure, I was awakened from deep sleep by a ringing telephone. It was Zel'dovich, with whom I had had only brief conversations in preceding days. He wanted to come to my hotel room to "finish discussing several points of physics." I agreed, he arrived within minutes, and I proposed that we go out and talk in the street, where "it is cooler and the air is fresh." "Perhaps that would be better," Zel'dovich replied. "I have a pencil and a pad of paper, so we can do physics there."

With this minuet for the sake of the bug completed, we strolled the back alleys of Jena, and talked about Sakharov. I had never seen Zel'dovich so upset. "If they can do this to Andrei Dmitrievich, what can they do to others?" he asked rhetorically. "Has the Academy of Sciences voted to strip Sakharov of his membership?" I wanted to know. Zel'dovich deflected the question: "In the Academy, Pontryagin [an eminent mathematician] gave a speech attacking Sakharov; Alexandrov [president of the Academy] defended him; and I was ready to defend him, too, but it was not necessary." Abruptly in the middle of our discussion, Zel'dovich broke off, shook my hand quickly, and ran back to his hotel, as though he suddenly had become frightened that our conversation was bugged.

What a contrast between these two friends, Sakharov and Zel'dovich: Sakharov, outwardly timid and shy, but with the courage to announce clearly his humanitarian and political convictions; Zel'dovich, outwardly vigorous and self-confident, but the epitome of political caution.

Moscow, June 1987

In December 1986 Mikhail Gorbachev invited Sakharov back to Moscow and encouraged him to return to his "patriotic work." Six months later some of my American friends went to the USSR for a conference on the future of space research, and returned with the following story: One morning Zel'dovich sat on the rostrum facing the audience of a plenary session, his jacket bedecked with his many state awards (ribbons, medals, . . .). It was a splendid sight; nobody else then alive possessed more high awards from the Soviet state than Zel'dovich, and Western scientists had never before seen him wear them. That afternoon, in a small, specialized session on space astrophysics, Zel'dovich arose to give a talk. The awards were gone; his jacket was bare. Before he could even begin speaking, a Russian scientist stood up and posed what obviously was a planted query: "Yakov Borisovich, this morning you were wearing your medals. This afternoon they are gone. Why?" "Andrei Dmitrievich Sakharov was absent this morning. Now he is sitting here in the audience. He had the same set of medals as I. He deserves his as much as I deserve mine. But his were taken away and have not been returned. It would be wrong for me to wear mine in front of him."

Moscow, August 1988

On December 2, 1987, Zel'dovich died of a heart attack, and Sakharov had but two more years to live. My last meeting with Sakharov was in his apartment in Moscow in June 1988. I went, with a close mutual friend, Vladimir Borisovich Braginsky, to discuss physics. I also went armed with a set of carefully formulated questions about Zel'dovich's contributions to the design of nuclear weapons. (My questions were intended to flesh out a description of the interrelations of Zel'dovich's weapons research and his astrophysics research, for a book I was writing).

Elena Georgievna Bonner, Sakharov's wife, greeted Braginsky and me at the door of the apartment and ushered us into the kitchen, where Sakharov joined us. I was shocked at how frail and tired he seemed. His hunger strikes had taken a tremendous toll. But his mind was still sharp, as our conversation ranged over cosmology, astrophysics, the nature of time, and the nature of fundamental particles.

In the midst of our conversation, Sakharov closed his eyes and went into a sleep-like trance. The room was silent for about two minutes, as Braginsky and I looked at each other in amazement and concern. Just as I was about to go seek help from Sakharov's wife, Sakharov opened his eyes, shook his head slightly, and said "You must excuse me. This happens to me sometimes nowadays." Seeing this stark evidence of failing health, I somehow was moved not to ask my questions about weapons research.

The answers, however, are now known. Elsewhere in this volume, Yu.

A. Romanov describes in detail, for the first time in any unclassified publication, the detailed roles of Zel'dovich and Sakharov in the 1940s and 1950s design of Soviet nuclear weapons. In reading this account, in reading Sakharov's *Memoirs*, and in reviewing my own memories, I cannot help but be impressed by the fecundity and complexity of the friendship between these two great men: Andrei Dmitrievich Sakharov and Yakov Borisovich Zel'dovich.

Sakharov: Man of Humility, Understanding, and Leadership

JOHN ARCHIBALD WHEELER

Princeton University
University of Texas at Austin

A New Way to Understand Gravity

A NEW AND DEEPER way to understand what we thought we already understood: that was Sakharov's great gift. Before Charles Misner, Kip Thorne and I ever met him, we already knew, studied, and profited from Sakharov's discovery[1] of yet another way to state the essence of gravity. He told us—so we stated in our 1973 book *Gravitation*[2]—that gravity is "an elasticity of space that arises from particle physics." Sakharov already in 1967 had identified the action term in Einstein's geometric theory of gravity "with the change in the action of quantum fluctuations of the vacuum [associated with the physics of particles and fields and brought about] when space is curved." In the Sakharov formulation the Newtonian constant of gravity expresses itself as a divergent integral over wave numbers. That integral has to be cut off, he pointed out, at a wave number of the order of the reciprocal of the Planck length.[3] This cut-off made, we have before us gravity as the metric elasticity of space. In brief, the sausage skin only then ceases to be floppy when it is filled with meat!

First Meeting with a Humble Searcher for Truth

My first meeting with awe-inspiring Andrei Dmitrievich Sakharov and his prodigy colleague Yakov Borisovich Zel'dovich came at Tbilisi in September 1968. Kip Thorne describes it in his contribution to this volume.[4] Never a word did either Russian or I ever say to each other about the nuclear devices on which we had worked, in our two countries, both during and after the war. Physics, pure physics, was the focus of the discussion with Sakharov. Never have I met anyone so senior who communicated more strongly the aura of a humble searcher for truth, one wanting to learn about the great mysteries—learn from nature, learn from the scientific literature, learn from discussion.

Last Discussions

My last meeting came at the supper Elena Bonner and he gave Boris L. Altshuler and me at their apartment Tuesday evening, May 26, 1987. Sakharov had come the day before to the opening session of the Fourth Moscow Seminar on Quantum Gravity,[5] and after my talk[6] had spoken to me and invited me to supper Wednesday night—Wednesday because he had to go to Leningrad on Tuesday. I had to excuse myself because my plane left Wednesday afternoon. Thereupon he put off his Leningrad trip to Wednesday and invited me for Tuesday evening, Academician Moisei A. Markov and he kindly arranging on the spot that I should have two suppers in succession at their two apartments the same evening!

Altshuler had worked much with Sakharov on gravitation and cosmology in general and Mach's principle in particular,[7] so that evening we might well have pursued modern cosmology. Instead, however, Andrei Sakharov drew me out on the subject of my own recent research, the motivating ideas of which I have recently published.[8] Altshuler helped to elucidate my views while Sakharov listened with attention, putting a question from time to time by way of clarification but never coming down to a final "I agree" or "I don't agree." His openness to new ideas was as evident then and there as it had been evident in my earlier visit and in his many writings. During an interlude, Altshuler told me details that I had never heard before of the ruthlessness with which Sakharov had been treated at Gorki and of the fateful December 16, 1986 phone call to him from Mikhail Sergeyevich Gorbachev that brought his release.[9]

Farewell Image

An undeserved blessing it will always seem to me that Elena Bonner and Andrei Sakharov could give so much of their evening to a lone American physicist when they were striving to the limit of their force for great causes. Everything spoke of the struggle: their serious countenances. Those piles of manuscripts from colleagues and unknowns in many places—did they not solicit Sakharov's judgment? Those piles of letters—did they not beg support for applications to emigrate or attend a foreign meeting? Every day pleas for help. Pleas from fellow workers for reform of the political system. Pleas soliciting, advice, assistance, support. Pleas for help from the families of dissidents dragged off to prison seventeen years ago or last week. Who else could they turn to? That one man flew the flag of hope to those who had been without hope.

On December 14, 1989, Andrei Dmitrievich Sakharov summoned up his spent strength to plead with fellow members of the Congress. Support political pluralism and a market economy, he told them. Speak for the people, "who have finally found a way to express their will."[10] A few hours later, he was dead.

Notes and References

1. A. D. Sakharov, "Vacuum Quantum Fluctuations in Curved Space and the Theory of Gravitation," *Soviet Physics Doklady (Doklady Akademii Nauk SSSR)* 177 (1967): pp. 70–71.

2. C. W. Misner, K. S. Thorne, and J. A. Wheeler, *Gravitation*, San Francisco: Freeman, 1973, pp. 426–428.

3. J. A. Wheeler, "On the Nature of Quantum Geometrodynamics," *Annals of Physics* 2 (1957): pp. 604–614.

4. K. S. Thorne, "An American's Glimpses of Sakharov," this volume.

5. M. A. Markov, V. A. Berezin, and V. P. Frolov, *Proceedings of the Fourth Seminar on Quantum Gravity: May 25–29, 1987, Moscow, USSR*, Singapore: World Scientific, 1988.

6. J. A. Wheeler, "Geometrodynamic Steering Principle Reveals the Determiners of Inertia," Ref. 5, pp. 21–93.

7. B. L. Altshuler, "Integral Form of the Einstein Equations and a Covariant Formulation of Mach's Principle," original Russian in *Zhurnal Eksperimental'noi i Theoretischeskoi Fizika* 51 (1966): pp. 1143–1150; English translation in *JETP* 24 (1967): pp. 766–773; also "Kaluza-Klein Ansatz for Quadratic-Curvature Theory: A Geometrical Way to Mass Hierarchy," *Physical Review D* 35 (1987): pp. 3804–3814 and references therein cited.

8. J. A. Wheeler, "World as System Self-Synthesized by Quantum Networking," *IBM Journal of Research and Development* 32 (1988): pp. 4–15 and "It from Bit" as published in two versions under the same title, "Information, Physics, Quantum: The Search for Links": the first, pp. 354–368 in S. Kobayashi *et al.* eds., *Proceedings of the Third International Symposium on the Foundations of Quantum Mechanics, Tokyo, 1989,* Tokyo: Physical Society of Japan, 1990; the second, pp. 3–28 in W. H. Zurek, ed., *Complexity, Entropy and the Physics of Information*, Reading, MA: Addison-Wesley, 1990.

9. Details in Sakharov's *Memoirs,* as translated from the Russian by Richard Lourie, New York: Knopf, 1990.

10. See Edward Kline, preface to Ref. 9, page xiii.

Tribute to Andrei Sakharov*

Sidney D. Drell

Stanford Linear Accelerator Center

Andrei, I always dared to hope—as did many of your friends and colleagues around the world—for this moment when you would be free to visit our shores and join us in our homes, our laboratories, our seminars, and in this great academy—which, since your election in 1973 as a foreign associate, is yours as well as ours. Still, as I look back over the arduous and, at times, tortuous path you had to travel to get here, this occasion seems to me to be as close to a miracle as I ever expect to witness. The recent changes in your country that have made possible your visit and this occasion tonight offer the further hope that our two great nations will embrace common principles of human dignity and mutual respect and that they will continue moving away from chilling confrontation toward constructive cooperation, the better to meet the challenges to the survival of humanity that you and your fellow board members of the International Foundation are addressing in your meetings this week.

Twenty years ago Andrei Sakharov published his remarkable essay "Reflections on Progress, Peaceful Coexistence, and Intellectual Freedom." The two basic theses which he developed in this essay are (1) the division of mankind threatens it with destruction and (2) intellectual freedom is essential to human society. His arguments remain as valid and com-

* Address at the National Academy of Sciences, Washington, D.C., November 13, 1988.

pelling today as they were when they first appeared. This essay publicly marked Sakharov's emergence from the laboratory where he had worked as a scientist—indeed, a great scientist. It was soon followed by further writings and speeches of great impact, and Andrei became recognized not only as a scientific leader in search of nature's principles for the properties of matter, but also as a moral leader in search of ethical principles for a humanity striving for peace, for progress, and for basic human dignity.

From 1968 up to the present Andrei has continued to speak out forcefully, courageously, persistently, and wisely on the main issues of our times: on problems of peace, the dangers of thermonuclear weapons, and the importance—and I quote from his 1975 book *My Country and The World* — "of disarmament talks, which offer a ray of hope in the dark world of suicidal nuclear madness." He risked everything and sacrificed much in his support of prisoners of conscience and his opposition to oppression wherever it occurs in the world. In his devotion to truth and human dignity and his defense of the freedom of the human spirit Andrei has become, in the words of his 1975 Nobel Peace Prize citation, "the spokesman for the conscience of mankind."

Human history has been inspired and ennobled by the occasional occurrence of figures of indomitable courage. Each of us has our own personal honor roll of those rare individuals whose lives have become morality plays with the dimensions of an historical epic, the theme of which is the struggle between conscience and principle on the one hand and raw political power on the other. Andrei stands tall in my honor roll of those giants who have been driven to do battle for principle in the manner described so eloquently by the young lawyer, Gavin Stevens, in William Faulkner's *Intruder in The Dust:*

> Some things you must always be unable to bear. Some things you must never stop refusing to bear. Injustice and outrage and dishonor and shame. No matter how young you are or how old you have got. Not for kudos and not for cash: your picture in the paper nor money in the bank either. Just refuse to bear them.

It is my great privilege to know Andrei Sakharov—and his equally courageous and wonderful wife Elena Bonner—as close personal friends. This friendship dates back to our first meeting in Moscow fifteen summers ago, when we were attending a working seminar on the substructure of elementary particles organized by the Soviet Academy of Sciences. But beyond friendship, I also take personal pride in the fact that Andrei and I are members of the same scientific community. As theoretical physicists, we are fellow members of the crew on that great adventure voyage of the human mind searching to discover what we are made of. We share this passion to understand nature. What are the elementary building blocks on the submicroscopic scale of distances hundreds of millions to billions of times smaller than the size of the atom? What are the forces that glue together the building blocks, or elementary constituents, of nature into the protons and neutrons and other forms of matter that we actually see in the laboratory?

Andrei is most widely known for his courageous leadership in the defense of human principles that we hold dear and as the father of the Soviet hydrogen bomb. But you should also know that he is a great scientist whose brilliant career as a theoretical physicist is distinguished by seminal research contributions to fundamental physics, including the behavior of plasmas and the properties of elementary particles.

In 1950 Andrei, together with Physics Nobel Laureate Academician Igor Tamm, an internationally honored and greatly admired former leader of Soviet physics and Andrei's teacher, wrote the pioneering paper in the controlled fusion effort in the Soviet Union. In this paper they introduced a confinement scheme for a hot plasma that is famous today under the name "tokamak". As a result of subsequent important work by other major figures in Soviet science, in particular the late Academician Lev Artsimovich, and including contributions by two of this evening's guests, Academicians Roald Sagdeev and Evgeny Velikhov and their colleagues, this is one of the most promising methods now being pursued around the world, including right here in the United States, for developing fusion as a practical source of energy.

Andrei also made a contribution of crucial importance to our quest to understand the evolution of our universe following its physical beginnings in the "Big Bang" of eighteen or so billion years ago. The problem he addressed is this: Physicists know that for each form of matter, there also occurs antimatter—for example, electrons and positrons; protons and antiprotons. Antimatter is a necessary consequence of joining the general principles of atomic theory—that is, the quantum theory—with Einstein's special theory of relativity—the theory on the basis of which we understand his all-too famous equation $E = Mc^2$. But we must wonder then what has happened to all the antimatter. Where did it go? In our universe—or all we can see of it as we peer far out into space to receive signals just arriving from distant events that occurred ten or more billions of years ago—why are the massive systems of stars and galaxies made almost exclusively of matter and not antimatter?

Andrei provided the clue for understanding this in 1968—the same year he published his "Reflections" essay. His was the leap of imagination to see that the absence of antimatter can be explained rather elegantly by joining a recent experimental observation that there is a very tiny difference between the behavior of matter and of antimatter with several general postulates that separately had been made in other contexts. The most intriguing of these postulates is that the proton, the nucleus of the hydrogen atom—long believed to be a stable particle of nature—may in fact decay just like other forms of subnuclear matter, albeit very, very slowly. This bold hypothesis is currently being tested in laboratories around the world. The experiments are very difficult and require massive equipment. No one has yet seen a proton decay, so the hypothesis has yet to be confirmed. But you can be sure that it is very comforting to know that our universe lacks antimatter because if we met a galaxy, or a star, or whatever made of antimatter, we would all go "poof." Collisions between little pieces of matter and antimatter would make nuclear explosions look, by comparison, like a pop-gun.

When the history books of the latter part of the twentieth century are written they will tell that this was a time when mankind was first able to begin writing a history of the evolution of the universe following the Big Bang that is based on solid experimental data and theoretical concepts. And in that chapter of history, as in other chapters of our times, Andrei's name will surely appear, this time as Andrei Sakharov, physicist.

Andrei's life in physics is clear evidence of the international character of science—true science. The "tokamak" idea of controlled fusion is of Russian parentage and is studied worldwide with free and eager exchange of new progress that is beneficial to all. Search for evidence of proton decay is being pursued with international collaborations on a world-wide basis in both hemispheres, east and west. Science knows no boundaries, and efforts to create barriers—whether to keep new ideas within or to prevent new ones from entering from the outside—have universally proved harmful to progress. The great nineteenth century Russian playwright, Anton Chekhov, said it best, as follows:

> There is no national science just as there is no national multiplication table; what is national is no longer science.

It is regrettable when, on occasion, governments need to be reminded of this basic fact. It may not be a law of nature, but it has proved to be a reliable rule of thumb, that national interests and true security are better served by keeping open the channels of communication of scientific achievements than by erecting barriers to stem the transfer of knowledge.

And, just as good science knows no geographic or political boundaries, modern-day scientists have increasing difficulty in defining a boundary line between work in the laboratory and a concerned involvement in the practical applications of scientific progress. Sakharov himself is one of the most important examples of this involvement and of the serious difficulties, and on occasion the painful disillusionment, that a scientist or a scholar may encounter when he or she reaches out of the private shell of the laboratory or the study and participates in society.

Sakharov has written in an autobiographical essay published in 1974 that "I had no doubts as to the vital importance of creating a Soviet superweapon—for our country and for the balance of power throughout the world," but tells of his concern for continuing bomb-testing throughout the following decade and of his involvement in a military-industrial complex "blind to everything except their jobs" and of his coming "to reflect in general terms on the problems of peace and mankind and, in particular, on the problems of a thermonuclear war and its aftermath." The involvement of scientists in war and weapons of death—as in other major issues of importance to the human condition—is in itself nothing new. Its distinguished honor roll of olden days includes such luminaries as Archimedes of Syracuse, Leonardo da Vinci, and Michelangelo. But never before have scientists dealt with weapons of absolute destruction, with weapons whose use could mean the end of civilization as we know it—if not of mankind itself. And never before has the gulf been so great between the scientific arguments—even the very language of science—and the political leaders whose decisions will shape the future.

The new fact that the fruits of our learning threaten the existence of all mankind presents an acutely heightened ethical dilemma to scientists. Our predicament is precarious because we have so little—if any—margin of safety. As much as any scientist I know, Andrei Sakharov has understood the special obligation of the scientific community to alert society to the implications of the products of scientific advances and to assist society in shaping the applications of these advances in beneficial directions.

Scientists who enter the political realm and participate in the public debate on the implications of scientific advances bear a special responsibility to speak accurately and responsibly on the technical challenges to society. Once again, Sakharov is a model for us all. He has spoken out courageously, passionately, and with outrage, when appropriate, on issues of social injustice and oppression; but, when speaking as a scientist on technical and factual issues, he has maintained the same high standards that we demand in our professional scientific lives. It is our obligation to do likewise. Unless we do, we will compromise—and lose—any effectiveness and credibility we bring to the debate as scientists.

By his actions, Andrei has been an inspiration to all of us. Constant in purpose, clear in vision, modest, and unflinching in his courage to speak out in circumstances of great personal danger, he has inspired support, admiration, and devotion from people of all stations and nations. I shall never forget the first evidence of that devotion which I saw when Andrei invited me to supper in his and Elena's modest apartment in Moscow during our first meeting in July of 1974. He reported that less than an hour before my arrival he had been visited by Moscow policemen bringing a protest from his neighbors about the disturbing noises from his apartment. What had triggered this protest was an event that had occurred the previous day. The La Scala Opera of Milan was visiting Moscow that week for performances at the Bolshoi Theatre—and two of its lead singers had arrived at Andrei's door unannounced to show their admiration and affection for him, which they expressed the best way they could—that is, through song in a private operatic recital.

Andrei, I can't sing in tune and, have no fear, I won't try. Instead, I will close by asking all your friends here tonight to join me in a toast expressed in the words of your friend Lev Kopelev, author, compatriot, and known to many of us as the mathematician Rubin who appears in Alexander Solzhenitsyn's great novel, *The First Circle*. Kopelev's beautiful tribute is:

> The majesty of his spirit, the power of his intellect and the purity of his soul, his chivalrous courage and selfless kindness feed my faith in the future of Russia and mankind.

Sakharov in His Own Words

Susan Eisenhower

The Eisenhower Group, Washington, D.C.

Roald Z. Sagdeev

University of Maryland, College Park
Academy of Sciences, Moscow

Few people in this century have been so esteemed for their original thought, humanitarian commitment, and moral courage as Andrei Sakharov. His extraordinary personal qualities continue to serve as inspiration to many millions of people throughout the world. Within the Soviet Union, particularly, Sakharov's voice is greatly missed.

Since his passing on December 14, 1989, some of the most difficult issues that will define the future of Soviet society continue to be examined and debated: economic reform and its "convergence" with market-based economies abroad, self-determination for the ethnic republics, and sweeping reforms of the governmental system, including establishment of a presidential structure—all matters that have reached deeper dimensions since his death. As a real testament to the power of his continuing presence, we have said more than once when confronted by these controversial issues that "Andrei would have objected" or "Andrei would have approved" or even "Andrei would have known."

Sakharov's sudden death shocked many people, especially his friends. Somehow we had grown accustomed to his persistent long hours and grueling work loads. We knew that his constitution was not strong, but we had hoped that the ravages of his forced exile in Gorki had not taken too big a toll.

Knowing how tirelessly he worked, we found it poignant that the epilogue of his recently published autobiography, *Memoirs*,[1] was written the day before he died. In it Sakharov makes a critical point somewhat abruptly and with characteristic directness: "The main thing is that my dear, beloved Lusia [Elena Bonner] and I are united—I have dedicated this book to her. Life goes on. We are together." There Sakharov's book ends.

Elena Bonner was his anchor, and as such, she played a pivotal role in his life. This is clearly and at times movingly depicted in Sakharov's reminiscences.

Memoirs is a book of epic proportions and obscure detail. Taken as a whole, Sakharov's story conveys a striking impression about how closely his life and times parallel the stages and developments of the first seventy-two years of the Soviet Union. In a sense, his story is both a reflection and personification of Soviet history:

Stage one: Like the young Soviet state, Sakharov lavishes unquestioning devotion on science and on the cause of national security—fixated on the next development after the atomic bomb and determined to get there in time to meet the challenge posed by the West.

Stage two: Issues of survival give way to rumblings of dissent and reevaluations of the basic set of human rights, while that which lives beneath the surface explodes into sharper and deeper conflict.

Stage three (to be described in the next book, a sequel called *From Gorki to Moscow and Beyond*[2]): *Perestroika* appears with the recognition that alienation doesn't ultimately change the human condition; only active work from within holds out promise. Like the maturing political scene in the Soviet Union itself, Andrei came to realize in his final years that more important than any protest on behalf of the human rights movement are actions to further the development of a state based on law.

In a Context of Turbulent Times

Extraordinary in its multidimensionality, the Sakharov phenomenon is virtually certain to attract the interest of generations of scholars, historians, and biographers. In sometimes exhaustive diary-like detail, Sakharov leaves an invaluable narrative that does much to explain his role within the context of the turbulent Russian record in the twentieth century.

In that sense, Sakharov's *Memoirs* is a priceless gift. It is honest, candid, thorough, and self-revealing. Sakharov must have had a profound feeling of responsibility to "set the record straight," not only as a witness to but as a key participant in many of the great moments in science as well as in Russian *and* world history. While his life certainly was influenced by events, he also helped shape events—many of them memorable. And while he brought his immense talent to each task he undertook, he also brought a remarkable reserve of personal courage.

Perhaps the most noteworthy of the many inner qualities that Sakharov reveals is his intense concentration and single-mindedness. His absorption with the hydrogen bomb project and later with human rights issues was so compelling that he complains, to his apparent sadness, that he did not have enough time to pursue "big science." The pages that describe his scientific work seem written with a profound sense of nostalgia. Despite his protestations, however, his brief and incomplete romance with big physics was extraordinarily fruitful, producing among many other things his invention of the magnetic confinement tokamak for controlled fusion experiments.

In addition, he was one of the first "heretics" to express serious doubts about one of the then-sacrosanct dogmas of physical science—baryon number conservation. His detailed account of how he pursued the goal of overcoming the philosophical limitations of Big Bang cosmology is impressive. These problems continued to haunt his scientific curiosity to the end of his life. Trying to overcome what he considered a major deficiency of modern cosmology—its failure to deal with the subtle interface with eternity or creation—he proposed many-sheeted models of the universe and even the reversal of time's arrow.

Independent of the final judgment by scientific purists, Sakharov's approach tells a great deal about his courage to reopen matters that are considered taboo in science. The Big Bang, he writes,

> was the moment of creation and so the question of what was before it lies beyond the limits of scientific research. However, an approach that places no limit on the scientific investigation of the material world and spacetime in my opinion is better and more fruitful, even though it leaves no room for an act of creation: The basic religious concept of the divine meaning of existence does not concern science and lies beyond its limits.

In an Ambivalent Russian Tradition

Despite his singularity as a modern scientist and thinker, Sakharov sprang from an ambivalent Russian tradition. Awakening from centuries steeped in serfdom and autocracy, nineteenth century Russia gave birth to a whole galaxy of dazzling intellectuals: writers and composers, artists and scientists. It was from this thin yet fertile layer of Russian intelligentsia that Sakharov's family came. And it was within this culture that Andrei's childhood was enriched.

From his grandfather, Ivan Sakharov, a prominent lawyer in prerevolutionary Russia, Andrei probably inherited his respect for social awareness and humanist principles. As a young boy, Andrei was greatly impressed with a collection of essays edited by his grandfather after the abortive 1905 revolution. The essays, all advocating the abolition of capital punishment, included Leo Tolstoy's powerful contribution, "I Cannot Keep Silent." "My grandfather's work on this book was an act of conscience and, to an extent, civic courage," Sakharov writes in *Memoirs*.

Sakharov's father, Dmitri, a physics teacher in private schools, had been educated at the University of Moscow, where the great Peter Lebedev taught. Dmitri Sakharov was an accomplished but amateur pianist who had won a gold medal from the famous Gnessin Conservatory. He enjoyed walking in the Caucasus, where he became acquainted with Igor Tamm, who would later be Andrei's mentor in graduate school and in bomb work, and who went on to share the 1958 Nobel Prize in Physics. Andrei writes that his father "had an enormous effect on me." In fact, Dmitri's literary output, including a book titled *Problems in Physics*, brought him sufficient money to be independent and provided him with some fame among educators. Andrei recalls a happy childhood during which "it was taken for granted that I would study physics at the university."

Despite the creativity and generosity of his family circle, however, Andrei writes that he "grew up in an era marked by tragedy, cruelty and terror." His uncle Ivan was arrested several times in the 1930s. The family eventually got news that he had died in prison when a letter his wife, Sakharov's Aunt Zhenya, had mailed to him "was returned bearing the inscription: 'Addressee relocated to the cemetery.'" Other relatives were arrested and sent to labor camps or shot.

Some of Andrei's ancestors were clergymen, and most of his other relatives were devoutly religious. Andrei was taught to pray by his mother, but he abandoned religion as a teenager. Having scaled the heights of scientific success, he confesses in his book:

> Today, deep in my heart, I do not know where I stand on religion. I don't believe in any dogma and I dislike official churches . . . or those tainted by fanaticism and intolerance. And yet I am unable to imagine the universe and human life without some guiding principle, without a source of spiritual "warmth" that is nonmaterial and not bound by physical laws. Probably this sense of things could be called "religious."

Perhaps the most tragic aspect of the 1930s was that the nation's youth were essentially oblivious to the true scope of the events that were unfolding around them. Like many others of his generation, says Sakharov, "I was content to absorb Communist ideology without questioning it." Only later perhaps did he sense that the dogma, officialdom, and intolerance he disliked so much were features of the system he had come to serve.

When World War II broke out, deep feelings of patriotism stirred the entire country. The war delayed Sakharov's political awakening, which would have been inevitable for someone with his intellectual curiosity and training. Driven by patriotic fervor to contribute to the war effort, he rejected suggestions by his professor, Anatoli Vlasov, a pupil of Tamm and author of the well-known "Vlasov equation" in plasma physics, that he pursue graduate studies. Instead, in no time at all, Sakharov found himself at an ammunition factory that was producing bullets for the battlefront. As insignificant a move as this seemed at the time, it brought the young Sakharov for the first time into the sphere of weapons technology. Once in this orbit Sakharov remained there many years before he finally reached escape velocity.

In a Secret Weapons Center

After the war he took up postgraduate studies in theoretical physics with Tamm. A few years later, they were both sent to a secret city called "the Installation" to work on thermonuclear weapons under Igor Kurchatov. The entire operation was supervised by Lavrenti Beria, Stalin's notorious KGB chief. There Sakharov's involvement was intensified by the nature of the mission itself:

> We were encouraged to throw ourselves into our work by the fierce concentration of a single goal, and perhaps also by the proximity of the labor camp and strict regimentation. . . . The rest of the world was far, far away, somewhere beyond two barbed wire fences. . . . It would require the passage of many years and radical upheavals for new currents to affect the shift in our view of the world.

The first revelation came when Sakharov faced a personal crisis over the nuclear weapons tests. Realizing that many lives would be adversely affected by the high levels of radiation released during the tests, he could not remain silent about what he regarded as the second unnecessary test of the so-called Big Bomb, which had a yield equal to sixty megatons. With the same drive and devotion he exhibited in his scientific work, he campaigned to bring this message to the Soviet leadership. At a gala banquet of the Central Committee Presidium, attended by prominent weapons scientists, including Sakharov, Premier Khrushchev rejected his pleas. "Leave politics to us," he declared as if proposing a toast. "We're the specialists. You make your bombs and test them and we won't interfere with you. . . . Remember, we have to conduct our policies from a position of strength. . . . Sakharov, don't try to tell us what to do or how to behave. We understand politics. I'd be a jellyfish and not chairman of the Council of Ministers if I listened to people like Sakharov!"

This may have been the genesis of Sakharov's future civil and political awareness. But Sakharov's transformation would not have been possible without the values that he harbored in a deep latent state from his rich moral upbringing. A few years later this development culminated in his famous essay, "Reflections on Progress, Peaceful Coexistence, and Intellectual Freedom."[3]

In No Sense Repentant

Those who hoped then and still do today that Sakharov would share with us his deepest feelings about the morality of his role as "father of the Soviet H-bomb" will not find them in *Memoirs*. If regret or remorse is found at all, it is not the type Dostoyevski described: no deep psychological self-analysis and self-castigation, based on the natural proclivity of the Russian soul to repent. Rather, Sakharov looks back with a sense of patriotic justification, for at that time the hydrogen-bomb was regarded as essential for national security, and Sakharov did everything he could for its success.

We will probably never discover his inner ethical impulses as the bomb's prime creator, or whether he ever worried about handing over such a mighty weapon to a totalitarian state. It might well be that after examining the complexities of human existence after World War II and during the Cold War, he deliberately decided to apply the "principle of causality" — in other words, that nothing from the past can be changed. This might explain why in the uncompromising dispute between U.S. nuclear weapons builders in the 1950s over development of the hydrogen-bomb, Sakharov obviously felt greater affinity with Edward Teller than J. Robert Oppenheimer, as embarrassing as this seemed then and even now to most of Andrei's colleagues and admirers.

Since repentance isn't touched on at all in the book, we found it impossible to know whether it was a sense of guilt that drove him later to take heroic stands against the repression of human rights or against the invasion of Afghanistan. Still, it may be that his courageous actions were simply impelled by his rare and inspired sense of self-confidence and humanitarian mission.

What we do know, we discover in his own words in *Memoirs*:

> Looking back on my life, I can see not only actions which are a source of pride, but others which were false, cowardly, shameful, foolish, ill-advised or inspired by subconscious impulses better not to dwell on. While admitting all this, in general terms, I don't want to linger on my failings—not out of concern for my reputation, but rather from a dislike for self-flagellation and public soul-searching. Moreover, I believe that no one really learns from other people's mistakes. It's enough to learn from your own mistakes and to emulate the virtues of others. I want these memoirs to focus less on me as a person and more on what I have seen and understood (or tried to understand) during my sixty-seven years of life. . . . After all, this book is a memoir, not a confession.

Notes and References

1. A. D. Sakharov, *Memoirs*, New York: Knopf, (1990).

2. A. D. Sakharov, *Moscow and Beyond: 1986 to 1989*, New York: Knopf, 1991 and (in Russian) Moscow: Chekhov Publishing, 1990.

3. A. D. Sakharov, *Sakharov Speaks*, New York: Knopf, 1974, p. 56.

Photographs:
Early Years Through Gorki

Overleaf: *In chapter 1 of his* Memoirs, *Sakharov describes the close family circle of his childhood. Born in 1921, he was four years older than the only other Sakharov child, his brother Georgi, who was called Yura (shown on the right together with Sakharov in this photograph taken in 1930). (Courtesy of Elena Bonner.)* ***Top left:*** *Nikolai Ivanovich Sakharov, Sakharov's great-grandfather, a priest in the village of Vyezdnoe, near Arzamas.* ***Top right:*** *Sakharov's paternal grandparents, Ivan Nikolaevich Sakharov and Maria Petrovna Domukhovskaya, about 1885. After attending school in Nizhny Novgorod—later renamed Gorki—Ivan became a successful lawyer and moved to Moscow.* ***Bottom:*** *Sakharov's parents, Ekaterina Alekseyeva Sofiano and Dmitri Ivanovich Sakharov, in the late 1950s. Dmitri taught physics and wrote a number of popular physics books.*

Top: *Engineer Sakharov in 1943. Sakharov worked in a large arms factory in Ulyanovsk on the Volga from 1942 to 1945.* ***Bottom:*** *Sakharov with Igor Kurchatov on the grounds of the Institute of Atomic Energy, summer 1957.*

Top Row: *Sakharov over time. Photographs from documents in about 1950 (left) and the early 1960s (middle) and in Gorki after the 1985 hunger strike (right).* **Bottom:** *Sakharov and his daughter Tanya with Yu. A. Romanov (left) and Yu. A. Zysin, in Sarov, mid-1950s. (See Romanov's chapter from this volume.)*

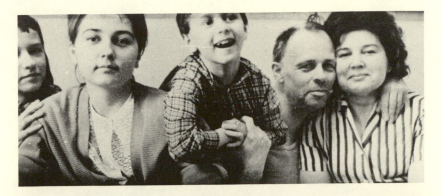

Top: Sakharov with his wife Klavdia Alekseyevna Vikhireva (right) and children (from left to right) Lyuba, Tanya, and Dmitri, mid-1960s. **Bottom:** *Igor Evgenievich Tamm, Sakharov's advisor at the Lebedev Institute, in May 1956. (Photo by Luis W. Alvarez.)*

Top: Sakharov and Elena Georgievna Bonner, mid-1970s. (AP/Wide World photo.) *Bottom: In their Moscow apartment, September 1979. (Photo by Jeri Laber, Helsinki Watch Committee.)*

Top: Outside the Lublino courthouse in Moscow during the trial of Yu. F. Orlov, May 1978. Sakharov is at the far left. Bottom: Alone together. Sakharov and Bonner, or "Lusia," in 1980, their first year of exile in Gorki. (Courtesy of Elena Bonner.)

Sakharov in his Moscow apartment, September 1979, four months before his arrest and exile to Gorki. (Photo by Jeri Laber, Helsinki Watch Committee.)

Scientific
Perspectives

Physics, the Bomb, and Human Rights

Sidney D. Drell

Stanford Linear Accelerator Center

Lev B. Okun

Institute of Theoretical and Experimental Physics, Moscow

AT THE TIME of his death from a heart attack on December 14, 1989, Andrei Dmitrievich Sakharov was recognized both as a great scientist and as a persistent and uncompromising fighter for human rights and political freedom for all. He lived to see his Russian homeland start on the path toward implementing the principles of democracy to which he had devoted the last two decades of his life. His leadership in the struggle of conscience and principle against raw political power earned him worldwide accolades as the conscience of humanity. Gentle and modest in person, but of unconquerable persistence in his commitment to principle and opposition to injustice, he had become, in the memorial words of a Russian commentator, both "the saint and martyr of *perestroika*." With the end of his life, the curtain fell on a morality play with the dimensions of a historical epic.

SAKHAROV WAS BORN in Moscow on May 21, 1921, into a family with the traditions of the Russian intelligentsia. His father was a physics teacher and was well known as the author of a physics textbook, which students still use. Andrei received his early schooling at home; in his autobiography he writes of having difficulty relating to his own age group. He graduated from high school with honors in 1938 and enrolled in the physics department of Moscow University. In October 1941, when the German army was approaching Moscow, the university was transferred to Ashkhabad, where he graduated with honors in 1942. He tells of gaining his first vivid impression of the life of workers and peasants during the difficult summer of 1942.

Sakharov's fellow students recollect that his ability to think and to formulate and resolve science problems was remarkable. They also remember that he was the only person in their hostel who, in that time of deprivation and hunger, could give his own last piece of bread to someone who badly needed it.

After graduating from the university, Sakharov worked from 1942 to 1945 as an engineer at a large arms factory in Ulyanovsk on the Volga, where he developed several inventions to improve the plant's inspection procedures. Sakharov tells of writing several theoretical physics papers during this period and sending them back to Moscow for review. In Sakharov's judgment those papers, which were never published, didn't really constitute original scientific work, but he wrote that "they gave me confidence in my powers, which is essential for a scientist."

During this period, in 1943, Sakharov married Klavdia Alekseyevna Vikhireva. They raised three children before her death in 1969.

Sakharov and Physics

In January 1945 Sakharov became a graduate student at the Lebedev Physical Institute. His adviser, Igor Tamm, greatly influenced his future. Academician Tamm (1895–1971) was an outstanding theorist who in 1958 shared the Nobel Prize with academicians Ilya Frank and Pavel Cherenkov for developing in 1937 the theory of what is now commonly known as Cherenkov radiation. He was a man admired for his character, integrity and warm personality. Outside of physics he is remembered in particular for his fearless fight against Trofim Lysenko and for his efforts to save and revive Soviet genetics.

Early Papers

Sakharov published his first research paper when he was twenty-six years old. He submitted it for publication in *Zhurnal Eksperimental'noi i Teoreticheskoi Fiziki (JETP)* in January 1947.[1] The paper estimated the cross section for the production of mesons as the hard component of cosmic rays in a model proposed by Tamm. (In this model, now completely obsolete, the charged mesons are pseudoscalars, while the neutral meson is a scalar). Sakharov considered meson production by photons and nucleons using the theoretical techniques developed in Walter Heitler's 1936 book, *The Quantum Theory of Radiation*. To estimate the cross sections, he considered several of the many noncovariant diagrams. He also estimated meson production in nuclei, and found that due to rather loose binding of nucleons the effective threshold is close to $2\mu c^2$ rather than μc^2, where μ is the meson mass.

In November 1947 he successfully defended his PhD thesis, "Theory of 0–0 Nuclear Transitions," and received the candidate degree. The main problem he discussed in the thesis was the ratio of the number of $e^+ e^-$ pairs to the number of single electrons knocked out of atomic shells (internal conversion electrons) in electromagnetic transition between two nuclear levels of the same parity, both having zero angular momentum. He considered two excited nuclei—RaC$'$ (Po^{214*}) and O^{16*}—for which controversial experimental and theoretical results existed at that time. His predecessors in the subject were J. Robert Oppenheimer, Julian Schwinger, Leonard Schiff (for O^{16*}), Hans Bethe, Hideki Yukawa and Shoichi Sakata (for RaC$'$).

In his thesis Sakharov also considered α decays of C^{12*} into Be^{8*} and Be^8, and tried to explain the drastic difference between the probabilities of these decays—the branching ratio for the latter is only 2 percent. To this end he introduced the notion of isotopic parity for a nucleus with equal numbers of protons and neutrons. Essentially what he meant was that the wavefunction of a system of nucleons had to be antisymmetric with respect to all degrees of freedom, including isotopic ones. For RaC$'$ he also took into account the large Coulomb field of the nucleus. In the approximation that he considered, the Coulomb field of the nucleus did not change the total probability of pair emission, only the angular distribution of the electron and the positron.

The third part of his thesis was a calculation of the Coulomb attraction between an electron and a positron in pair production. This effect, as stressed in the thesis, becomes detectable only for those pairs in a very narrow kinematic region where the electron and the positron fly in the same direction—within, say 1°—and their relative motion is nonrelativistic. The last part of the thesis was published in a modified form as a separate paper in *JETP* in 1948.

When you read Sakharov's thesis, which has seventy-one pages, you are impressed by how carefully all the steps are explained, all the intermediate formulas written down, and numerical coefficients derived. He liked to write as clearly as possible. His friends recall that to handwrite formulas into a typed text was a pleasure for him.

In 1948 Sakharov also published a second paper in *JETP* and authored two reports of the Lebedev Institute. The *JETP* paper analyzed the optical method of measuring plasma temperature. When electrons are in thermodynamic equilibrium and deexcitation is negligible, the relative intensities of selected optical atomic lines are a measure of their temperature; otherwise these intensities give the so-called excitation temperature, which has no simple physical meaning. Sakharov also discussed molecular spectra, remarking that the linear relation between temperature and the logarithm of the intensity remains valid beyond the region where it is supposed to work. Many years later he frequently would say that physical laws tend to be approximately valid far beyond the expected limits of their validity.

One of the two Lebedev reports mentioned above presents a calculation of the decrease in the intensity of a synchrotron's electron beam due to scattering on gas molecules in the initial period of acceleration, when the energy is under 1 MeV. The second report is much more interesting. Titled "Passive Mesons," it is a reaction to the discovery of the pion and the muon (he called the latter "passive meson 200") and to a paper by F. C. Frank. Frank considered exotic nuclear cold fusion reactions catalyzed by the formation of "mesotronic hydrogen," which could give a free "shake-off mesotron" with an energy of 4 MeV. Frank tried to interpret in these terms the 4-MeV secondary particles (muons from pion decay) that were observed by Cesare M. G. Lattes, Giuseppe P. S. Occhialini, and Cecil F. Powell.

Sakharov's report contained the first explicit consideration of the muonic mesoatom and pioneered the idea of cold muon-catalyzed DD fusion. Sakharov's estimate of the Coulomb-barrier factor was more optimistic than Frank's by a factor of a thousand. But his conclusion was pessimistic: "With usual mesons 200 the meson catalysis reaction is impossible." Later work (including Sakharov's) has shown that the pessimistic verdict was premature. Today muon-catalyzed fusion is a field of intense research, with perhaps a promising future. Sakharov returned to the topic of muon-catalyzed fusion in his next open publication, coauthored with Yakov B. Zel'dovich, which appeared in *JETP* in 1957.

Plasma Physics

In July 1948, by a special government decision, Sakharov was enlisted in classified work on atomic weapons, as a member of Tamm's group. He was one of the creators of the Soviet nuclear bomb and is often referred to as "the father of the Soviet hydrogen bomb" (more of this later). During the next eight years Sakharov received the highest state honors for his important contributions: Hero of Socialist Labor, twice (in 1953 and 1956—he received it again in 1962), the Stalin prize (1953), and the Lenin prize (1956). He also received a doctor's (DSc) degree (1953) and was elected to full membership in the Soviet Academy of Sciences (1953). At thirty-two years of age, he was one of the youngest members ever elected.

The only paper by Sakharov during this period that has been declassified is his report, written in 1951 and published in 1958, on the "Theory of the Magnetic Themonuclear Reactor" (in fact it was part II of a paper on this subject; parts I and III were written by Tamm). This was the opening and main paper in four volumes of declassified reports that the Soviet Academy published in Russian on the eve of the 1958 Geneva Conference on Peaceful Applications of Atomic Energy. The title of these volumes, as given in English translation in the proceedings of the conference, was *Plasma Physics and the Problem of Controlled Thermonuclear Reactions*. Although Sakharov's paper grew out of military research on high-intensity sources of neutrons, it opened new vistas in mankind's search for clean sources of energy for peaceful purposes. The first description of this plasma physics work was presented by Igor Kurchatov, head of the Soviet weapons project, in his talk at Harwell in 1956, when he came to the United Kingdom accompanying Nikita Khrushchev. The main idea was that of confining a

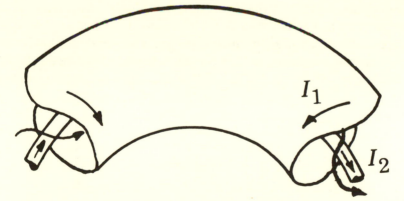

Toroid diagram that Sakharov used to illustrate his scheme for a magnetic thermonuclear reactor. Currents I_1 in an external coil and I_2 in an axial ring produce magnetic lines of force that have a spiral shape. (From Proceedings of the 1957 Geneva Conference on Peaceful Applications of Atomic Energy, *vol. 1, Elmsford, New York: Pergamon, 1961. Reprinted by permission.)*

hot plasma in a toroidal magnetic field. (See figure.) Sakharov's paper is the seed from which the tree of tokamaks and other, similar installations has grown.

Research on themonuclear fusion is now being carried out in many countries. Several large tokamaks are under construction in the Soviet Union, the United States, Western Europe, and Japan. It is expected that a deuterium–tritium reactor will start to produce energy early in the next century. Unfortunately it will also produce a lot of radioactivity. A much cleaner deuterium–helium-3 reactor would be much more difficult to construct.

Sakharov published no scientific research papers between 1958 and 1965. This was a period when he grew increasingly concerned about the accelerating course of the arms race and the dangers of radioactive fallout from continued testing of nuclear weapons in the atmosphere. He published an analysis of the harmful consequences of radioactive pollution in 1959 and was actively involved in initiatives in the Soviet Union leading to the Limited Test Ban Treaty of 1963 (a topic to which we shall return).

In 1965 Sakharov and eight coauthors published a short paper on the experimental development of magnetic cumulation, or compression. Sakharov had first put forward in 1951 the idea of creating ultrastrong magnetic fields by converting the mechanical and thermal energy released in a chemical explosion. There were two types of magnetic cumulators: MK-1 and MK-2 (in Russian the word *cumulator* starts with *k*). In the MK-1 scheme the magnetic flux was compressed in a tube by coaxial implosion from outside. In MK-2, which was developed in the years 1952–56 and reached much higher magnetic fields, the electric current in a solenoid was compressed by an explosion running inside the solenoid from one end to the other, and a magnetic field was ejected into a coaxial line and compressed there. (See figure.) In this way a twenty-five megagauss magnetic

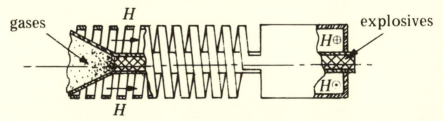

The MK-2 magnetic cumulation generator. The propagating explosion shorts and shortens the helix, decreasing its inductance. This increases the current in the helix and increases the magnetic energy. (From A. D. Sakharov et al., Doklady Akademii Nauk SSSR 165: 1965, p. 65. [Soviet Physics Doklady 10: 1966, p. 1045.])

field was created in 1964. Subsequently, in 1966, Sakharov published a short review titled "The Principles and Characteristics of Magnetoimplosive Generators." The prospects that this breakthrough opened have proved varied and bright. Ultrastrong magnetic fields are used in the study of electrical, optical, and elastic properties of various materials. They can be used for accelerating particles and projectiles. Regular international conferences are devoted to the topic of megagauss fields. The most recent such conference, Megagauss V, was held in July 1989 in Novosibirsk.[2]

Cosmology and Baryon Asymmetry

The papers on magnetic cumulation were a kind of farewell to the classified work of the 1950s. In 1965 Sakharov entered a new field: He published his first paper on cosmology. The problem he dealt with was the formation of primordial astronomical objects from an initially homogeneous distribution of matter. He assumed that at the beginning the homogeneous matter was at zero temperature. The mechanism he considered was the gravitational instability of a uniform expanding universe. He generalized previous studies by taking into account quantum fluctuations. He also discussed later stages of evolution, when stars formed galaxies. This "cold" model was abandoned rather soon as a result of Arno Penzias and Robert Wilson's 1965 discovery of the 3-K background radiation, but even in 1980, commenting on this paper, Sakharov wrote, "It is still possible that the earliest stages in the development of the universe should still be described by the cold model."

In his next paper, written a year later, Sakharov already discussed the "hot" model of the universe known as the "Big Bang" and tried to consider the energy density of the hot photon gas at a number density higher than its Planck value.

His next publication—four pages in *JETP Letters* in 1967—is one of the boldest and most famous physics papers of the century. Its aim was to explain why the matter in the universe is built of protons, neutrons, and electrons, while antiprotons, antineutrons, and positrons are so rare that we can observe antimatter only when it is produced in high-energy collisions, mainly in particle accelerators. This particle–antiparticle disparity is usually referred to as the "baryon asymmetry of the universe," protons and neutrons being the lightest of all baryons. Sakharov made the elegant assumption that originally the universe was neutral and had no baryon asymmetry. He then had the brilliant insight to realize that an asymmetry would build up following the Big Bang, via nonstationary processes during the expansion of the early universe, if his novel idea of proton instability were combined with the violation of particle–antiparticle symmetry (CP symmetry), which James Cronin, Val Fitch, and their collaborators had discovered experimentally in 1964 in decays of kaons. According to Sakharov, some hypothetical processes violate baryon number conservation and CP symmetry on the Planck scale. Assuming the existence of several types of vector bosons with leptoquark quantum numbers whose emission transforms a quark into a muon, Sakharov introduced a tri-linear nonrenormalizable self-interaction of these leptoquarks that violates the conservation of the baryon and lepton numbers but conserves their difference.

Many features of this model became characteristic of grand unification models proposed in the 1970s, and the discovery of proton decay became, and remains today, the goal of several very-large-scale underground detectors. The estimate of the proton's lifetime given by Sakharov was about 10^{50} years. Grand unification models started with proton lifetimes of 10^{30} years but have been revised, as lower experimental limits now reach to 10^{32} years. It appears that it will take at least ten years to add an additional factor of 10 to this limit. (The difference between the 10^{50}-year and 10^{30}-year lifetime estimates stems from the fact that Sakharov considered the processes to occur on the Planck scale, while in modern grand unification theories baryon nonconservation occurs at energies five orders of magnitude lower. The proton lifetime is proportional to the fourth power of this energy scale.)

The paper on baryon asymmetry was accompanied by a four-page letter containing a specific model of CP violation that fits the observed effect of CP violation in neutral-kaon decay and that can be used to compute the effect of CP violation in other processes. In contrast to grand unification models, in Sakharov's model the high-energy scale of baryon nonconservation was very high, but the mass of leptoquarks was low—on the order of the W-boson mass. Consequently, the leptoquarks would effectively induce the CP violation in $K \leftrightarrow \overline{K}$ transitions and cause some appreciable effects violating μ-e universality. Sakharov was disappointed when, shortly after his paper was published, experimental data were reported on the decay of K^0 into two neutral pions that purported to show a difference from this particle's decay into two charged pions. This was contrary to his predictions. Later it would turn out that these neutral-pion data were wrong, but by that time Sakharov would be absorbed by other interests.

Sakharov continued to work on the baryonic asymmetry of the universe until the end of his life. The words "Baryonic Asymmetry of the Universe" served as the title of a *JETP* paper published in 1979 and of his last talk at a physics conference—the 1988 Alexander Friedmann Memorial Symposium in Leningrad. In 1979 he compared his approach with that of grand unification and worked out in detail the kinetics of baryon-nonconserving processes in the expanding universe. The main concerns of his Friedmann talk were the inflationary universe and the role of baryon nonconservation, and whether instantonlike transitions might wipe out the "grand" baryonic asymmetry at a later stage of the universe's evolution, namely, at the electroweak phase transition around 1 TeV. The talk demonstrated how closely he was watching recent developments in particle physics and cosmology.

Quark Model

For Sakharov, the years 1965–67 were ones of extremely intense activity in several directions. In addition to his seminal work on the baryon asymmetry of the universe, he constructed with Zel'dovich in 1966 linear mass formulas for mesons and baryons in the framework of the naive quark model. Their main interest at the time was a model in which a baryon consists of four quarks and an antiquark (today $4q\bar{q}$ would be classified as a crypto-exotic meson). However, they also considered three-quark baryons.

Sakharov's interest in linear mass formulas persisted for many years. In 1975 he generalized them to predict the masses of charmed mesons and baryons, which were unknown at that time. In February 1980, at the beginning of his exile to Gorki, he reduced the number of phenomenological parameters in the formulas to six: three masses for the ordinary, strange and charmed quarks; separate additive constants for mesons and baryons; and a common spin-spin coupling constant b, which in the case of baryons had a semiempirical factor of $\frac{1}{3}$ in front of it. With the new set of parameters he succeeded in reproducing the observed patterns of meson and baryon masses. Moreover, in a second paper, received by *JETP* nine days later, by comparing the ratio of the respective mass differences between the vector and pseudoscalar particles caused by quark magnetic and chromomagnetic interactions, Sakharov determined, in the framework of his nonrelativistic quark model, the ratio of electric and gluonic charges.

The naive nonrelativistic quark model evidently does not address the most profound problems of modern physics. But Sakharov was not snobbish: He loved physics in every form. To think about a puzzle was fun for him.

The Book of the Universe

Returning to the mid-1960s we find two papers by Sakharov devoted to the origin of the gravitational force. Here he considers this force as a "metric elasticity" of space. This elasticity is a reaction of space to its curving and is caused by quantum effects of vacuum polarization. In this approach the Lagrangian of the gravitational field is assumed to be originally equal to zero; it becomes nonzero as an effective Lagrangian resulting from one-loop diagrams of virtual particle–antiparticle pairs. Zel'dovich applied a similar idea to the electromagnetic field. Sakharov himself returned to his original idea in 1970, 1974, and 1975, trying to overcome problems caused by quadratically divergent integrals (a cutoff at the Planck scale was assumed to provide the correct value of the Newtonian coupling constant). In 1974 Sakharov remarked that his approach was incompatible with the scalar–tensor modification of general relativity. In the 1980s several theorists in the West—Stephen Adler and Anthony Zee, for example—continued this effort. From a pragmatic point of view, this "null Lagrangian" approach may be considered as a mathematical expression of a kind of composite model in which gravitons and photons are bound states of particles and antiparticles.

Starting from his first paper on the baryon asymmetry of the universe, Sakharov again and again returned to the tantalizing problem. What was before the Big Bang? Already in 1965 he proposed the hypothesis of cosmological CPT invariance, considering a "pre-universe" that represents a CPT reflection of our universe with respect to the moment $t = 0$.

In 1969 he considered this cosmological reflection in connection with the possible existence of stable neutral particles ten times heavier than protons; he assumed them to be more abundant than protons and to form what we now call "dark matter." In an article with the deceptive title "Antiquarks in the Universe," he proposed searching for these particles. In the same year, in a preprint titled "A Multisheet Cosmological Model of the Universe," he generalized the idea of a "pre-universe" by considering an infinite (or semi-infinite) series of collapsing and exploding universes. In 1972 he combined the cosmological CPT reflection with topological considerations concerning the possible origin of baryonic and leptonic quantum numbers.

Sakharov continued his physics research during the seven long years of his confinement in Gorki, a time of great stress and virtual isolation from his scientific colleagues. In three $JETP$ papers (1980, 1982, and 1984) he discussed various aspects of "multisheet" cosmology with and without cosmological CPT symmetry. In particular, in 1984 he discussed the possibility of quantum creation of an infinite number of universes, some of them possessing not one but several time-like coordinates. In all three papers black holes attracted his attention. He discussed their role in smearing out inhomogeneities in density. In 1986 he wrote a special $JETP$ letter on the evaporation of mini black holes, pointing out the role of evaporation of "shadow world" particles—that is, particles that interact with ordinary matter only gravitationally. He concluded his 1988 Friedmann Memorial talk by discussing the role of the false vacuum in the multisheet model of the universe.

Sakharov's cosmological views were an important part of his personality. Here is the end of his 1975 Nobel Peace Prize lecture:

> I support the cosmological hypothesis that states that the development of the universe is repeated in its basic characteristics an infinite number of times. Further, other civilizations, including more "successful" ones, should exist an infinite number of times on the "preceding" and the "subsequent" pages of the book of the universe. Nevertheless, this *weltanschauung* cannot in the least devalue our sacred aspirations in this world, into which, like a gleam in the darkness, we have appeared for an instant from the black nothingness of the ever-unconscious matter, in order to make good the demands of Reason and create a life worthy of ourselves and of the Goal we only dimly perceive.

Sakharov and the Bomb

Just as Sakharov spoke from his brilliant mind as an uncommonly creative scientist, so he also spoke and acted from his heart and conscience in his courageous and persistent battle for human rights, for intellectual freedom, and for peace. He committed himself fearlessly and relentlessly on both the individual and the global scale in his opposition to human injustice and in his political and educational efforts to reduce the threat of nuclear holocaust.

Evolution of Views

Sakharov wrote about how his social and political views evolved during the period from 1953 to 1968—the year he published his first "nonphysics" paper, a remarkable and wide-ranging essay that was printed first in the West, under the title "Reflections on Progress, Peaceful Coexistence, and Intellectual Freedom." Following the publication of this and subsequent powerful writings and speeches, Sakharov became recognized worldwide as not only a great scientist but also a moral leader of a humanity striving for peace, for progress, and for basic human dignity.

Sakharov described his original satisfaction with having played so prominent a role in the development of the Soviet hydrogen bomb as stemming from a need to create, in the interest of peace, a balance to the "capitalist bomb." He wrote:

> A few months after defending my dissertation for the degree of candidate of science, roughly equivalent to an American PhD, which occurred in the spring of 1948, I was included in a research group working on the problem of a thermonuclear weapon. I had no doubts as to the vital importance of creating a Soviet super-weapon for our country and for the balance of power throughout the world. Carried away by the immensity of the tasks, I worked very strenuously and became the author or coauthor of several key ideas.

However, he also wrote of becoming increasingly involved during the 1950s with a military–industrial complex "blind to everything except their jobs," and he told of coming "to reflect in general terms on the problems of peace and mankind and, in particular, on the problems of a thermonuclear war and its aftermath." Sakharov's concern about the harmful effects of radioactive fallout from atmospheric testing of nuclear bombs grew out of his involvement in the Soviet weapons program and led him to "an increased awareness of the moral problems engendered by such activities."

His first collision with the Soviet establishment can be traced back to 1955. After a nuclear test, he expressed the hope that such weapons would never be used, and in response Marshal Mitrofan Nedelin, who headed the test, used a parable to tell him, in effect, that this was none of his business.

Sakharov convinced Kurchatov to try to persuade Khrushchev not to carry out a gigantic nuclear test. But the attempt failed. In 1961 Sakharov himself wrote to Khrushchev, insisting on the continuation of the nuclear test moratorium, and failed again. In 1962 he again addressed Khrushchev, this time to prevent a large-scale nuclear explosion in the atmosphere. Again his arguments were ignored. But finally the Soviet government approved his idea of a treaty banning nuclear tests in the atmosphere, outer space, and underwater. Sakharov wrote about his satisfaction that he was able to use his position to present to a key Soviet official an important idea that may have been instrumental in bringing about government support for such a treaty: This was his suggestion that the Soviet government set aside the controversial question of underground testing. The major nuclear powers signed the Limited Test Ban Treaty in 1963.

Nuclear Arms Control

During the 1970s and 1980s Sakharov repeatedly spoke out strongly on the gravity of the threat of nuclear holocaust and on the most urgent need to control nuclear arms. In 1975 he wrote:

> The unchecked growth of thermonuclear arsenals and the buildup toward confrontation threaten mankind with the death of civilization and physical

annihilation. The elimination of that threat takes unquestionable priority over all other problems in international relations. This is why disarmament talks, which offer a ray of hope in the dark world of suicidal nuclear madness, are so important.

Later, during the first year of his exile to Gorki, he wrote further, in *The New York Times Magazine* of June 8, 1980:

> Despite all that has happened, I feel that the questions of war and peace and disarmament are so crucial that they must be given absolute priority even in the most difficult circumstances. It is imperative that all possible means be used to solve these questions and to lay the groundwork for further progress. Most urgent of all are steps to avert a nuclear war, which is the greatest peril confronting the modern world. The goals of all responsible people in the world coincide in this regard, including, I hope and believe, the Soviet leaders.

Both during his exile in Gorki and following his return to Moscow in 1987, Sakharov gave close attention to the strategic nuclear arms talks and stated carefully reasoned positions on the pressing issues. In particular he frequently spoke out with concern about the U.S. Strategic Defense Initiative and its potential to destabilize the nuclear balance if deployed. He made one of his final comments on nuclear weapons during his first visit to the United States, in November and December 1988. In remarks at an occasion honoring Edward Teller, Sakharov drew parallels between his and Teller's "lifelines" and expressed his respect for Teller's guiding principles. He then commented, with respect to his work building the hydrogen bomb:

> I and the people who worked with me at the time were completely convinced that this work was essential, that it was vitally important. At that time our country had just come out of a very devastating war in which I personally had not had a chance to take direct part, but the work in which I became involved was also a kind of war. In the United States, independently, the same kind of work was being carried out. The American scientists in their work were guided by the same feelings of this work being vital for the interests of the country. But, while both sides felt that this kind of work was vital to maintain balance, I think that what we were doing at that time was a great tragedy. It was a tragedy that reflected the tragic state of the world that made it necessary, in order to maintain peace, to do such terrible things. We will never know whether it was really true that our work contributed at some period of time toward maintaining peace in the world, but at least at the time we were doing it, we were convinced this was the case.

The world has now entered a new era, and I am convinced that a new approach has now become necessary. And I think in each case when a person makes a decision, he should base that decision on an absolute conviction of his rightness, and only under such circumstances can we ever find mutual understanding. And under such circumstances and in doing so, it is very important, and essential in fact, to find out all the points of difference as well as the points of coincidence and the points where the views are the same. There are certain issues on which Dr. Teller and I have views that coincide; for example, we are both concerned with how to insure the safety of thermonuclear energy. On the other hand, there are other spheres in which we disagree on matters of principle. One such issue is the issue of the space race, antiballistic missile defense. I consider the creation of such a system to be a grave error. I feel that it would destabilize the world situation. It is a system that would require enormous cost, both to establish and deploy such a system as well as to establish a system that would counteract it—the offensive system that would be able to counteract such a system.

Sakharov and Human Rights

During the 1960s Sakharov became involved in an ever-expanding circle of issues of principle that took him beyond the debate over nuclear weapons policy. In 1964, as a young member of the Soviet Academy of Sciences, he opposed a political effort to let a mediocre assistant of Lysenko, the discredited charlatan of a biologist, into the Academy. Election to the Academy is by secret ballot. During the debate preceding the election, Sakharov protested against this new candidate, and indeed against Lysenko. This was no small step for him to take, as Lysenko, whom Stalin had made the "chief of biology" and who had destroyed genetics as a science in the Soviet Union, was close to and influential with Khrushchev, then the Soviet premier. At the end of the debate, which had been forced by Sakharov, the candidate was turned down for membership. It is reported that Khrushchev was so furious he threatened to abolish the Academy. (This did not occur; Khrushchev was dismissed from office in October 1964.)

Beginning to Struggle

Sakharov's strong humanitarian convictions, his compassion for the persecuted, and his devotion to human dignity and freedom of the human spirit led to his first public appeals, in 1966, for victims of repression.

That year, he and twenty-one other prominent personalities signed an appeal to the Twenty-third Communist Party Congress condemning attempts to rehabilitate Stalin. He also sent a telegram to the Supreme

Soviet of the Russian Federation protesting a new clause in the criminal code dealing with "spreading deliberately false slanderous concoctions, defaming the Soviet state and social system." Sakharov saw that this clause gave the authorities a pretext for prosecuting people for their convictions. On December 5, Constitution Day, he took part for the first time in the annual human rights demonstration in Pushkin Square.

In 1967 he wrote a letter to Leonid Brezhnev defending Alexander Ginzburg and three other human rights activists. He also talked to Brezhnev about Lake Baikal, in an effort to prevent industrial development on its shores, which would pollute this unique reservoir, the world's largest body of pure water. The Soviet Academy did not support him in this effort, and the lake became badly polluted and is still being polluted today.

In 1968, as mentioned above, Sakharov published in the West his first "nonphysics" paper—his remarkable "Reflections on Progress, Peaceful Coexistence, and Intellectual Freedom." In this essay he develops two basic themes: That the division of mankind threatens it with destruction, and that intellectual freedom is vital to human society. Sakharov repeated these two themes over and over during the next twenty-one years of his life. In his autobiography Sakharov wrote:

> These same ideas were echoed seven years later in the title of my Nobel lecture: "Peace, Progress, and Human Rights." I consider the themes to be of fundamental importance and closely interconnected. My 1968 essay was a turning point in my life. . . . After my essay was published abroad in July 1968, I was barred from classified work and excommunicated from many privileges of the Soviet establishment.

In the Soviet Union the essay was widely distributed through *samizdat*. About eighteen million copies were printed throughout the world. (All Sakharov's political writings were originally published in the West, in English; only recently have they started appearing officially in the Soviet Union, in Russian.)

Sakharov commented frequently that although his intellectual passion for physics remained as strong as ever, he realized that as a result of the accident of his fame as the father of the Russian hydrogen bomb, he had acquired a moral obligation to use his notoriety—the fact that people listened and the press reported when he spoke—to act and speak out in defense of human rights, in which he believed so deeply. He said that he could not turn his back or walk away from helping those less famous or fortunate. Thus, Sakharov wrote that "after 1970, the defense of human rights and of victims of political repression became my first concern."

In March 1970 he was joined by Roy Medvedev and Valentin Turchin in a letter to the Kremlin leadership analyzing many failures of the Soviet system "caused by the antidemocratic traditions and norms of public life" that had started with Stalin and were continuing. They pointed to pollution and environmental damage, censorship and imprisonment of writers, alcoholism, red tape, errors of policy, and technological backwardness. Their proposals for democratic reforms, including amnesty for political prisoners, the end of censorship, and an end to the labeling of citizens by nationality, went unanswered. Persisting in his cause, on November 4, 1970, Sakharov, together with Valery Chalidze and Andrei Tverdokhlebov, founded the Moscow Committee for Human Rights and focused more heavily on mashalling worldwide public opinion in the human rights struggle.

Sakharov was joined in his campaign for human rights by Elena Bonner, whom he married in 1971. He met Bonner, a physician, during a rally with dissidents, and for the next eighteen years she was constantly at his side as an equally courageous and determined battler. It was she who went to Oslo in November 1975 to accept the Nobel Peace Prize when Soviet authorities refused to grant Sakharov a visa.

Hunger Strikes and Gorki

The summer of 1974 marked the first of Sakharov's hunger strikes. During the period 1974–85 Sakharov undertook four serious, health-threatening hunger strikes. In each instance he used the hunger strike as a means of drawing attention to an injustice being suffered by others and mobilizing world opinion to bring pressure to right the wrong.

His first hunger strike was timed to coincide with the Moscow summit of President Richard Nixon and General Secretary Brezhnev in June 1974. With world press attention centered on the summit events in Moscow, Sakharov announced a hunger strike of finite duration (it lasted one week before it had to be ended because of its impact on his health) to call attention to the plight of the many minority groups in the Soviet Union whose members had no rights whatsoever to emigrate back to their native countries and rejoin their families. Although this strike received wide attention in the world press, it brought about no immediate change of policy. Sakharov emphasized its theme again in his 1975 Nobel Peace Prize address, and on many subsequent occasions.

His second hunger strike occurred over a three-day period in May 1975 and was occasioned by Soviet refusal to permit Bonner to travel to Italy for a needed eye operation. Bonner's health problems were a constant concern to Sakharov during these years. Moved by the political impact triggered by this hunger strike, including selective boycotts by Western scientists, the Soviet authorities relented, and Bonner was permitted to travel to Italy, where the surgery was performed successfully. It was on this same trip to Italy that she continued on to Oslo to accept the Nobel Peace Prize for Sakharov.

Sakharov's third hunger strike was a severe ordeal that started in November 1981 and lasted for seventeen days. By then Sakharov had already been exiled to Gorki for almost two years for protesting the Soviet invasion of Afghanistan during Christmas week 1979. The cause of this strike was the refusal of the Soviet authorities to permit Liza Alekseyeva to emigrate to the United States to join her fiancé, Alexei Semyonov, who is Bonner's son and was Sakharov's stepson. Sakharov was very deeply troubled by the suffering of this young couple, which he attributed to his own activities as a dissident and not to any fault of their own. News reports on the course of this hunger strike were fragmentary in the West. However, it soon became apparent from what was learned in the West, and from his personal appeals to several friends near the end of the strike, that his life was in grave danger. There was an enormous worldwide outpouring of support for him and of rage at his oppressors, who finally relented.

Sakharov's fourth and final series of hunger strikes started in May 1984, shortly after Bonner had also been sentenced to be confined to Gorki in a further effort to break off their communication with the outside world. The goal this time was to gain permission for her to travel to the West for urgently needed heart bypass surgery. These hunger strikes continued intermittently for eighteen months, and the impact on Sakharov's health was life threatening. He was kept in a hospital facility for about three hundred days. In October 1985, Sakharov once again achieved his goal, and a successful sixfold heart bypass operation was performed on Bonner in Boston in January 1986.

Sakharov's Legacy

It was Sakharov's remarkable achievement during the troubled decade of 1974–85 to show to a world strained by violence, by hate, by rigid ideologies, that there is hope in the power of the human spirit and will. He moved governments and people alike and gave faith for the future through, in the beautiful words of his friend and compatriot Lev Kopelev, "the majesty of his spirit, the power of his intellect and the purity of his soul, his chivalrous courage and selfless kindness."

When Mikhail Gorbachev came to power in 1985 with his new thinking, a convergence began to develop between the stated basic policy goals and aspirations of the Soviet government and the principles Sakharov had long espoused: free expression, democratic ideals, cooperative security arrangements with the West, and arms control. Sakharov's exile to Gorki as a dissident became an anachronism. By the end of 1986 the full rights of Soviet citizenship were restored to him, and he returned to Moscow and emerged as a citizen-hero and subsequently a member of the People's Congress. By the time of his death he had become a leader in the newly revitalized movement for freedom and democracy in the Soviet Union. Just how powerful his voice had become as the conscience of the Soviet Union—and all mankind—was evident in the tremendous outpouring of respect and the deeply felt, sincere grief at his death.

Sakharov was and is a model for all scientists who enter the political realm and participate in public debate on the implications of scientific advances. He spoke out courageously, passionately and, when appropriate, with outrage on issues of social injustice and oppression. But when addressing technical issues relevant to public policy, he recognized the special responsibility scientists bear to speak accurately and maintain the same high standards we demand in our professional scientific lives. He was an inspiration to all who knew him or knew of him. Constant in purpose, clear in vision, modest and unflinching in his courage to speak out in circumstances of great personal danger, he inspired support, admiration, and devotion from people of all nations.

Sakharov's voice is now sorely missed, but his spirit continues to energize and guide the quest he led for more than two decades—the quest for justice, human dignity, and freedom everywhere in this world.

Notes and References

1. All of Sakharov's scientific papers were originally published in Russian, most of them in *JETP* and *JETP Letters*; twenty-four of these papers appeared in English. See A. D. Sakharov, *Collected Scientific Works*, New York: Marcel Dekker, 1982.

2. See *Physics Today*, June 1990, p. 36.

The Father of the Soviet Hydrogen Bomb

Yu. A. Romanov

All-Union Scientific Research Institute of
Experimental Physics

In 1948, a small group of theoreticians was formed at the Lebedev Physical Institute under the leadership of Igor Evgenievich Tamm, with the special government-assigned task of studying the possibility of building thermonuclear weapons. Only three years earlier, the bloodiest war in the history of humanity had ended, but already Churchill's famous speech at Fulton declared that "the old doctrine of the balance of power" was no longer valid, and this was the beginning of the "cold war." Our country, worn by the suffering and deprivations of war, and wanting to establish military parity, immediately started to develop nuclear weapons and prepared to test its first atomic bomb, whose enormous power had been demonstrated by the Americans at Hiroshima and Nagasaki. It was known that efforts in the U.S. were directed toward construction of the hydrogen bomb based on the fusion of the heavy isotopes of deuterium (D) or deuterium and tritium (T). The particular feature of this bomb was that its explosion energy was determined largely by the quantity of thermonuclear fuel present and could amount to megatons. In the explosion of the atomic (fission) bomb, the energy released was limited by many factors, in particular by the need for large quantities of expensive fissionable materials. The separation and availability of deuterium was much simpler and cheaper than the separation of the isotopes of uranium and production of plutonium.

In 1942, Edward Teller provided the initiative to construct a hydrogen bomb in the U.S. In the USSR, according to my knowledge, this problem was posed in 1946 in a special document submitted to the government by I. I. Gurevich, Ya. B. Zel'dovich, I. Ya. Pomeranchuk, and Yu. B. Khariton. Soon thereafter, at the Institute of Chemical Physics of the Soviet Academy of Sciences, a small group of collaborators was formed (A. S. Kompaneyets and S. P. Dyakov) under the leadership of Zel'dovich. This group began to study the problem. Due to the extreme secrecy, no information was available about the progress of this similar work in the U.S. However, as we know today, at the end of the 1940s the state of this research was approximately the same in each country.

It was clear that to sustain a thermonuclear reaction, a temperature on the order of a few tens of millions of degrees was necessary, and that this temperature could be reached only by using an atomic bomb as the ignition device. However, if it was simply surrounded by deuterium, this would not result in a significant increase in the explosive power. The reason is that the dissipation of matter at high pressure and the decrease in temperature due to the heat transfer would make the fusion reaction rate too slow, and in such an arrangement only a few percent of the deuterium nuclei would react. The situation would improve significantly if tritium were used instead, since the rate of the DT reaction at a given temperature is about a hundred times that of the DD reaction. However, tritium is not found in nature, and must be produced in nuclear reactors by bombarding lithium with neutrons. Tritium, therefore, is expensive. It is also radioactive with a half-life of 12.6 years, which means that it must be continuously replenished. Thus the construction of the hydrogen bomb was not only a complex technical and industrial problem, but it also required the solution of many basic, purely scientific problems. The group led by Tamm was organized to solve these problems. Tamm was a scientist with a world reputation, and a man with a great spirit, exceptional honesty, and high principles.

The group was located on the third floor of a house on Myuski Street, in three small rooms, and of course behind closed doors. One of the rooms was Igor Evgenievich's office. This had a large desk, a school blackboard for discussions, and, over the board, a portrait of L. I. Mandelshtam — Tamm's teacher and friend. Next to this office was V. L. Ginzburg and S. Z. Belenki's room, and the third room was assigned to Igor Evgenievich's student Andrei Sakharov, who had just a short time before defended his doctoral thesis. In this room some space was also assigned to me (I started my doctoral work at the Physical Institute in June 1948). Here I got to know Andrei Dmitrievich, with whom I had the privilege to work until 1955.

At twenty-seven this simple, modest, childlike man already enjoyed authority in scientific circles. He distinguished himself through the clarity and correctness of his thought, and the conciseness of expression of his ideas. His doctoral thesis was devoted to theoretical problems of nuclear physics. He dedicated himself with energy to the new problems of national defense, offering all his creative power to this problem of importance for the country.

During the first months, we began to familiarize ourselves with the new field of technical physics; we studied the published literature, went to the Institute of Chemical Physics to meet Zel'dovich and his colleagues, became familiar with their work, and studied the problems confronting us on the drawing board. In this way we laid the foundations of a new science.

It may seem impossible, but after only a couple of months, Andrei Dmitrievich formulated some basic ideas which determined the direction of the entire problem's development.

Until that point, Zel'dovich's group considered liquid deuterium (possibly mixed with tritium) as fuel for the thermonuclear facility. Sakharov proposed a heterogeneous construction—named the "layer cake" by him—with alternating layers of light elements (deuterium, tritium, and their chemical compounds) and heavy elements (U^{238}). It turned out that similar suggestions were made in 1946 by Teller, but originally the American scientists adopted a different path which proved to be a dead end.

What are the advantages of such a "layer cake"? First of all, it permits the realization of the "fission–fusion–fission" principle necessary for increasing the explosive energy. Neutrons produced by the DT reaction have energies larger than the fission threshold of U^{238} and lead to its fission. As a result, additional energy is released. More importantly, because of the low thermal conductivity of uranium, the thermal flux emitted by the bomb is reduced. Finally, the light elements situated in the immediate vicinity of uranium will be compressed many times. This last phenomenon was called "sakharization" in the circle of scientists involved in the development of the weapon. The physical cause of sakharization is extremely simple: at superhigh temperatures matter is nearly completely ionized, and equalization of the pressures in the light and the heavy substances assures the equality of the concentration of electrons within them.[1] This means that the light substance will become compressed, which in fact was exactly what was needed in order to increase the rate of the fusion reaction. If lithium is also included in the layered system, under the action of neutrons it would be converted very effectively into tritium which, as already mentioned, participates in the fusion reaction.

The idea of using within the layers the isotope Li^6 was credited to Ginzburg. He affectionately named the lithium deuterate (LiD) "Liddy," although in the reports that were usually written by hand the substance was labeled conventionally. I. V. Kurchatov clearly described the great promise of the use of Li^6, and efficiently organized its production. As a result, the Soviet Union was the first to use it in the hydrogen bomb.

The work on the project received increasingly higher priority and required Andrei Dmitrievich's presence at "the Installation"—the All-Union Scientific Research Institute of Experimental Physics, where in 1946 the most important research efforts related to the construction of nuclear weapons were concentrated. On March 17, 1950, Sakharov flew on an LI-2 transport airplane to the institute to accept a permanent position. I flew on the same airplane. We faced five years of intensive work together.

IN 1949, WHEN HE ARRIVED at the Installation by official appointment, Andrei Dmitrievich was already familiar with the results of the first tests of the atomic bomb. After this, the construction of the hydrogen bomb began to take a realistic shape. The main leadership was provided by Kurchatov, while the scientific leader and the chief designer was Khariton.

The development of hydrogen weapons required the participation of specialists in the most varied fields. Without modeling the process of thermonuclear burning it was not possible to obtain any reliable results. For this it was necessary to devise methods to calculate the gas-dynamic, thermal, and other physical phenomena in a design with complex geometry. At the end of the 1940s a series of research groups was established to develop numerical methods for solving these problems of mathematical physics. The leaders of these science groups were N. N. Meiman, K. A. Semendyaev, and A. N. Tikhonov. However, the situation in the field of numerical techniques was significantly less developed in our country compared to the U.S.: the fastest computer at our disposal was a keyboard Mercedes computer obtained from Germany. Specific calculations were performed by many calculators, who were girls, and the schedule for each calculation was rather lengthy—from weeks to half a year. In 1951 the scattered groups of mathematicians were united under the leadership of M. V. Keldysh in a special institute in Moscow, called the Department of Applied Mathematics. The institute recruited such prominent mathematicians as I. M. Gelfand, K. I. Babenko, and others.

In 1953 the first electronic computer built in our country, the *Strela* (arrow), was commissioned and started to perform calculations for the project, under the leadership of Tikhonov and Semendyaev. With their help, various designs were developed, and significant corrections were made to the initial evaluations.

Intensive experiments related to the kinetics of neutron processes in complex assemblies were conducted, simulating the structure of the layered system. These problems were worked on by scientists from our institute (Yu. A. Zysin, A. I. Pavolvski), from the Lebedev Institute (I. M. Frank, I. Ya. Barit), and also from Dubna (V. A. Davidenko, I. S. Pogrebov), which at that time was called the Hydrotechnical Laboratory (probably because of the proximity of the Volga-Moscow channel), although the only hydrotechnical facility there was the cooling system of the proton accelerator. (At present, it is the Joint Institute for Nuclear Research.) Some non-nuclear experiments were performed by K. I. Shtchelkin, A. D. Zakharenkov, who used regular TNT charges to establish the basic gas-dynamics parameters of the selected bomb design. At the Semipalatinsk testing site, high priority work was performed to prepare for studies of the effect of such an explosion on various arms and military equipment.

In general, intensive preparations were made for the first hydrogen bomb test in the USSR, scheduled for 1953. Such a powerful ground explosion had never occurred in our country before.

What happened in the U.S. during this period? Today, we know more about the development of thermonuclear weapons in the U.S., and can compare it with our own work.[2]

The American hydrogen bomb project was not a lightning-fast program, as was described in 1949 by Teller. The first computer calculations were carried out only at the end of 1949. One after another, the concepts that proved to be unpromising were abandoned and so, their authors, Teller and S. Ulam, were in a state of great pessimism.

In January 1950 President Truman decided to intensify work on the construction of the hydrogen bomb. This was triggered by the first successful test of the Soviet atomic bomb in September 1949.

During this period in Los Alamos, where the work on thermonuclear weapons was conducted, it was decided to use a deuterium-tritium mixture for the thermonuclear ignition inside the "initiator"—the fission bomb. This design was just, in fact, a more powerful atomic bomb, in which its TNT-equivalent was increased. The idea was confirmed during the testing in 1951 performed under the code-name "Greenhouse," in the explosion named "George."

1951 was the year of enlightenment for the American creators of the thermonuclear weapon. In February, Ulam and Teller formulated a series of basic ideas which accelerated significantly the progress of the development of the thermonuclear weapon.[3] In one month, they proposed to use the fission–fusion–fission scheme to enhance the energy released. The tests named "Mike" (1952) and "Bravo" (1954) confirmed the validity of the suggested designs.

On August 12, 1953, at the Semipalatinsk testing site, the first test of the

Soviet hydrogen bomb was performed. This test confirmed the expected characteristics of the device and determined the effect of the explosion on the various pieces of military equipment and weapons. The construction of the bomb used Sakharov's basic principles, for which he was rightfully called "the father of the hydrogen bomb."

Analyzing the results of our first test, Hans Bethe noted that this was not a real hydrogen bomb, since it did not yet burn a large amount of the thermonuclear fuel.[4] Indeed, the "actual" hydrogen bomb was exploded in our country later, in 1955. However, our bomb in 1953, in contrast with the American bomb called "Mike," which weighed sixty-five tons, was not a fixed installation but could be transported by an airplane. Exactly at that time, S. P. Korolev started the work on the construction of a missile that could transport it. Subsequently, thermonuclear devices became significantly lighter, and the design developed by Korolev served as the basis for the rocket which took the first man into space.

AFTER THE ENTHUSIASTIC reception of the successful test, after his election as member of the Academy of Sciences, and after being awarded the title of Hero of Socialist Labor and the Laureate of the State prize, Andrei Dmitrievich again resumed work on the thermonuclear problem. Not all the projects from the end of 1953 and the beginning of 1954 were brought to realization. In the early spring of 1954, in discussions with Zel'dovich, new ideas were born, similar to those reached by Ulam and Teller in 1951. It is amazing how similarly scientists think, even without sharing information about each others' work. Scientific research has its own internal logic, and with such a concentration of the best minds in each country, the progress in development had to proceed more or less in parallel.

I remember how Andrei Dmitrievich gathered the young collaborators in his small room (my period of work at that time—almost six years—was longer than that of the other participants) and started to talk about the remarkable properties of materials with high atomic number as excellent reflectors of high intensity, short-pulse radiation. Without numerical calculations and with the help of amazingly simple models based only on arguments of similarity, he was able to reach quantitative results reflecting quite accurately the factual aspects of the problem. He was talking quite laconically, and I—being used to his style—often had to explain the meaning of his ideas. He could explain very complex problems on the back of an envelope. Where and when he managed to think of all these problems, we could only imagine. Moreover, he tried to transform his ideas into concrete designs, discussing at a professional level all the technological problems in the factory, including the details of experimental techniques with the laboratory researchers and the calculation procedures with mathematicians. His breadth of knowledge was complemented by his nonstandard approach to problems. This all-encompassing approach was unique.

The preparation for testing of the "actual" hydrogen bomb went amazingly fast. All the scientific, technical, and technological problems were successfully solved within one and a half years after the basic ideas were suggested by Zel'dovich and Sakharov. This was possible not only because of the strong scientific leadership, but also because of the efforts of an experienced group of young and energetic scientists and engineers. Their part in the establishment of the "nuclear shield" makes a detailed historic-scientific analysis of this subject an immediate necessity.

Problems of only secondary importance in this project did not exist. I remember vividly the hotly debated question of how to paint the airplane so that the bomb, dropped on a gigantic parachute, would not burn it. Such problems were many, and they were solved quickly and at a high professional level.

On November 22, 1955, with the successful test of the hydrogen bomb dropped from an airplane, the initial period of development of thermonuclear weapons was completed. For the success of this work, many of the participants received high awards. Sakharov was granted the second star as Hero of the Socialist Labor and, together with Kurchatov, Khariton, and Zel'dovich, he received the newly established Lenin Prize. On the reverse side of each medal a number was engraved, from one to four. Andrei Dmitrievich received his third Hero star for the testing of the superpowerful hydrogen bomb, performed in 1962, at the island Novaya Zemlya, the "New Earth" testing ground.

Following somewhat different paths, after failures and successes, the U.S. and USSR constructed the modern thermonuclear weapon at almost the same time. Its further development was directed toward improvements and specific use.

FROM THE MEMOIRS OF YU.A. ROMANOV

IN 1955 I WAS ASSIGNED to work in a newly organized institute, where I led a small group of theoreticians. The many hundreds of kilometers that separated me from Andrei Dmitrievich did not damage our friendly relationship, and we always remained friends, addressing each other with the familiar form of "you."

I was always delighted to be together with his hospitable family. Both he and his wife Klava lived a very modest life; they did not consider it necessary to wear elegant and expensive clothes, although from 1950 on their monetary incomes were more than sufficient for this. The unspent money, in amounts of hundreds of thousands of rubles, was transferred by the Sakharovs to social needs. He was very strict regarding any evidence of dishonesty or disorder, although he was a man of delicate and soft nature and, as one says, could not even kill a fly.

I remember the following episode. Andrei Dmitrievich's family used to travel quite often to Moscow, while he remained alone at his home, immersed in his scientific thoughts, but little concerned with domestic order. When mice appeared in his kitchen, his neighbors suggested that he call the appropriate service for rodent extermination. "Never," answered Andrei Dmitrievich, and began to leave for them pieces of bread and cheese.

Another funny incident happened in the summer of 1950. One Sunday Andrei Dmitrievich, Valentin Nikolaevich Klimov, and I went to the woods which surrounded the city. By mistake, we came rather close to a fence guarded by soldiers. "Stop, I will shoot!" we heard a voice shout. We stopped. "Who are you, inmates or free ones?" The fact was that in the city there were many "prisons." A big truck drove up to us. "Get in!" We climbed into the truck. "Sit down on the floor," said the leader. At the same time, three rather skinny fellows, in sports outfits and somewhat advanced in years, were rocking in the truck (which was riding on a bumpy road) with their palms on the floor, as if to soften the pain of their uncomfortable position. We arrived at the military barracks. "Get out and stand by the wall!" sounded the order. We were then led into a big room, where an extraordinary committee of state security was already gathered. They all probably knew us, but adopting a stern attitude, they asked each of us in turn our first name, family name, patronymic, place of birth, and place of work. After this interrogation they said that the rules for walking should not be infringed, and let us go.

One should admit that during those years the security officials were very concerned about the scientists. Being concerned for the scientists' health and life, and also responsible for the "security" of their secret thoughts, the officials permitted only a few scientists to take vacations in the "big city." Those who did not leave were paid a special bonus in addition to their monthly salary. In the difficult postwar years, all measures were taken to assure the successful work of the scientists in defense of our country.

Notes and References

1. For details, see V. I. Ritus, "Who Else if Not Me?" in this volume.
2. R. Rhodes, *The Making of the Atomic Bomb*, New York: Simon and Schuster, 1986; C. Hansen, *U. S. Nuclear Weapons: The Secret History*, New York: Crown, 1988.
3. The core of these ideas is discussed in the books by R. Rhodes, *op. cit.*, and C. Hansen, *op. cit.*
4. See Hans Bethe, "Sakharov's H-bomb," in this volume.

"Who Else If Not Me?"

V. I. RITUS

Lebedev Physical Institute, Moscow

IN THE BEGINNING OF 1989 the Lebedev Physical Institute of the Soviet Academy of Sciences (FIAN) was preparing to elect the Scientific Council of the Institute. According to the new, democratic rules, a brief resume of each candidate was drawn up and displayed in the hall for everyone to see. Among them was the resume of Andrei Dmitrievich Sakharov, written with my participation:

Candidate for Membership in the Scientific Council of the Physical Institute, Department of Theoretical Physics

Sakharov, Andrei Dmitrievich, born in 1921, senior scientist at FIAN, member of the Soviet Academy of Sciences, internationally recognized theoretical physicist, known for his distinguished work in the field of thermonuclear fusion, elementary particle physics, and cosmology.

Sakharov's main results and fields of research:

1. Physical concepts and calculations that led to the invention and construction of nuclear weapons.

2. Pioneering ideas on plasma confinement and ground-breaking calculations of controlled thermonuclear fusion devices.

3. Ideas and calculations on the generation of very strong magnetic fields by compression of the magnetic flux emerging in an implosion.

4. Research on quantum field theory, elementary particle theory, and, in particular, on muon-catalyzed nuclear reactions (together with Zel'dovich).

5. Treatment of gravitation as the metric elasticity of space. Gravity originates as a result of energy variations of quantum vacuum fluctuations during deformation of space, analogous to the way usual material elasticity results due to energy variations of intermolecular bonds during deformation.

6. Work related to cosmology, in particular, the baryon asymmetry of the universe.

Sakharov is known for his outspoken social activity. He is a Nobel Peace Prize winner, one of the founders and trustees of the International Foundation for the Survival and Development of Humanity, member of the Presidium of the Soviet Academy of Sciences, member of the Scientific Council of FIAN, member of several Academies of Science in the U.S., France, and many other countries.

This brief outline also demonstrates the evolution of Sakharov's scientific activity: from work of tremendous practical significance, he moved on to basic studies of the principles of creation of the universe, in which he formulated profound pioneering ideas.

His work on the hydrogen bomb was undoubtedly exceptional in all respects. It brought Sakharov recognition of his talent as a theoretical physicist, first among the Russian elite physicists, and then throughout the entire world. Based on this work, he was elected a member of the Academy of Sciences, was granted the title of Hero of the Socialist Labor and was a Stalin Prize winner (which included a half million rubles, an unheard of amount at that time), not to mention additional government gifts such as a *dacha* and a car.

The time has come to explain the basic idea of this work, and to provide my impressions of Sakharov during those tense years when I worked under his supervision (1951–55) and later when, his clearance lifted, he returned to FIAN and we again became collaborators in the same department—the I. E. Tamm Department of Theoretical Physics.

AFTER MY ARRIVAL at "the Installation,"[1] two days were spent waiting for my clearance for the theoretical department. At that time I met all the theoreticians except Sakharov and Tamm, who was in Moscow. When I arrived at the department, Sakharov emerged from his room, walked toward me with a broad smile, and rubbed his hands energetically, as if savoring the pleasure of our acquaintance in advance. Later I learned that this habit was merely a sign of his good mood.

He was a tall man, with a slight belly, a round face, and long, dark, slightly receding hair combed to one side. I can still hear his soft voice roll-

ing his r's. We introduced ourselves. Suddenly, everyone disappeared.
Sakharov led me to the blackboard, took a piece of chalk in his left hand,
and, with the words "the object is designed in the following way," he drew
a large circle. He is an original, I thought; he wants to introduce me to the
layout of the city, and for economy he draws a centrally symmetric map.
Sakharov proceeded to draw a smaller circle, perfectly concentric with the
first, and uttered a few more sentences in which I could hardly find any
logic. A couple of minutes later I realized that he was talking about a totally
different object—the hydrogen bomb.

Although the basic principles of the design of the hydrogen bomb are
now well know,[2] it is appropriate to mention Sakharov's basic idea. The
main task was to make use of the energy released during the explosion of a
fission bomb to heat and fuse heavy hydrogen (deuterium or D). That is, to
achieve the thermonuclear reactions,

$$D + D \rightarrow p + T + 4MeV,$$
$$D + D \rightarrow n + He^3 + 3.3MeV,$$

which, due to their energy release, are capable of sustaining themselves. It
appeared that, in order to achieve this goal, a layer of deuterium had to be
placed in the regular atomic bomb between the fissioning substance (a hollow sphere of uranium-235 or plutonium-239) and to surround it by a
chemical explosive whose implosion transforms the fissioning substance
from the subcritical state to the supercritical state. It turned out, however,
that in this process deuterium was not heated sufficiently and the thermonuclear reaction did not take place.

We recall in this connection that the rate of the DD reaction is deter-
mined by its cross section $\sigma_{DD}(\upsilon)$ of this reaction, which depends on the relative velocity of the colliding nuclei and the deuterium concentration n_D.
In fact, in a unit time each deuteron can collide with $\sigma_{DD}(\upsilon)\upsilon n_D$ other deuterons. After averaging over the thermal (Maxwell's) distribution of veloci-
ties, this collision frequency, or the average reciprocal lifetime of the deu-
teron, $\overline{\sigma_{DD}(\upsilon)\upsilon}n_D$ depends only on the temperature and the concentration of
deuterium, and determines the fraction of deuterium "burnt" during the
explosion Δt:

$$\frac{\text{number of burnt deuterons}}{\text{total number of deuterons}} = \overline{\sigma_{DD}(\upsilon)\upsilon}n_D\Delta t.$$

In order to increase the fraction of burnt deuterium, Sakharov proposed
to surround the deuterium with a layer of unenriched, natural uranium
(mostly U^{238}) which would moderate the separation and, more important,

significantly increase the concentration of deuterium. In fact, at temperatures reached after the explosion of the fission bomb primer, the material surrounding it is nearly fully ionized. The pressure of such a gas is equal to nkT, where n is the total concentration of nuclei and electrons. Here it is very important to recall that the uranium nucleus is surrounded by ninety-two electrons, while that of deuterium is surrounded only by one. This is the essence of the trick. From the equality of pressures and temperatures at the boundary between the deuterium and uranium, we find that the concentration of the deuterium nuclei is

$$n_D = \frac{Z_U + 1}{Z_D + 1} n_U = \frac{Z_U + 1}{2A_U M} \rho_U \sim \frac{1}{4M} \rho_U.$$

That is, it is proportional to the density ρ_U of uranium, with a proportionality factor which depends only weakly on the material of the surrounding layer (Z is the atomic number of the material, A is the mass number, and M is the atomic mass unit). Thus the uranium envelope, whose density is twelve times greater than the density of standard explosives, is more than ten times the density of deuterium and therefore increases the rate of the thermonuclear reaction by a similar amount. Such a method of reaction increase was called "sakharization" by our collaborators.

The increased rate of DD reactions leads to significant production of tritium (T), which fuses with deuterium in the nuclear reaction

$$D + T \rightarrow n + He^4 + 17.6 \text{ MeV}$$

which has a cross section a hundred times larger than that of the DD reaction and releases five times more energy. Moreover, the nuclei of the uranium envelope rapidly undergo fission under the action of fast neutrons generated in the DT reaction and significantly increase the power of the explosion.[3] This result suggested the use of uranium as an envelope, instead of any other heavy element (such as lead).

The power of the thermonuclear reaction could be increased significantly if some of the deuterium was replaced by tritium at the outset. However, tritium was very expensive, as well as radioactive. V. L. Ginzburg therefore proposed the use of Li^6 instead of tritium, since Li^6, bombarded by neutrons, generates tritium in the reaction

$$Li^6 + n \rightarrow He^4 + T + 4.8 \text{ MeV}.$$

In fact, a charge in the form of lithium deuteride (LiD) radically increased both the power of the thermonuclear reaction and the energy released by fission in the uranium envelope, which was several times greater than the thermonuclear energy release.

That was the physics underlying our first thermonuclear weapon.[4]

In parallel with this primary activity, Sakharov worked intensively on the idea of the magnetic thermonuclear reactor. Such a reactor was envisioned by him as a solenoid filled with deuterium and bent into a torus, which has the shape of a donut. The deuterium was heated by strong discharge currents that passed through the windings of the torus. These currents also generated a magnetic field inside the torus which prevented the plasma from colliding with the walls of the torus. It is amazing how close the dimensions and other parameters of these facilities, calculated by Sakharov, are to those of the tokamaks built many years later, both in the Soviet Union and elsewhere.[5]

The third important idea formulated by Sakharov during those years was the generation of very strong magnetic fields by compression of magnetic flux inside a solid metallic cylinder. The cylinder was compressed by cylindrical implosions. The intersection of the moving side walls of the cylinder by magnetic lines of force generated a current in the walls which, in turn, generated an additional magnetic field inside the cylinder. By this process the magnetic flux $\Phi = \pi R^2 H$ inside the cylinder remained constant. As a result, the strength of the field increased in inverse proportion to the square of the radius of the cylinder.[6]

Later, it was found that a similar idea had been suggested at approximately the same time by Ya. P. Terletskii. I had the impression that Sakharov was slightly upset by this news.

The experimental studies on the compression of magnetic flux, started at Sakharov's initiative, led in 1964 to record high values of magnetic fields on the order of twenty-five megagauss.

ALL THESE YEARS, Sakharov worked with an exceptional intensity, arriving at the department before everyone else, and leaving last. This even though he had a family (wife Klavdia Alekseyevna and two small daughters, Tatyana and Lyubov) and we were all five to eight years younger than him.

Even now, I cannot forget the intensity of his work. Once when I entered his office, he was sitting in his chair with his head in his hands, looking at a drawing.[7] He turned his head toward me, and I saw several of his long, dark hairs fall on the drawing. No wonder that most people saw him later in quite a different way.

In addition to his own work and participation in many meetings in which very important decisions were made, Sakharov spent much time supervising the work of his collaborators. I remember that Yu. A. Romanov and I were calculating the probability of a very rare process in a macroscopic system, making extensive use of the probability theory. We wrote a draft manuscript and gave it to Sakharov. On the third or fourth page, he noticed an error in our logic. We scratched our heads, corrected that part of the paper and also those that followed. Sakharov read further—again finding an error, showing once more our insufficient mastery of the probability theory. We again corrected the final part of the paper. But Sakharov found yet another error, this time the last one. We were not embarrassed, because the only people who knew about these errors were the three of us. Sakharov's comments had been soft and tactful, but his level was so much different from ours! In that particular instance, we were ready to participate in a meaningful discussion and quickly grasped his comments. Difficulties sometimes arose when unclear problems were discussed. Each of us expressed our views, but Sakharov's arguments were generally difficult to understand—his way of thinking was unorthodox. Usually we were seeking a solution based on well-known methods, while he grasped the problem intuitively and made his way to its solution as a whole, and not in separate steps.

BECAUSE SAKHAROV worked so intensively, we seldom saw him at leisure, but here are a few "non-working" episodes:

One time, at the beginning of their residence at the Installation, Sakharov and Romanov took a walk through the forest outside the town and came to barbed wire—the boundary of the Installation. The soldiers immediately took them into custody, summoned a truck by telephone, sat them on the floor of the truck in handcuffs and with stretched legs, and delivered them in this position to the security gate. During the trip their legs got numb and their knees hurt. It turned out that this was a typical security measure to prevent the escape of inmates. This was truly a beginning with many implications!

Within three weeks of my arrival, Sakharov turned thirty years old (May 21, 1951). In the evening, about twenty people gathered at a party in his cottage (he and his family occupied half of a two-story wooden house—three rooms and a kitchen). Klavdia Alekseyevna had baked a huge pie and decorated it with thirty candles. Although I had heard of such traditions, I saw it then for the first time. I enjoyed the evening very much. It was a delightful party full of wit, spirit, and wine. Perhaps for that reason, some time later I felt the need to go out on the street and breathe some fresh air. It was a warm night full of stars. Suddenly I heard steps behind me, and saw Sakharov approaching me. "Volodya, how do you feel?" he asked. I was moved by his concern. We strolled for a while and returned to the house.

In the midst of our activity, the department (more precisely, Igor Evgenievich Tamm and Sakharov) was assigned an automobile with a female driver. Although it was only a twenty minute walk from our home to work, we used the car frequently. Usually, the first to arrive was Sakharov. The second trip brought the rest of us. Igor Evgenievich arrived on the third trip, much later. One time I decided to go to "the factory" (the experimental station), and I told Sakharov that I would release the car as soon as I arrived there. We forgot about Igor Evgenievich! He had to walk to work. Arriving at Sakharov's office, he gave Sakharov a verbal thrashing. Sakharov took it quietly, saying nothing about my blunder. This scene was rather unpleasant but instructive for all of us. Later, I witnessed Igor Evgenievich apologize to Sakharov for his rash judgment.

In the green corner of the Installation (on the territory of the "general's cottage," reserved for important visitors) a volleyball court and a tennis court were built. Strangely, these were seldom used. Once we forcefully persuaded Sakharov to play tennis. Klavdia Alekseyevna also came to watch us. Sakharov's opponent served the ball. He followed it with his eyes, his thoughts elsewhere, and then suddenly reacted, swinging his racket and meeting empty air like Don Quixote.

"Klava, you saw me return the ball?"

"Adik, I think you missed it."

"Yes, but if I had hit it, what a smash it would have been!"

One time, I was sent to see Landau's group in Moscow, which was working on numerical solutions of mathematical problems set up by our group. Some preliminary results were urgently needed. This was the first time I met Lev Davidovich Landau and he took me to his group, saying, "Now I will introduce you to our boys." I was then twenty-five, and talked uninhibitedly for two hours with "the boys," who I thought were older than me (one of them was bald, while the other still had some hair on his head). I remember that they were very interested to know about Sakharov, trying to understand what sort of physicist he was and with whom he could be compared. In my opinion, no other physicist in the USSR was more gifted at that time.

At the same time, I had to accomplish a rather delicate mission. The fact was that Sakharov and I had been studying the problem in which I was interested. More precisely, he had drawn the basic sketch and I had checked it and added the necessary details. It turned out that Sakharov had forgotten to write an important term in the partial differential equation, and I had not noticed this error. Later when we noticed, I had been very upset and wanted to send the correction to Moscow, but he said that the people there were well qualified, that they were familiar with the equation, and that they would correct the error. Indeed they did.

The two "boys" were obviously flattered when I told them about Sakharov's comments. Before I left, they briefly had a discussion—who should sign my permit. It turned out that one of them was E. M. Lifshitz and the other I. M. Khalatnikov.

Soon after Stalin's death, to the frequently asked question "What will happen now?" Sakharov replied: "Nothing, of course. Everything will go the same way. A complex system is governed by its own internal laws and supports itself." He added that each individual person, even one in a high position, influences only his immediate environment. In general, during those years, Sakharov was politically passive.

In our department was V. N. Klimov, a collaborator who was younger than Sakharov and apparently a member of the Communist Party. (He died tragically in the mountains before he reached age thirty.) Valya used to read the newspapers "with the pencil in his hand"; he read between the lines and made fun of the contradictions and lies spread in the press at that time. Sometimes he even stretched the law. He was often summoned to the *gorkom* (we called it *politotdel*, "the political division"), where they lectured him and, thank God, let him go. We all truly understood him, but regarded his activity with some amazement, considering it useless and dangerous. I think that Sakharov felt the same way about this matter, although I never heard him either endorse or condemn it. In fact, for many of us Valya was the first to think "differently." We even thought of him as a human rights protector. Remember, that was a time when Beria was in power.

AFTER THE SUCCESSFUL TEST of the first Soviet hydrogen bomb, Tamm left the Installation and devoted himself totally to his work at the theoretical department of FIAN, where I moved in 1955. Therefore, except for a few occasional meetings, my relationship with Sakharov was interrupted until 1969, when he also returned to the theoretical department. During the years 1956–69, Sakharov continued to work on the problem of improving thermonuclear weapons, and for this work he was awarded two more stars of the Hero of Socialist Labor. He also played increasingly more attention to non-secret projects—muonic catalysis of nuclear reactions (1957), the baryon asymmetry of the universe (1967), the relationship between gravity and elementary particles (1967), and $K^0 \leftrightarrow \overline{K^0}$ transitions, which we now describe as transitions with the exchange of two W bosons (1967).

In recent years, in view of the search for the proton decay, Sakharov's work on the baryon asymmetry of the universe has become widely recognized, since it included the first prediction of such a decay.[8] Sakharov worked from the Big Bang model of a hot, expanding universe, and demonstrated that in order for the observed baryon asymmetry of the universe to occur, the following three conditions must be satisfied:

1. Interactions in which baryon number is not conserved must exist.

2. The particle–antiparticle symmetry (C) and the combined parity (CP) must be violated in these interactions.

3. The universe must be far from thermal equilibrium.

Since reactions that change baryon number have never been observed, Sakharov assumed that such interactions between quarks and leptons occur through the participation of intermediate bosons having fractional charge and extremely large mass (on the order of the Planck mass). Such reactions, therefore, can occur only at enormous energies, or when the temperature of the universe was near to or higher than the threshold for generation of the intermediate bosons. This also means that such X bosons can decay through channels with different baryon numbers, B_1 and B_2, and with relative probabilities r and $1-r$. The decay of a boson–antiboson system $X + \overline{X}$ will then lead to a system with a nonvanishing baryon number,

$$\Delta B = rB_1 + (1 - r) B_2 - \bar{r}B_1 - (1 - \bar{r}) B_2 =$$
$$= (r - \bar{r}) (B_1 - B_2)$$

if the probabilities r and $\bar{r}$ of the partial, charge-conjugate channels are different. This difference, of course, could be due to the nonconservation of C and CP symmetries.

However, if the universe at such temperatures is in thermal equilibrium, then the number of baryons must necessarily be equal to the number of antibaryons. This is a corollary of the CPT theorem, according to which the mass M and the lifetimes of the particles and antiparticles must be the same, and their distributions must be proportional to $\exp(-M/kT)$. Since the universe is not stationary, and since it leaves thermal equilibrium very rapidly, this circumstance makes Sakharov's mechanism for the violation of its baryon symmetry valid.

In 1967 Sakharov published a very interesting article titled "Vacuum Quantum Fluctuations in Curved Space and the Theory of Gravitation."

In order to understand its meaning, it is important to recall that, according to Einstein, gravity is the curvature of space caused by the presence of matter; that is, by the presence of real particles and fields (which have some energy density). The curvature is proportional to the energy density, and the proportionality coefficient is Newton's gravitational constant G, divided by the velocity of light raised to the fourth power:

$$\text{curvature} \sim G/c^4 \text{ x energy density}$$

This is the famous Einstein equation.

In his work, Sakharov asserted that this equation has a dynamic interpretation: that the curvature multiplied by c^4/G is the change in the energy density of the vacuum due to the curvature of space. Therefore, in Sakharov's view there is hope that with quantum field theory it is possible to find the energy of the quantum vacuum fluctuations as a function of the curvature of space. In the first approximation, this function should be linear with respect to the curvature, with a proportionality coefficient completely determined by the very short wavelength part of the quantum fluctuation spectrum. On the other hand, according to Einstein, this coefficient is c^4/G. The gravitational constant is thus determined by elementary particle physics at very high momentum.[9]

During the years 1956–69, two significant events occurred in Sakharov's personal life: one of them happy, the birth of a son; and the other tragic, the death of Klavdia Alekseyevna. Those years were also marked by a profound evolution of his socio-political opinions.

The testing of thermonuclear weapons continued with ever increasing frequency and greater energy release. The tests damaged nature and required the evacuation of thousands of people whose health and life were endangered. Sakharov's participation in the research and testing of these weapons posed a series of acute moral problems for him. He began to lobby actively for the end of nuclear weapons testing, and this brought him into conflict with Khrushchev and other high-ranking officials. Although nuclear parity had been reached, production of nuclear weapons above this level began to become a tool of political blackmail and domination, and threatened the peace and life of all of mankind. Sakharov concluded that in order to eliminate the threat of self-destruction of humanity, it was necessary for our country to reach an understanding with the democratic countries of the West, and to hold general human values above ideological values. He expressed this idea in his paper "Reflections on Progress, Peaceful Coexistence, and Intellectual Freedom," which was published abroad in 1968.

The authorities removed Sakharov from his classified work. He returned to FIAN and found himself heading the human rights movement in the country. At the same time, he participated regularly in the seminars of the theoretical department, attended the meetings of its Scientific Council, and sometimes talked about his work. We had the opportunity to discuss both physics and political ideas with him, the latter, of course, in private settings. At that time, unorthodox ideas were blossoming; in our conversations we discussed such concepts as *glasnost*, pluralism, alternative choices, multiparty systems, and convergence.

Many of us shared Sakharov's convictions, although we considered some of them too far-reaching. We had an abiding fear for the fate of ourselves and our department. Although scientific colleagues in the department, even during the most vicious campaigns, did not sign any letters defaming Sakharov, in reality we did not help him. I can say about myself that I, along with some of my colleagues, signed the petition written by Sakharov in defense of Zh. Medvedev (his name was familiar to me), and was very pleased upon learning that he was released from the psychiatric hospital. This apparently was one of the rare cases, if not the only one, when the voice of society was listened to. However, I did not sign the petition in defense of the participants of the so-called airplane case. With an uneasy feeling I gave Sakharov three reasons why I did not sign the petition: one should not endanger the life of other people for the sake of one's own goals; I did not know the people who were involved or the details of the case; and I did not have any immunity against the repression of the authorities. All but the last reason applied to Sakharov too, who had immunity from repression by virtue of his high position. Having signed the petition himself, he probably thought his team should do the same and rely on his protection. As to the immunity, he said a doctoral degree was sufficient to confer it. I still feel that I made the right decision, but why then do I feel the pangs of conscience?

We had a long, candid discussion in his old apartment in Stchukino (near the Kurchatov Institute), during which he said that he was ready to sacrifice himself, bearing in mind the possibility of being exiled.

I talked with Sakharov about his human rights activity many times. I felt that he should limit his activities and concentrate on speaking and writing programmatic articles about global problems that concern all of humanity as well as our country, and that he should carefully think about all these matters. I thought his actions in defense of other individuals and on some particular problems were open to orthodox criticism, and must have cost him much time, energy, and nerves (even if only for collecting reliable information and writing many petitions). In some way, I managed to share these thoughts with Elena Georgievna. She replied, "Yes, I also tell him about this all the time." But the range of activities which attracted Sakharov progressively increased.

One time, in answer to my question why a certain telegram to Pinochet about Pablo Neruda was worded so critically, he answered that the text was already prepared at the time they asked him to sign it, that one could always find pretexts if one wanted, but the important point was that the goal was accomplished. I then felt that he simply had no fear: it was important to achieve the goal; he did not think of the harm that might come to him.

Another time I asked him why he defended a particular case, which I considered to be hopeless. "Who else if not me?" he asked. Yes, he had followers, but only a few of them had the courage to conquer their fear. In fact, he acted as any normal man should act, and his example taught us this lesson.

THE INVASION OF AFGHANISTAN troubled the entire Soviet Union. Everyone I talked with expressed indignation about this action. But only Sakharov and a few others spoke out openly about the invasion. The authorities' reaction came immediately—deportation to Gorki, and withdrawal of all his state awards.

My first visit to Sakharov in Gorki (together with I. V. Andreev, a researcher in our department) took place in January 1983. We easily found the house, the front entrance, and the apartment by the description of the previous visitors. With great excitement, we vigorously shook hands with the guard, shaking the snow off our clothes at the front door. Hearing the noise, Sakharov came out smiling and we entered his apartment. After ten minutes, the door bell rang, and we heard the lively request of the guard: "Andrei Dmitrievich, please allow me to see the passports of your visitors." He probably thought that we were KGB officials, or he was simply a decent man. In the afternoon the head of the nearby post office brought Sakharov letters, including some from abroad. We appreciated the fact that her conversation with Sakharov was also very polite. The letters were written by some unknown people, one a priest, all connected in some way with human rights organizations.

We told Sakharov all we knew, and something about our work. During the day, Sakharov made arrangements for dinner (this was usually prepared by Elena Georgievna, but she was then in Moscow). We brought the food with us in a special bag; it was prepared by chef Sakharov, leaving us the sophisticated work of washing the dishes. After dinner, he declared one hour of rest; he stretched out on a bed, and suggested that we do the same. I was unaccustomed to taking naps during the day and soon found myself wandering through the apartment, unwittingly looking for possible bugs. I did not notice anything suspicious. By chance, I saw on Sakharov's desk the beginning of a memorandum about the Arab–Israeli conflict. Later, he showed me Pais' book about Einstein, which mentioned Einstein's serious interest and involvement in the well-known Wallenberg case. Sakharov told me the details of this case. Strangely enough, despite *glasnost*, in a recent Russian translation of this book (1989) Wallenberg's name is not mentioned.

During my second visit (February 9, 1984), after exchanging news about scientific problems, Sakharov demonstrated his skills in the use of a small computer sent to him from abroad. In particular, he programmed and solved the problem of the motion of Mercury around the sun, taking into account the effects of general relativity, and thus numerically determined the velocity of Mercury's perihelion shift. Working with the "clever" computer brought him real pleasure. After dinner, which passed in the same spirit as the previous one, he told me about a matter that bothered him: he had sent a letter to Andropov, asking him to grant Elena Georgievna permission to travel abroad for medical treatment, but after three months he had not received an answer. "I'll wait one more week, and then I'll declare a hunger strike," he said. I tried to persuade him not to do this, asking him to wait, telling him that because of Andropov's prolonged absence, rumors were circulating about a severe illness, that changes at the top were possible, and hence changes in the attitude towards him.

By coincidence, Andropov died the same day, but he was replaced by Chernenko. Sakharov sent another letter, this time addressed to Chernenko. There was no reply for a long time, and then they notified him that an answer would be given after the May Day celebration. As we know (see the magazine *The Flag*, 1990, No. 2), on May 2, 1984 Elena Georgievna was arrested and later she was sentenced. The hunger strike declared by Sakharov on the day of her arrest, his admission to hospital, and the subsequent barbaric treatment by the doctors and KGB agents changed him beyond recognition.

After these events, I met Sakharov on the day of his return to Moscow, in December 1986. Although I was glad and excited to see him, it was hard for me to look at his exhausted face, his sunken affectionate eyes, his stooping shoulders, and his emaciated body. If in spirit he emerged a victor, the physical trauma proved to be incurable.

ONE OFTEN HEARS THE QUESTION: How could such a great humanist like Sakharov be involved in building thermonuclear weapons and, what is more, for a regime as inhumane and nondemocratic as that of Stalin and Beria? Or another question: What impelled him to turn away from that successful work on nuclear weapons to the problems of peace and disarmament, to the defense of human rights? I think that the answers to these questions are related to the evolution of Sakharov's creative spirit. He was first of all a very gifted physicist and inventor. At that time he considered his ideas about building the thermonuclear bomb and a thermonuclear reactor exclusively as great scientific and technological advances, and not as the solution to problems of military and political conflicts. Testing the validity of these ideas and seeing their realization were a confirmation of his creative pride. Despite the propaganda, we did not fear a real threat from the U.S., but the spirit of competition (who will do it faster and better?) undoubtedly prevailed, as it always does in any scientific endeavor, especially since we were behind initially. In the mid-1950s, when these ideas were accomplished, the physics problems solved, and promising directions identified, the interest of the prominent scientists began to shift in other directions. They had acquired enormous prestige and realized the power of their inventive potential. At this time, Sakharov saw that his creation, in the hands of a small group of power-hungry people, was becoming a tool for the spread of geopolitical domination. In a way, this was a challenge from the autocracy to the creators of scientific-technological progress. We are fortunate that this call was accepted by a man with an enormous intellectual power, the highest humanitarian principles; a man of conscience and duty. And he gave all his strength to find a way out of the crisis. Could someone other than he have done it?

Notes and References

1. After I graduated from the physics department of Moscow State University in 1950, I continued my graduate studies. Meanwhile, M. A. Markov recommended to Tamm that I be included in the group that was organized in a research center outside Moscow to work on Sakharov's idea. At the beginning of May 1951, when I was sent there, I thought that here was the location of the large secret accelerator about which rumors were circulating in Moscow.

2. "Nuclear Weapons," *Great Soviet Encyclopedia* 51 (*Bolshaya Sovietskaya Entziklopediya*), Moscow, 1958, pp. 320–321; "The Nuclear Explosion," *Encyclopedic Dictionary of Physics (Fizicheskii Entzikpedicheskii Slovar)*, Moscow, 1984, pp. 917–918.

3. Recall that natural uranium consists of 99.3 percent U^{238} and 0.7 percent U^{235}. In contrast with U^{235}, which can be split by both fast and slow neutrons, U^{238} is split only by fast neutrons with an energy larger than 1 MeV.

4. See Yu. A. Romanov, "The Father of the Soviet Hydrogen Bomb," in this volume.

5. See I. N. Golovin and V. D. Shafranov, "The Origin of Thermonuclear Fusion," in this volume.

6. See A. I. Pavlovski, "Magnetic Cumulation," in this volume.

7. He was protected by one of his two bodyguards, nice young men who did not bother us but who were on duty around Sakharov twenty-four hours a day.

8. See A. D. Linde, "Inadmissable Questions: Courage or Insanity?", in this volume.

9. See S. L. Adler, "Sakharov and Induced Gravitation," in this volume.

Sakharov's H-bomb

HANS BETHE

Cornell University, Ithaca

ANDREI SAKHAROV'S MEMOIRS are deeply moving. Some of the excerpts also give new insight into the development of the Soviet hydrogen bomb, although Sakharov scrupulously avoided revealing the details: "I shall remain silent about some aspects of my life and work in that period . . . I consider myself bound for life by a pledge not to divulge state and military secrets, a commitment I undertook of my own free will in 1948."[1]

Still, it is clear that Sakharov's ideas were the basis for both the first and second Soviet hydrogen bombs, tested on August 12, 1953, and November 22, 1955, and he was deeply involved in their development. He first joined Igor Tamm's hydrogen bomb research team in 1948, and in 1950 moved to "the Installation," the remote site where Soviet weapons were designed. There he remained until 1968, when his essay "Reflections on Progress, Peaceful Coexistence, and Intellectual Freedom" was published in the West. Soviet authorities had earlier employed various sanctions to discourage him from expressing the political views they deemed unacceptable. But "Reflections" was the final straw; Sakharov, who was in Moscow on the day it was published, was never allowed to return to his office at the weapons complex.

In the early days, the peasants living near the test site were told that "a 'test model of communism' was under construction." To Sakharov the place was "a curious symbiosis between an ultramodern scientific research institute and a large labor camp. . . . The workshops, the proving grounds, the roads, even the housing for the Installation's employees had been built by prisoners who were escorted to work by guard dogs."[2]

The 1953 test of a big boosted fission bomb at Semipalatinsk was cele-brated by the scientists and hailed by Stalin's successor, Georgi Malenkov. But Sakharov clearly indicates that it did not provide the answers necessary for further development. Instead, it was the 1955 test, based on what he called his "Third Idea," that "crowned years of effort." That second test "solved the problem of creating high-performance thermonuclear weap-ons" and opened the way for a whole range of devices with remarkable capabilities.[3]

Sakharov's discussion confirms what we concluded from analyzing the radioactive debris collected after the Soviet tests—that only the second model, detonated in 1955, was a true hydrogen bomb. Our continuing analysis of debris from Soviet atmospheric tests through 1963 indicated that all subsequent devices tested by the Soviets were based on the 1955 design.

In the United States, the test that "opened the way" occurred on Novem-ber 1, 1952, when a weapon based on the work of Edward Teller and Stan-islaw Ulam was detonated. All further U.S. hydrogen devices were based on the Teller–Ulam principle.

Thus it was three years after the first U.S. test before the Soviets' first test of a corresponding design. This refutes the conventional wisdom—still frequently offered—that the interval between successful U.S. and Soviet H-bomb tests was barely ten months, from November 1952 to August 1953, and that it was high time for the U.S. government to decide in 1950 to pursue H-bomb development.

Sakharov says his Third Idea was not stimulated by analyzing the debris from our 1952 test, as I suggested as a possibility to Daniel Hirsch and William Mathews. Knowing his scientific excellence and his devotion to the project, I now believe that he probably developed the idea independently.

In the late 1940s and early 1950s, nuclear pioneers Robert Oppenheimer and Teller engaged in a heated debate over the urgency and practicality of developing a U.S. thermonuclear bomb. Teller urged the government to move quickly, while Oppenheimer advised against working on a thermo-nuclear weapon. Sakharov concluded that on technical grounds Teller was "of course" right to believe that a practical design would be found sooner or later. But, says Sakharov, "Oppenheimer's position was not without merit. Oppenheimer apparently believed (and had impressive evidence to back his view) that the designs that had been concocted for a hydrogen bomb were not very promising." Not then, but later on, Sakharov grew to sympathize with Oppenheimer: "Striking parallels between his fate and mine arose in the 1960s, and later I was to go even further than he had. But in the 1940s and 1950s my position was much closer to Teller's, practically a mirror image."[4]

Sakharov considered Teller's colleagues unfair and mean-spirited because many later ostracized him. He implies that the scientific community's reaction was due to Teller's championing of an unpopular idea, and he defends Teller's position on H-bomb development as "taking a stand on principle."

This is an argument I cannot accept: Teller lost the affection and respect of many scientists not in 1950 when he pushed for H-bomb development, but four years later when Oppenheimer's loyalty was questioned by the Atomic Energy Commission. Teller's scientific colleagues regarded his testimony during the AEC investigation as an unwarranted personal attack that contributed to Oppenheimer's loss of his security clearance.

In any case, claimed Sakharov, the argument in 1950 over the H-bomb go-ahead was meaningless. "Hindsight shows the situation [in the Soviet Union] was already out of control by the time the Teller–Oppenheimer dispute erupted, and neither side could then have pulled back." Sakharov dismissed the suggestions of Oppenheimer's colleagues on the General Advisory Committee, I. I. Rabi and Enrico Fermi in particular, that the United States try to conclude an agreement with the Soviet Union not to develop the H-bomb. Nothing could have changed Stalin's and Beria's minds. "Stalin, Beria and company already understood the potential of the new weapon, and nothing could have dissuaded them from going forward with its development. Any U.S. move toward abandoning or suspending work on a thermonuclear weapon would have been perceived either as a cunning, deceitful maneuver or as evidence of stupidity or weakness. In any case, the Soviet reaction would have been the same: to avoid a possible trap and to exploit the adversary's folly."[5]

Perhaps a total suspension of development was unrealistic. But such a criticism could not have been applied to Vannevar Bush's ingenious proposal in 1952, which Barton J. Bernstein described in the Fall 1989 issue of *International Security*. Bush proposed that the United States complete research on a hydrogen device, but not test it. The United States, said Bush, could declare publicly that it was ready to test the device, but would refrain from doing so as long as no other power tested one.

Such a policy might have saved the world from a thousand-fold escalation of the explosive power of the atomic bomb. And the policy would have been self-policing, since a test in the megaton range can be detected all around the world. Because an H-bomb is a very complicated device, no country would put the weapon into its arsenal without having tested it. It is unfortunate that Bush's proposal was rejected by the U.S. government.

How the Soviets would have reacted is, of course, unknowable. But in March 1953 Stalin died, and a much less hard-line government came into power.

Notes and References

1. Andrei Sakharov, *Memoirs*, New York: Knopf, 1990, p. 101.

2. *Memoirs*, p. 113.

3. *Memoirs*, p. 193.

4. *Memoirs*, pp. 99–100.

5. *Memoirs*, p. 99.

The Origin of Controlled Thermonuclear Fusion

I. N. GOLOVIN

V. D. SHAFRANOV

Kurchatov Institute of Atomic Energy, Moscow

In the field of controlled thermonuclear fusion, A. D. Sakharov not only proposed the basic idea of the method, based on which one can hope to achieve such reactions, but he also performed extensive theoretical studies on the properties of high-temperature plasma and its stability. This work assured the success of the experimental and technical studies which received recognition throughout the entire world.

I. E. TAMM

IN APRIL 1956, Academician I. V. Kurchatov, a member of an official Soviet governmental delegation, delivered a lecture at the British nuclear research center in Harwell titled "On the Possibility of Producing Thermonuclear Reactions in a Gas Discharge."

By that time, thermonuclear fusion reactions had already been produced in the first hydrogen bombs (first at the end of 1952 by the Americans in the huge device "Mike," and later in transportable devices—on August 12, 1953, in the USSR, and in March 1954 in the U.S.). Burning of thermonuclear fuel in bombs was achieved by heating it to hundreds of millions of degrees with an atomic (fission) bomb. In his speech at Harwell,

Kurchatov talked about the controlled, or rather slow thermonuclear reaction in a very small amount (fractions of a gram) of heavy hydrogen (deuterium).

In order to achieve the heating and thermonuclear burning while continually replacing the burnt hot fuel, it was necessary to prevent collisions of the hydrogen nuclei (moving at velocities of thousands of kilometers per second) with the walls. "One of the ideas related to this problem," said Kurchatov in his lecture, "involves the use of magnetic fields for confinement of the hot plasma. Academician Sakharov and Academician Tamm were the first to suggest this idea in 1950." In this way a vast international community heard about Andrei Dmitrievich Sakharov for the first time.

Igor Evgenievich Tamm (who in 1950 was a corresponding member of the Soviet Academy of Sciences) was already a well-known physicist, renowned for his work in solid state physics, nuclear forces, elementary particles, the theory of Cherenkov radiation, and for the classic university textbook *The Theory of Electricity*. Sakharov, on the other hand, was known only within a narrow circle of physicists. However, an observant reader who noticed that Sakharov was elected Academician at the end of October 1953, at the age of thirty-two (having passed through the rank of corresponding member at the same time as Tamm), and that this nomination coincided with the announcement of the first thermonuclear weapon test in the USSR, could guess that this was a new, bright talent, one of the main creators of the thermonuclear bomb. And yet now he was revealed as the originator of the idea for the magnetic confinement of plasma as well.

Thirty-four years have passed since Kurchatov's speech at Harwell. The solution of the problem of controlled thermonuclear fusion (CTF) turned out to be far from simple. During this period the field—which was once top secret—has developed into a broad international collaboration, and today plasma physics and controlled thermonuclear fusion are two crucial areas of research. Many versions of magnetic plasma confinement have been tested—the pinch systems (self-compressed discharges) which Kurchatov talked about at Harwell, open magnetic confinement systems with magnetic mirrors, stellarators of American origin, and other systems. And what has been the outcome? The basic direction of CTF research worldwide has now become the development of the tokamak system, the key elements of which—a toroidal magnetic field and a toroidal electric current generated within the plasma—were proposed by Sakharov in 1950. The great successes of Soviet physicists in this field (heating the plasma to temperatures of ten million degrees, and the observation of neutrons of clearly thermonuclear origin) took place around 1970—twenty years after the birth of the idea. After another two decades, at the largest tokamak JET (the Joint European Torus), a deuterium plasma was obtained with a temperature of 300 million degrees. The quality of confinement was such that if the deuterium was replaced with a mixture of deuterium and tritium, the power released by the fusion reactions would be greater than that consumed to heat the plasma (so far experiments with tritium have not been performed because of its radioactivity). Similar results have also been obtained at the American tokamak, TFTR. These are important stepping stones on the road to accomplishing Sakharov's concept of a magnetic thermonuclear reactor. At present, in Garching, Germany, with the joint forces of scientists from Western Europe, the USSR, the U.S., and Japan, an International Thermonuclear Experimental Reactor (ITER) based on the tokamak is being developed. Such is the current scale and results of the activity initiated forty years ago by Andrei Dmitrievich Sakharov.

The Birth of the CTF Program

Beginning in 1948, Sakharov, a young researcher in the theoretical department of the Lebedev Physical Institute, having defended his doctoral thesis a short time earlier under the supervision of Tamm, took part in the work on the development of thermonuclear weapons. In the eyes of those around him, he was already a mature scientist who distinguished himself with his bright mind, deep understanding of the laws of physics, and unusual creativity. It was known that, while working at a munitions factory during World War II, he worked out two minor theoretical problems (that work later amazed Tamm by the originality of the solutions). He possessed a rare combination of theoretical and practical, engineering-level thinking, making a number of inventions in the field of production quality control.

There was no evidence then that thermonuclear weapons were being developed anywhere in the world, but some American popular magazines raised the fear that a "superbomb" could possibly be built. Igor Evgenievich and his collaborators, having worked on the theory of nuclear forces many years earlier, knew that the fusion of the hydrogen isotopes deuterium (D) and tritium (T) into helium nuclei would release about five times as much energy (per unit of mass) as that released in the fission of uranium. It did not seem possible to greatly increase the explosive power of the uranium bomb, but wouldn't it be possible to use its explosion to trigger a detonation in a mixture of deuterium and tritium? To answer this question, the theorist again had to become an inventor. The young Sakharov had a special kind of mind; he mastered the complex problems of theoretical physics with ease, and also had a capacity for practical thinking. Soon, inspired by the basic ideas formulated by a group of theorists led by Tamm, he proposed such a highly precise model of the hydrogen bomb that, after complete calculations of the reaction rate, radiation intensity, fragment emission and the gas dynamic processes, a bomb design could be presented to the engineers. Sakharov's model was approved and in 1949 he and Tamm worked in the secret design office headed by Yu. B. Khariton. There, with youthful enthusiasm, Sakharov devoted all his energy to the construction of the weapon, convinced that the military dominance of the U.S. over the USSR was a threat to world peace.

From time to time, the research centers received for evaluation inventions originating in all parts of the country. Often, the more ambitious the invention was in its objective and importance, the more naive it was. After the possibility of a hydrogen bomb was published in the U.S., such proposals were also received in these research centers. One such proposal, sent in 1950 to the central committee of the Party by O. A. Lavrentiev, a twenty-four year old who was performing his military service in Sakhalin, came to Tamm and Sakharov's department.[1] The young sergeant, with a high-school education, proposed to achieve the conditions for thermonuclear reactions in a way similar to that occurring in the sun, by replacing the gravitational forces that prevent the expansion of the solar matter with electrical forces. Positive and negative potentials applied to a system of grids should prevent the escape of the electrons and the positively charged nuclei.

The proposal was not at all naive! Sakharov was enthusiastic about the problem proposed by the young man with no special education, but he saw that his idea could not be realized: the field intensity between the grids would have to be prohibitively high (higher than 10^6 V/cm), and the conductors would be unavoidably bombarded by high-energy particles and would be destroyed. Sakharov considered whether it would be possible to protect the conductors by passing an electrical current through them. In fact, the magnetic field of the current could protect the conductors against the bombardment of the plasma particles, but this field was not constant (it increased with decreasing distance to the conductor). Therefore, the charged particles would drift along the direction of the current, stopping at the walls of the vacuum chamber at the points where the conductors passed through it. As a result, they transferred their energy to the wall. The desired thermal insulation could not be achieved.

Lavrentiev's letter, however, made Sakharov think further about other ways of achieving controlled thermonuclear fusion, for it could be used not only to generate energy, but also to produce weapons. Indeed, tritium would be formed, as a result of fusing deuterium nuclei, and tritium was necessary for the thermonuclear bomb. Moreover, by bombarding thorium with neutrons from the DD reaction, one could obtain uranium-233 which, like uranium-235, can be used in an atomic bomb. There were then only a few nuclear reactors producing tritium and fissile materials. A successfully constructed thermonuclear reactor could rapidly solve the fuel problem for both the atomic and thermonuclear bombs. No wonder, therefore, that these problems were discussed with great concern by Tamm's group, and were brought before Ya. B. Zel'dovich and Yu. B. Khariton for their judgment.

Sakharov understood that this idea could have practical significance only if the thermonuclear reaction could be made self-sustaining. First of all, it was necessary to assure good thermal insulation of the plasma (whose temperature would be enormously high) from the walls. Couldn't a magnetic field be used for insulation? Indeed, in a uniform magnetic field a charged particle would move in a spiral, winding its trajectory around the same bundle of magnetic lines of force. Transitions from one bundle to another could occur only as a result of particles colliding and scattering off each other. The necessary high plasma temperature could be produced by ionizing the deuterium gas and then heating it with high-frequency radiation directly in this magnetic field, inside a chamber surrounded by current-carrying coils.

Andrei Dmitrievich discussed his ideas with Tamm. The idea was strikingly simple; use the restricted motion of charges in the direction perpendicular to the magnetic lines of force. Indeed, what physicist didn't know about the circular orbits of accelerated beams of particles in cyclotrons and other cyclic accelerators? Only now, the magnetic field had to be built not along a unique orbit, but throughout the entire volume of the plasma. The radius of curvature of the trajectory of a particle had to be minimal (for nuclei it had to be on the order of a fraction of a centimeter, and for electrons it had to be several tenths or several hundredths of a millimeter), which meant that the strongest possible magnetic field was needed. In order to avoid plasma losses in the longitudinal direction, the chamber and the magnetic field had to be constructed in the shape of a torus.

Intensive theoretical work began. Tamm solved the kinetic equations for the plasma in a magnetic field, and derived the formulas describing the heat and particle fluxes from the high-temperature plasma. These derivations were necessary for the design calculations of the magnetic thermonuclear reactor. The behavior of plasma at the chamber walls was studied: The recombination of charged particles there resulted in the formation of cold neutral atoms. The great danger of "toroidal drift" of charged particles was acknowledged, as was their continuous displacement along the main axis of the toroid, due to the intrinsic nonuniformity of the toroidal magnetic field. Sakharov found several possible ways to compensate for this drift (called at that time "drift stabilization") by forming the magnetic lines of force in the shape of a spiral, by using a current-carrying ring suspended inside the toroid, or by inducing a current inside the plasma itself. This second solution has been adopted in the current construction of the tokamak. After a few years, G. I. Budker proposed a different method of eliminating longitudinal losses: instead of using a chamber in the shape of a torus, he suggested increasing the magnetic field at its ends, which creates a magnetic containment system with magnetic mirrors. Both these systems were developed. At that time, basic problems related to the construction of a controlled thermonuclear reactor with magnetic plasma confinement were still unsolved.

Andrei Dmitrievich and Tamm made the first calculations of the parameters of "small" and "big" models for a thermonuclear reactor, ignoring the effects of the curvature of the toroid and without the axial current. In the "small" model, the reactions occurred only with continuous energy consumption; the "big" model had a self-sustained thermonuclear reaction. The calculations showed that for thermonuclear reactions with intensities of practical interest, the plasma's temperature had to be higher than 32 keV (350 million degrees), and its particle density had to be 10^{14} cm^{-3}. Below 32 keV, no thermal insulation would help, since the bremsstrahlung radiation of the electrons would dissipate more energy than that released by the nuclear fusion. With a magnetic field of 50 kG (Sakharov showed that copper coils with appropriate cooling could be used to obtain such a field), then the condition for a self-sustained reaction could be achieved in a toroidal chamber of radius not less than two meters. Under these conditions the heat flux at the chamber walls would be 10^{14} (!) times smaller than in the absence of a magnetic field. This figure could have discouraged researchers involved in other activities and would have paralyzed any further analysis. But the task of constructing a thermonuclear weapon thousands of times more powerful than the atomic bomb also shattered the imagination. Sakharov, therefore, mentioned this factor of 10^{14} quietly, as if it were an ordinary one, and continued the analysis.

Returning home to Moscow for a short respite, Tamm and Sakharov discussed these problems with their collaborators at the Lebedev Institute; V. L. Ginzburg, S. Z. Belenki, and E. S. Fradkin.

Tamm calculated the deterioration of the thermal insulation in the toroidal magnetic field with a current passing through the plasma, as compared to the case of a cylindrical reactor model. The possible deterioration did not appear to be catastrophic. Seventeen years later, detailed calculations by

A. A. Galeev and R. V. Sagdeev led to new concepts in physical kinetics, namely, the "neoclassical" theory of transport processes in toroidal, high-temperature plasma.

Also considered were the problems of energy loss from the plasma due to initially "cold" atoms which collided with the walls, became high-energy atoms as a result of charge exchange, and subsequently left the plasma unimpeded. Ten years later these processes near the wall became the main problems associated with construction of the reactor.

More and more troublesome was the problem of plasma stability. Wouldn't the hot plasma be brought outside by convection fluxes, similar to the way warm air rises in the earth's atmosphere? Wouldn't wave processes occur in the plasma, increasing the heat transfer?

The volume of work began to snowball, but the basic problem—the rapid development of thermonuclear weapons—was left to Sakharov and Tamm for its solution. Stalin imposed more stringent deadlines. The chief of the First Central Office of the USSR Council of Ministers, B. L. Bannikov, proposed that Kurchatov's collaborators at LIPAN—the Laboratory for Measuring Instruments, now the Kurchatov Institute of Atomic Energy—who worked on the electromagnetic separation of uranium and lithium isotopes be brought into the controlled thermonuclear fusion project.

Before submitting the proposal for a new project to the authorities, Kurchatov decided to submit it to the leading physicists for approval. At the end of January 1951 he organized a meeting with Tamm, Sakharov, Khariton, Ya. B. Zel'dovich, I. N. Golovin, L. A. Artsimovich, N. N. Bogolyubov, and M. G. Meshcheryakov. At the meeting, the idea of magnetic thermal insulation received general approval. In February, Kurchatov prepared the draft of the government decision, and sent it to Beria for Stalin's signature.

March passed, and nobody knows how long it would have taken for the letter to be signed, if Argentina's President Juan Peron hadn't announced that on February 16, 1951, a German physicist, R. Richter, achieved controlled thermonuclear fusion in a laboratory in Huemel. Later, it became clear that this claim was erroneous. But at that time, Peron's announcement compelled our authorities to make the decision (indeed, "a prophet is not without honor, but in his own country"). By mid-April, the project was discussed in Beria's office. The decision was made to nominate Artsimovich as leader of the MTR (magnetic thermonuclear reactor) program, and A. M. Leontovich as leader of the theoretical studies. On May 15, 1951, with Stalin's signature, the Central Committee of the USSR Communist Party and the USSR Council of Ministers issued the decision to organize the work on controlled thermonuclear fusion. That was the beginning of Soviet CTF research.

In the beginning, Sakharov periodically would come to LIPAN with new ideas about the experimental setups. One time, it was an idea to use a copper shell to keep the current in equilibrium; another time, a proposal involved using in the reactor a mixture of deuterium and tritium, in which the reaction would be induced much more easily than in deuterium alone. Yet another time, he arrived with a detailed report on work performed under his supervision by D. N. Zubarev and V. N. Klimov, on the interaction of the thermonuclear plasma with the vacuum chamber wall. When the date scheduled for the testing of the hydrogen bomb approached, he came to LIPAN less and less often.

One should mention that at the same time England and the U.S., under total secrecy, started to conduct research work on pinches. The information on Richter's apparent success stimulated the Princeton astrophysicist L. Spitzer to invent the "stellarator"—a toroidal magnetic system with compensation of the toroidal drift of the charges, without inducing the current inside the plasma. A little later, at the Livermore Laboratory in California, H. York and R. Post proposed to confine the plasma by using nontoroidal magnetic systems with "magnetic mirrors" at the ends, (similar to Budker's "Probkotron").

After many years of studying various systems of magnetic confinement (opened for discussion in 1958), preference was given to the tokamak—a toroidal system based on Sakharov's idea. During the first years of its development, the groups led by I. N. Golovin and N. A. Yavlinski worked on this problem at the Kurchatov Institute. Later, the studies in this field were led by L. A. Artsimovich.

From MTR to ITER

The basic studies of Tamm and Sakharov on controlled thermonuclear fusion, known as the "Theory of the Magnetic Thermonuclear Reactor," were summarized in 1951 in reports, and were published in 1958. These were the first three articles in a four-volume series *Plasma Physics and Controlled Thermonuclear Fusion*, edited by Academician A. M. Leontovich, which was completed for the Second Geneva Conference on the Peaceful Applications of Atomic Energy, where for the first time a wide exchange of information between the controlled fusion programs of the USSR, the U.S., and U.K. took place. Even today, after four decades of most extensive research in this field, involving a huge army of physicists, it is remarkable to see the high scientific level of the first theoretical works. They not only formulated the groundbreaking ideas and performed the first calculations, but also defined the major problems on which the "thermonuclear" physicists had to work for many years to come.

Tamm authored the first and the third parts of "The Theory of MTR." Here he mainly considered the basic problems of the theory of magnetically confined plasma, and evaluated (in the first part) the parameters of the "small" MTR model (with a low plasma density).

One could get an idea about the content of the second part of "The Theory of MTR," written by Sakharov, from the following introduction to it.

The properties of a high-temperature plasma in a magnetic field were discussed in a paper by Tamm, in which he demonstrated the possibility of the realization of a magnetic thermonuclear reactor (MTR). In this paper we shall consider other questions concerning the theory of MTRs:

1. Thermonuclear reactions. Bremsstrahlung radiation. 2. Calculations for the "big" model. Critical radius. Local phenomena near the wall. 3. Magnetization power. The optimum design. Efficiency of production of the active substances. 4. The drift in the inhomogeneous magnetic field. Suspended current. Inductive stabilization. 5. Plasma instabilities.

Let us discuss the most interesting results of this work, from today's perspective. The parameters of the "big" reactor are still impressive: the large radius of the toroid was twelve meters, the radius of the plasma was two meters, and the intensity of the magnetic field was 50,000 G. At a plasma temperature of 100 keV (1.1 billion Kelvin), 150 grams of deuterium would burn in twenty-four hours. This corresponds to the production of about 100 grams of tritium in twenty-four hours, or eighty times more than if uranium-233 were used. (This refers to Sakharov's idea regarding the production of atomic fuel—in particular, for atomic power plants—as the first stage in an MTR.) Later, this idea was adopted in the hybrid reactor projects, which are currently being seriously considered in China and in many other countries.

Close attention was given to the phenomena occurring near the vacuum chamber walls. Sakharov showed that the thermal flux directed from the plasma toward the wall gives rise to a temperature gradient (hot plasma near the cold wall) which is not dangerous to the wall.

In the fourth chapter, in addition to considering stabilization of the drift caused by the toroidal magnetic field's inhomogeneity by using a suspended current-carrying ring, Sakharov formulated the idea on which the tokamak is based.

Another method to achieve stabilization of the drift, which is technically unacceptable and should therefore be carefully studied, consists in inducing an axial current directly inside the plasma. In this method, it is not clear whether the high-temperature plasma is destroyed at the time the induction current is reduced to zero.

Sakharov himself did not have the opportunity to work on his own ideas in the field of controlled thermonuclear fusion. The development of the research in the USSR first focused on pinches. (Since one needs an axial electrical current inside the toroid, the decision was made to avoid any external longitudinal magnetic fields, solving the problem of plasma confinement by magnetic fields.)

Various modifications of the magnetic confinement of the plasma were suggested and submitted for experimental tests at that time. These included open traps with magnetic mirrors with probes, high-frequency confinement, and so on. The most interesting aspects of this research were the plasma instabilities and the anomalously large thermal and particle losses as compared to the theoretical predictions. Similar difficulties were also encountered in the experiments related to excitation of currents directly inside the plasma in the toroidal magnetic field. Gradually, however, the researchers realized the importance of cleaning the discharge chamber walls and correcting the transverse magnetic field (which confined the toroidal plasma) with currents directed along the wall and at right angles to it, and an optimal technology was developed for obtaining a macroscopically stable plasma, with acceptable levels of anomalous heat and particle losses. The transfer of the bulk of peaceful research in CTF to tokamaks in the 1970s made possible their development to the current level, where experimental tokamak reactors can be developed.

Forty years after the birth of the idea of the magnetic thermonuclear reactor, the basic ideas of such reactors and of plasma confinement by magnetic fields underwent a series of modifications.

The enclosure of the system inside a toroid, taking into account the limitations imposed by requiring stabilization of the plasma, resulted in a lower attainable ratio of the plasma pressure to the pressure of the external magnetic field. If in the Sakharov model it is close to one, in the present tokamak systems it is one order of magnitude smaller.

In the toroidal plasma, the theoretical, and, even more, the real thermal conductivity and plasma diffusion rate turned out to be signficantly larger than those in Sakharov's model.

The mechanism of the heat flux to the chamber walls also changed. The idea of energy output through the elements of the chamber—not across but along the magnetic lines of force—was confirmed. For this purpose, between the plasma and the chamber walls a region is created where the magnetic lines of force (and also the heat flux from the central plasma) hit special receiving plates. The temperature in this region is much higher than that near the wall in Sakharov's model. This is because the plasma near the wall has significantly lower density than in Sakharov's model, and at the given heat this flux uniquely determines the temperature. To decrease to safe levels the energy of the particles that bombard the plates, conditions were created (by using an inert gas "cushion") for strong particle recycling. In this system, a charged particle that hits the wall recombines as a neutral particle and returns to the plasma, where it becomes ionized. This process is repeated many times, and the energy of the "hot" particles is transferred to the plates in small portions.

A total change of approach has also occurred concerning the deuterium used as fuel in mixture with equal quantities of tritium. The use of tritium obtained from the fission reactors was suggested for the startup of the reactor, after which it could be obtained from the lithium-containing "blanket" that surrounds the thermonuclear reactor. The use of the deuterium–tritium (DT) mixture, with an ignition temperature an order of magnitude lower, eliminates the additional energy losses through bremsstrahlung radiation. Because of the lower temperature of the plasma, despite the increased real thermal transfer as compared with that assumed in the "big model," the DT reactor performs at parameters close to those of the ideal DD reactor. For example, in the ITER project, the volume of the plasma was approximately equal to that of the Sakharov's "big model."

A solution was found for the problem that troubled Andrei Dmitrievich, namely the unavoidable vanishing of the induced current, which would result in loss of the thermal insulation of the plasma. Tokamak currents have already been sustained for prolonged periods of time by using high-frequency radiation. In 1988, Sakharov was invited to a seminar at the Kurchatov Institute, and having learned about the progress of CTF research, said in his calm voice, "I didn't know about this successful achievement of the current by using the mechanical action of high-frequency waves on the electrons."

New understanding has been reached in the problem of radiation hazards from thermonuclear reactors. In 1950–51, it was found that the thermonuclear reactions themselves emit negligibly small amounts of radioactivity. However, in the 1970s, attention was focused on the neutron-induced radioactivity of the reactor's structural materials. Although the biological hazard of a thermonuclear reactor is calculated to be two orders of magnitude smaller than that of a fission reactor, researchers—in addition to developing the neutron-rich DT reactors—are investigating the possibility of constructing almost totally hazardless "low-radioactivity" reactors that use as fuel a mixture of deuterium and helium-3. Tamm and Sakharov did not consider this possibility because of the lack of reserves of helium-3 on Earth. However, as a result of the progress of space exploration, it is no longer beyond our reach to try to obtain it on the Moon, where rich reserves of this isotope have been discovered.[2] Thermonuclear reactors thus have the potential of becoming ecologically clean and nearly totally hazardless energy sources.

Controlled fusion research was given a significant boost by the progress in the development of superconductivity and computer technology. The progress in superconductivity eliminated the problem of high-power losses in sustaining the magnetic field (the "magnetization power," in Sakharov's terminology), which for the "big" model equalled half the power released in the thermonuclear reactions. Four tokamaks using superconducting magnets have already been approved (in the USSR, France, and Japan). The ITER project also considers the use of superconducting coils for generation of the magnetic field.

The CTF research, even when it was conducted under the strictest secrecy, developed in parallel and nearly at the same time in a number of countries. In spite of this, the pioneering work of Sakharov and Tamm played an important role in the development of this area not only in the USSR but also in the whole world.

It was the systematic study of the Sakharov system—developed at the Kurchatov Institute in the 1950s and 1960s and called "tokamak" in 1957 by Golovin and Yavlinski—that led in the 1960s and 1970s to a change of direction in research resulting in the achievement of plasma parameters that made it possible to develop the experimental thermonuclear reactor based on the tokamak concept. No matter which direction further developments take, the tokamaks have already played a major role. They demonstrated that it was possible to produce a stellar material on Earth for the accomplishment of controlled thermonuclear fusion, and raised hope that mankind could master thermonuclear energy.

Sakharov received his highest recognition as a scientist mainly for his work on the hydrogen bomb. Compared with his role in the peaceful development of fusion power, this side of his activities may in the future seem merely incidental. He will then remain in the memory of our grateful offspring not as the designer of weapons of terrible power, but as the founder of the ecologically clean and plentiful energy source of the future—energy to serve a new human society, based on Reason and Humanity, for which he struggled and to which he offered without reserve all his strength.

FROM THE NOTES OF I. N. GOLOVIN

To INVOLVE LIPAN in the research on controlled thermonuclear fusion reactions, B. L. Bannikov named V. I. Pavlov as the leader of the PGU, or First Main Division, a department of the KGB. Pavlov was then the leader of the design office where Tamm and Sakharov were working. Kurchatov himself, who was renowned for his work on the hydrogen bomb, used to spend much time on business trips, leaving Moscow for weeks, and sometimes for months. Therefore, Pavlov appointed me as Kurchatov's first deputy:

"Igor Nikolaevich! Come visit me. You will meet your dear old teacher Igor Evgenievich and Andrei. They will tell you a remarkable story."

"I am always glad to see Igor Evgenievich, but who is Andrei?"

"Don't you know Andrei? Andrei Sakharov? Like you, he is also one of Tamm's students, an exceptional young man. He is one of us. A brilliant mind!"

That's how the young Sakharov was characterized by the KGB general."

A meeting between Pavlov, Sakharov and myself took place on October 22, 1950, in Pavlov's office on New Razanski street in the PGU building.

Sakharov talked slowly and deliberately about the results of his and Tamm's calculations. Pavlov noted that Tamm and Sakharov's first priority was to work on their main project, and to spend no more than one-third of their time on other problems. He suggested that I discuss the setup for the forthcoming experiments with the experts who built electromagnets for isotope separation. I left them, astounded by the bold proposal, which described plasma in a way far different from the customary diffusion plasma in gas discharges.

Ten days later Kurchatov returned and I related this exciting piece of news to him. Kurchatov immediately invited Tamm and Sakharov to his office, carefully studied their proposal, and with great enthusiasm promised his full support. Immediately, at Tamm's suggestion, the project was named "the MTR problem"; i.e., the magnetic thermonuclear reactor. Regarding it to be closely related to the hydrogen bomb, they classified it top secret.

Kurchatov immediately requested that all publications on the MTR be sent to him. Tamm already had prepared a report in 1951, which was the first paper in the four-volume series entitled *Plasma Physics and Controlled Thermonuclear Fusion*, published in 1958. In addition to this report, there were only two other reports by V. L. Ginzburg devoted to the analysis of the properties of a plasma formed in gas discharges placed in a magnetic field (published in unclassified literature in the *Proceedings of the FIAN Institute*).

BY MID-APRIL 1951, an excited D. V. Efremov, at that time the Minister of Electrotechnic Industry, burst into Kurchatov's office holding a newspaper that had sensational news: the German scientist Richter, who had emigrated to Argentina, had achieved thermonuclear fusion and a release of neutrons in a gas discharge in deuterium!

Kurchatov immediately wrote a letter to Beria about this discovery, mentioning the delay in the project. Beria responded immediately, and in several days he called Sakharov, Tamm, myself, and Pavlov to his office in the Kremlin to attend a meeting of a special committee (the highest authority, under Beria's leadership, charged with the problem of developing nuclear and thermonuclear weapons). In the office, the members of the committee (Kurchatov, Bannikov, Zavenyaghin, Pervukhin, and others) were already assembled. Sakharov talked briefly about his proposal and mentioned that Tamm had performed the basic calculations on MTR. Tamm became excited and, asking for permission to speak immediately after Sakharov, began to explain in an emotional state that the basic ideas and much of the merit belonged to Sakharov. Beria impatiently lifted his hand and interrupted Tamm, saying, "Nobody will forget Sakharov," and asked him to sit down.

When Kurchatov added that he wanted the leaders of the theoretical and experimental physics departments to approve Leontovich and Artsimovich, General Meshik, who was sitting on the right of Beria, told him with a theatrical whisper that Leontovich was known for his free-thinking. Beria replied in a loud voice, "He'll be watched; there will be no leaks." Kurchatov also asked that the MTR Council be approved, with him as the head of the project and Sakharov as his deputy.

On May 5, 1951, the decision was signed by Stalin. The controlled thermonuclear fusion project received the status of one of the most important government programs.

Notes and References

1. Lavrentiev later attended Moscow State University, and after graduation, he worked at the Physicotechnical Institute of the Soviet Academy of Sciences in the field of CTF.
2. For details, see L. J. Wittenberg, J. F. Santarius, and G. L. Kulcinski, "Lunar Source of He^3 for Commercial Fusion Power," *Fusion Technology* 10 (1986): p. 159.

The Fate of an Unpublished Report

S. S. GERSHTEIN

Institute of High Energy Physics, Protvino

L. I. PONOMAREV

Kurchatov Institute of Atomic Energy, Moscow

IT IS KNOWN that in general half of all published scientific papers are not cited. Of the other half, after ten years only 20 percent are still cited, and after fifteen years only 5 percent. However, there are some publications which are constantly referred to, even twenty and thirty years after their publication. This recognition separates the classic papers from the rest in any field of intellectual endeavor.

Andrei Dmitrievich Sakharov was able to do even more: his paper of 1948, titled "Passive Mesons," was never published, but even now it is cited in the literature related to muon catalysis. To some extent, it even influenced the direction of the lives of the authors of this paper.

According to a logic that totally escapes the modern reader (but in complete agreement with the customs of that time), his report was immediately classified. The first citation of that work dates back to 1957, to a joint paper authored by Ya. B. Zel'dovich and A. D. Sakharov, titled "Reactions Produced by μ-mesons in Hydrogen,"[1] and later, in 1960, in a review paper by Ya. B. Zel'dovich and S. S. Gershtein titled "Nuclear Fusion Reactions in Cold Hydrogen."[1] Until now only a few have known the specific content of Sakharov's paper: they talked about it, citing secondary or even more remote sources.[2]

In the spring of 1989, we discussed with Sakharov our desire to publish

Title page of Sakharov's unpublished 1948 paper "Passive Mesons," probably in Sakharov's handwriting.

this landmark paper. He gave his approval, admitting, however, that he did not know where it could be found. After Andrei Dmitrievich's sudden death, the report was found in the archives of FIAN (the Lebedev Physical Institute of the Soviet Academy of Sciences). It was declassified and at last we had in our hands the yellowish pages of the manuscript which, to a certain extent, anticipated by decades the development of a very interesting field of physics.[3]

Today's reader finds it difficult to imagine the conditions in which many scientists from Sakharov's generation had to do science: continuous control, bodyguards, notebooks with numbered pages to be used *only* for calculations, however trivial, and much more. At that time it was considered natural. But uncontrolled thoughts could penetrate even these barriers: two notebooks belonging to Zel'dovich have been spared. While at "the Installation" in 1957 he made a number of calculations in them regarding various processes of muon catalysis. (They also contain Zel'dovich's brief summary of Sakharov's classified report.)

From these notes, one can see the influence Sakharov had on Zel'-

dovich, and how highly Yakov Borisovich regarded his rare intuition as a physicist. On many pages one can see notes like: "ADS: charge exchange between identical particles," "ADS: three particles," "ADS's profoundest idea," etc. One of the notebooks also contains the manuscript of a joint paper written by Zel'dovich and Sakharov, which was published in 1957 after the experimental discovery of muon catalysis by L. Alvarez et al. We will talk more about this paper below, but let us first go back to the report of 1948.

In it, Sakharov for the first time analyzed comprehensively what would happen if a negatively charged muon (μ^-) was stopped in deuterium, and he reached the following conclusion. The muon, together with two nuclei of deuterium (D), could form a DDμ muonic molecule, i.e., a molecule in which an electron is replaced by a muon. As a result, the nuclei are brought together so closely ($\sim 5 \times 10^{-11}$ cm) that they nearly instantaneously (10^{-9}s) undergo a fusion reaction, $D + D \rightarrow He^3 + n$ (or $T + p$), with a release of a relatively large amount of energy (3.3 and 4 MeV, respectively). The liberated muon could then form another muonic molecule, in which a fusion reaction would again occur, and so on. Such a process would continue until the muon, which acts as a catalyst of the fusion reaction, could no longer participate.

In order to evaluate the boldness of Sakharov's idea and the swift effect it had on the new scientific discoveries, one must recall the scientific background against which this work was performed. This will also account for the title of the report.

According to Yukawa's hypothesis formulated in 1935, the short-range nature of the nuclear force stems from the fact that the interaction between

Excerpt from Ya. B. Zel'dovich's notebook showing calculations on muon-catalyzed fusion.

nucleons occurs through the exchange of a particle with a mass equal to 200–300 electronic masses, which he called a meson. A particle with approximately this mass was detected in 1936–38 in cosmic rays at sea level. However, subsequent studies showed that the observed particle (now called μ-meson or the muon) could not be the Yukawa particle, since it interacted very weakly with the nuclei of matter. This was confirmed, in particular, by the fact that it traveled freely through the entire atmosphere, a distance ten times greater than that possible for a particle with the properties predicted by Yukawa without being scattered or absorbed by the atomic nuclei. On the other hand, it was found that at high altitudes cosmic rays contain, in addition to the so-called hard component, which penetrates through the atmosphere, a soft component, which interacts strongly with the atomic nuclei and is absorbed by them.

Amazingly, the masses of the particles in the hard and the soft components were approximately equal. Since at that time the accuracy of measurements of this important characteristic of the particles was not high, it was assumed that the same particle was observed in the hard component and the soft component. We had, it seemed, an insoluble paradox: Why does the same particle behave differently at high altitudes and at sea level? This paradox was solved in 1947, when C. Powell, C. Lattes, and G. Occhialini recorded on a photographic emulsion an event in which at the stopping point of one charged particle there emerged a new track corresponding to a charged particle with a kinetic energy of about 5.5 MeV and mass approximately equal to the mass of the stopped particle. The authors correctly interpreted this event as being the decay of the particle predicted by Yukawa (the π-meson or pion, in the current terminology) into a muon and something else. Pions are generated in the interactions of cosmic-ray particles with the nuclei of the elements that make up the atmosphere, and they decay into a lighter charged particle and a neutral particle which leaves no track in the photoemulsion.

In the present-day notation this is the decay of charged pions into a muon and a muonic neutrino,

$$\pi^{\pm} \rightarrow \mu^{\pm} + \nu\mu.$$

Assuming that a muon, in contrast with a pion, does not interact strongly with the nuclei (it is "passive"), the difference between the hard component and the soft component of cosmic rays could be understood. But more importantly, the discovery of an unexpected particle, the muon, became the starting point of a whole series of discoveries which have led to the understanding of the universality of weak interactions and, finally, to the formulation of a unified theory of electroweak interactions.[4] But in 1947, all these discoveries were yet to be made. It was necessary to analyze other possible explanations of the observed phenomenon, and confirm that a new particle had indeed been discovered.

AN ENGLISH PHYSICIST, F. C. Frank, made such an attempt to interpret the event observed by Powell, Lattes, and Occhialini, without the introduction of a new particle. One of the discussed possibilities could be stated as follows: A negatively charged meson, having been stopped in the emulsion, can bind a proton and a deuteron into a muonic molecule about 10^{-11} cm in size. In such a muonic molecule the Coulomb barrier repelling the nuclei is much smaller than in the usual electronic molecule. The fusion of a proton and a deuteron into a He^3 nucleus, which produces an energy of 5.5 MeV, must therefore proceed rather rapidly. If this energy is transferred to the meson, then a new track belonging to a 5.5 MeV meson will run from the point at which the meson originally stopped. This process is indeed very close to the one observed experimentally. It should be mentioned that Frank himself rejected this possibility, assuming that the amount of deuterium in natural hydrogen is too small to account for the sizeable yield of such a reaction. His conclusion, therefore, was that there seemed to be no explanation of the observed event other than the one given by Powell et al.

Curiously, the reason Frank gave for rejecting the considered fusion reaction in the muonic molecule $pD\mu$ is not correct. It was indeed this reaction that Alvarez, who discovered muon catalysis, subsequently observed in a liquid-hydrogen bubble chamber. This reaction cannot occur in a photoemulsion, because a negatively charged muon is usually captured by nuclei of heavier elements. We can now definitely say, moreover, that the event Powell and his coworkers observed was the decay of a positively charged pion, since a negative pion that stops in matter is absorbed by nuclei nearly instantaneously and does not have time to decay.

Despite these stipulations, even Frank's hypothesis played an important role in the subsequent development of muon catalysis. At this time, the muon had already been known for ten years, and muonic atoms had been predicted some time earlier, but no one had thought of considering the formation of muonic molecules and the rate of fusion reactions in them.

Frank's work attracted the attention of Sakharov who, considering a practical way to realize heavy-hydrogen fusion reactions, directed his thought in a different direction. Assuming it quite likely (as he wrote in his report) that there are two kinds of mesons ("active" and "passive"), he studied the behavior of the passive mesons stopped in pure deuterium, and came to the conclusions that were mentioned in the beginning of this article. This is how he formulated them:[5]

The content of this note refers to an article in [section left out],[6] which discusses the experiments of Powell et al. [a gap]. Let us assume that a passive, negatively charged meson with a mass [section left out] 200 enters a heavy hydrogen gas which is confined, for example, in a high-pressure vessel. With the passage of time [section left out], it settles in the K orbit near one of the deuterons, forming a "mesic atom" D-M 0.25×10^{-10} cm in size. Diffusing between the D nuclei like a neutron, the mesic atom finally settles on another deuteron, forming a mesonon[7] D-M-D (in a time of [a gap]). Finally, a mesonon is an unstable entity, since during the zero-point fluctuations of the mesonon, the deuterons can overcome the potential barrier that separates them, giving rise to the reaction (in a time [section left out]) . . .

The meson is then released and the process begins again.

Using the Wentzel-Kramers-Brillouin method, it is easy to calculate the time [a section left out] (by using the experimental probability of the DD-reaction at above-the-barrier energies).[8]

On the basis of the calculations, Sakharov concluded that the time of the nuclear reaction in the DDμ muonic molecule is on the order of 10^{-9} s (modern calculations give exactly this value). Further, he absolutely correctly stated that the most critical time in the process is the time at which the mesonon forms from the mesoatom. In its evaluation, Sakharov considered that the mechanism of formation of the mesonon was the radiative transition of a meson through the field of two deuterons, not noticing that much more probable was the conversion transition with transfer of the mesomolecule's binding energy to the atomic electron.[9] Based on this, he concluded that "with the usual mesons the 200-meson-catalyzed reaction is not possible." This may explain the fact that until the experimental discovery of muon catalysis in 1956, Sakharov was no longer involved in this problem.

Sakharov completed this work, as already mentioned, immediately after the discovery of the $\pi \rightarrow \mu$ decay. At that time, the nature of the muon and the neutral particle produced with it had not yet been determined, and the universality of weak interactions was not known. Sakharov used only the hypothesis of the nuclear "passivity" of the muon. In the first part of the paper he therefore argued that the neutral particle, which forms along with the muon, has a mass and is nuclear-active. It can be inferred from the text that he meant the π-meson, which decays into two gamma rays. Sakharov correctly maintained that these particles play an important role in the explanation of the properties of Auger showers observed in cosmic rays, "which were earlier considered a classical cascade phenomenon." Today it is difficult to determine the mass he proposed to give to the neutral pion, based on the measured energy of the passive muon in the $\pi \rightarrow \mu$ decay. What is important is that in considering the generation of the passive mesons, he assumed that they could be generated either as a result of the decay of the active mesons, or in pairs in electromagnetic interactions. Noting that in cosmic rays this second possibility plays a negligible role compared with the nuclear and disintegration processes (as in the case of heavy-particle accelerators), he writes; "It should be emphasized, therefore, that it is fundamentally important to carry out experiments with electron accelerators, which enable us to solve the problem of the existence and properties of passive mesons (charged mesons which can therefore be produced in pairs)."[10]

Sakharov's words indeed sound prophetic if one recalls that about thirty years later, scientists using electron–positron colliding beams (about which he couldn't speculate in 1948) discovered the tau lepton, a heavy particle which in his terminology is also passive. Sakharov's remark about the promising future of electron accelerators is only one example, characteristic of his entire scientific creativity, of his attempts to connect his theoretical results with experimental research. At that time, an electron synchrotron was being constructed at FIAN. His direct interest in the construction of this accelerator is documented in another unknown report found in FIAN's archives, titled "Influence of Scattering on the Intensity of the Beam in a Synchrotron," and dated June 1948.

BUT LET US return to muon catalysis. Under the imposed conditions of secrecy, Sakharov's work on this problem was not known even to many of his collaborators. Even Zel'dovich, who published a paper in 1954 on the possibility of muon catalysis of nuclear reactions in deuterium, did not know about it. Sakharov himself, as already mentioned, returned to this problem after the discovery in 1956 on the pD fusion reaction induced by a muon (i.e., the reaction discussed by Frank). This discovery raised a whole series of problems which Zel'dovich and Sakharov jointly solved in 1957.

Muon catalysis was, in fact, discovered "by accident." Alvarez and his group used a bubble chamber filled with liquid hydrogen to study the interaction of negative K⁻ mesons. In these experiments they observed, in particular, the resonances which played an important role in the classification of hadrons (later, Alvarez was awarded the Nobel Prize for this work). The bubble chamber was bombarded with K mesons from the accelerator, and the negative μ mesons entering the chamber were an undesirable background. The experimenters noticed, however, that in a few cases the stopped muons looked unusual: a few millimeters from the point at which the muon stopped, another muonic track started. The length of this track indicated that the energy of the muon was about 5.5 MeV. What appeared to happen was that the muon slowed down in the chamber, stopped, and then somehow gained energy again. It occurred to them that the muon obtained its energy as a result of a pD fusion reaction (which characteristically releases this amount of energy) occurring in a muonic $pD\mu$ molecule. This explanation, as Alvarez recalls, was offered almost immediately by E. Teller. He also explained the existence of a "gap" between the stopping point of the muon and the beginning of the new track. The stopped muon forms, along with the proton, a muonic atom $p\mu$, which diffuses freely through matter until it encounters a deuterium atom. As a result of such an encounter, the muon goes over to the deuterium atom, forming the mesic atom $D\mu$, which in this case acquires additional energy and travels a certain distance without leaving any tracks in the chamber because of its neutrality. After it stops, the mesic atom $D\mu$ forms, along with the hydrogen nucleus, a muonic molecule $pD\mu$, in which the nuclear fusion occurs. Subsequent experiments with higher deuterium concentrations confirmed this hypothesis.

It was not clear, however, what would be the probability for the capture of a muon by a deuteron in the hydrogen, after observing the process even at such low concentrations of deuterium as that in natural hydrogen. The large probability that the energy released in the reaction $p + D \rightarrow He^3$ transferred to the muon in the muonic molecule $pD\mu$ also required an explanation. The results of the calculations carried out by Zel'dovich and Sakharov[11] answer both these questions. It should be noted that these exceptionally elegant calculations were based solely on dimensional analysis, but they proved to be much more accurate than the approximate calculations performed independently by other researchers.

Sakharov subsequently demonstrated sustained interest in muon catalysis. In 1958 he gave the scientists at the Joint Institute for Nuclear Research in Dubna (V. B. Belyaev and B. N. Zakhariev) a thick pile of papers with calculations of the interaction potential of nuclei in muonic molecules. This example shows that in his scientific activity, he did not avoid the dirty work.

In 1963, learning from Zel'dovich about the new aspects of the mesomolecular processes and their relationship with experimental studies of the weak interaction processes of muons, Sakharov agreed to be the official opponent in the defense of the doctoral thesis of one of the authors (S. S. Gershtein). With a dedication rarely encountered today, but characteristic of this man, he carefully studied the thesis, and more than one-and-a-half months before the defense he returned his review. His observations later played an important role in refining calculations of mesomolecular levels, resulting, in particular, in the discovery of a highly excited level in the DTμ molecule.[12]

Andrei Dmitrievich Sakharov lived to see that his rather short (five pages) classified report led to the development of a new field of physics which today involves fifty laboratories in fourteen countries, on topics which attract international conferences and which have generated the publication of a special journal.

Notes and References

1. Ya. B. Zel'dovich and A. D. Sakharov, *JETP (Zhurnal Eksperimental'noi i Teoret-icheskoi Fiziki)* 32 (1957): pp. 947–949; Ya. B. Zel'dovich and S. S. Gershtein, *Soviet Physics—Uspekhi (Uspekhi Fizicheskikh Nauk)* 71 (1960): pp. 581–630.

2. For example, J. D. Jackson, the first to study the meson catalysis cycle in a mixture of deuterium and tritium, said at one of the conferences in 1984 that he knew about Sakharov's report from a Western physicist who visited the USSR, and who heard of it from a Russian colleague, who heard of it from his teacher, who in turn heard of it from his teacher, who had seen the report (the chain is explained like this: G. Fiorentino— L. I. Ponomarev— S. S. Gershtein— Ya. B. Zel'dovich).

3. The authors mention with pleasure the participation of V. Ya. Fainberg, who responded promptly to our inquiry and found the manuscript in the FIAN archives, and M. V. Keldysh, who was instrumental in its declassification.

4. The story of the unexpected discovery of the muon, during the search for Yukawa's anticipated particle, the pion, has been repeated. In the mid-1970s, during the search for mesons containing the charmed C-quark, the tau-lepton was unexpectedly discovered. This particle represents the third generation of leptons (the electron represents the first generation, and the muon, the second).

5. In the copy of the report found at FIAN, some equations and numerical evaluations are missing.

6. There is no doubt that the gap corresponds to the citation of Ch. Franck's paper in *Nature* (1947, vol. 160, pp. 525–27).

7. This is Sakharov's term for the muonic molecule "DDμ". Most probably, this is a misprint and "mesonon" should be read as "mesoion." The term "mesoion" is closer to the object under consideration than is the currently adopted term "muonic molecule." The symbol D-M-D underlies the fact that the meson (M) binds two deuterium nucleons (D) together.

8. The phrase "above-the-barrier energies" is not precise. In reality, as will be shown in the following paper, Sakharov correctly used the experimental data for the below-the-barrier DD reactions at energies of the order of 10 keV. For the accelerated deuterium nuclei would be a more correct phrasing.

9. This conclusion was reached by Ya. B. Zel'dovich in 1954 (*Soviet Physics Doklady (Doklady Akademii Nauk SSSR)* 95, (1954): p. 493–496.

10. Apparently, Sakharov attributed to this confirmation a particular importance, since in the report this sentence is underlined.

11. Ya. B. Zel'dovich and A. D. Sakharov, *op. cit.*; Ya. B. Zel'dovich and S. S. Gershtein, *op. cit.*

12. We intentionally do not dwell on the subsequent development of the muon catalysis and its possible practical applications, since this problem is thoroughly covered in the publication *Nature*. See: L. I. Ponomarev, "The Muon Catalysis of the Nuclear Synthesis Reactions", *Nature* 9 (1979): pp. 8–20; Yu. V. Petrov, "Hybrid Nuclear Reactors and Muon Catalysis", *Nature* 4 (1982): pp. 62–72. See also: "Cold Synthesis or the Third Way Toward the Generation of Atomic Energy," *The Future of Science* 21 (1988): pp. 33–58.

Assessing Radioactive Hazards

V. I. KOROGODIN

Joint Institute for Nuclear Research, Dubna

DURING THE LAST YEARS of his life, A. D. Sakharov devoted much of his concern to the problems of radiation hazards. His brilliant, persuasive, speeches against the testing of nuclear weapons are well known, as is his position on the Chernobyl accident. However, it is less known that he took the same humanitarian position thirty years ago, when there was no nuclear energy and therefore no radiophobia in the country. At that time, Sakharov already felt his responsibility toward mankind; he had already started the struggle to limit the testing of nuclear weapons and to evaluate quantitatively the possible victims of the tests.

The problems related to radiation hazards were made the object of careful studies by the end of the 1940s and the beginning of the 1950s, particularly in relation to the atomic bombardments of Hiroshima and Nagasaki, the increase and broadening of the geographic distribution of sites used for testing of nuclear weapons, and the development of nuclear technology. For biologists and medical doctors, this problem was not unexpected: the research on radiation genetics and the radiobiology of living organisms, which was already a few decades old, permitted a correct formulation of the basic aspects of radiation hazards and allowed one to foresee the direction of their development.[1]

As early as 1927, G. Müller of the U.S., at the Fifth International Conference on Genetics, announced to the scientific community that ionizing radiation may cause genetic modifications (mutations) in fertile mice and drosophila. Later, it became known that the mutagenic action of ionizing radiation was universal—the mutation rate for genes and chromosomes was increased by irradiation, in all living systems, from microscopic organisms to man. By the 1930s, the basic laws of radiation-induced mutation were clarified. It was established that the frequency of new mutations increased directly proportional to the radiation dose. This means that the genetic action of the radiation did not have any threshold: no matter how small the doses were, or how low the frequency of exposure may have been, it inescapably produced some types of mutations, increasing the "mutation load" of the irradiated population. As a result of such mutations, the mortality of the irradiated organisms' descendants (down to the very remote ones), who received these mutations "by inheritance," increased. In the drosophila and the mice, which were mostly used in this study, the "doubling doses" were determined (the doses that resulted in a doubling of the mutation rate as compared to background radiation).

According to the first calculations of the doubling dose in man, based on the observations made in the 1950s, this quantity oscillated within wide limits (from 3 to 150 rad), but the most credible was considered the dose of 15–30 rad.[2] The doubling dose for man means that, if about 70,000 out of 1 million newborns on Earth have defects due to the annual spontaneous radiation dose, then under additional exposure to a dose of 15–30 rad the number of descendants with defects increases to about 140,000 per million. A characteristic of radiation-induced mutagenesis, therefore, is its "nonthreshold" property; i.e., the frequency of mutations per unit dose does not depend either on the dose or on the time distribution of the irradiation. Another characteristic property is that the genetic defects occurring in cells of irradiated humans appear with certainty in some form even in the most remote descendants, up to a few tens of generations, so that the results of even one single exposure will extend over hundreds or thousands of years.

By the mid-1950s, it became clear that some nonthreshold radiation effects were observed not only in the descendants, but also in the irradiated organisms themselves. In experiments performed on laboratory animals and also on humans irradiated in the course of their profession or for medical treatment, the incidence of malignant tumors due to mutations in the somatic system was monitored. The nonthreshold level of the carcinogenic effect of radiation stems from the fact that it is based on a mutation effect. However, the malignant tumors may appear only many years (up to ten or more) after the irradiation event. This circumstance, together with large individual variations in the sensitivity of organisms to irradiation, and the relatively low frequency of "radiation induction" of tumors (about a few cases per hundred people, for a dose of 100–200 rad) does not allow one to establish a reliable relationship between the frequency of cancer and the irradiation dose, and all such evaluations have had only a probabilistic character.

The nonthreshold effects which occur even for small doses (10 rad) should also include the increased sensitivity to stress, and to various types of diseases related to destruction of the immune system. Such effects of small doses are least studied, basically for two reasons. First, experiments on living animals are difficult, and their results do not extrapolate well to humans. Second, observations collected on humans irradiated with small doses require a careful selection and a good definition of the control group. In each particular case, it is not possible to decide whether the lowered sensitivity to diseases is due to irradiation or to other causes; therefore, the conclusions are less reliable.

Such was the scientific background when Sakharov published his paper titled "Radioactive Carbon from Nuclear Explosions and Nonthreshold Biological Effects."[3] Although the author was far from radiobiology, the ideas formulated by him were correct and have remained in force until the present. What are these ideas and what is their importance today?

During the explosion of all types of atomic weapons, including the so-called clean (without fission fragments) hydrogen bomb, a large number of neutrons is released in the atmosphere, which are absorbed by nitrogen in the air in accordance with the reaction,

$$n + N^{14} \rightarrow p + C^{14},$$

forming the long-lived carbon isotope, C^{14}. Falling into the water basins and the tissues of living organisms, in particular, the organism of man, the radioactive isotope of carbon "disintegrates and causes radiation damage measured by the dose of 7.5×10^{-4} rad per megaton of explosive power." The average half-life of the isotope is 5,570 years, and its effects could extend up to 8,000 years.

By evaluating the possible effects of such an additional irradiation of man (compared to the natural background), Sakharov used the concept of "nonthreshold biological effects of radiation." That is, he considered the frequency of mutations that cause various anomalies in descendants, various new malignancies, including leukemia, and the destruction of the immune system that result in an increase in the incidence of these diseases and an acceleration of aging. According to Sakharov's calculations, the probable human death rate caused by these effects is 5×10^{-4} per rad, while the test of a bomb with 1 megaton power would add 6,600 human deaths over a period of 8,000 years. This was, as Sakharov mentioned, a lower estimate; in reality, the number of victims could be significantly larger.

Without discussing the accuracy of these evaluations (even today we do not have reliable data at our disposal), let us consider two particular features of Sakharov's approach to the problem of radiation hazard.

Nonthreshold Effects

First, the evaluation of radiation damage based on the nonthreshold effects. That is, the negative effects of small doses—those for which no symptoms of radiation disease occur (which would result in various injuries of the major organs and disruption of the function of the small intestine).

Unfortunately, the biological effects of small doses on mammals and humans have so far not been studied systematically. Classical radiobiology, and consequently radiation medicine, devoted much attention to the mechanisms and effects of large doses of radiation (hundreds and thousands of rad) on an organism. At such irradiation doses, the tissues or the organisms die within a few hours, weeks, or months. Here the successes are very high: today we know the laws of incidence of the severe effects of radiation and how they work at the molecular and tissue level. Another characteristic of the classical approach is the necessity of using highly homogeneous experimental subjects and samples. During such studies, the concept of a threshold of the radiation effects was developed. According to this concept, in order to observe severe effects, it is necessary that the radiation dose exceed a certain threshold (e.g., a few tenths of a rad). From a pragmatic point of view, the threshold concept played a positive role, especially in the early stages of development of nuclear technology, when the staffs of nuclear facilities were unavoidably exposed to irradiation. The threshold concept allowed one to establish the tolerance level of irradiation for individuals of "category A" (5 rem per year)[4], which did not immediately threaten their health. Regarding the low dose effects of radiation on category A humans, due to the relatively small sample, it is very difficult to evaluate them reliably; therefore, they are virtually neglected.

However, classical radiobiology and radiation medicine still treat the action of small radiation doses on animals and humans and the problem of individual differences in radiation sensitivity. The study of these problems needed the development of special research methods: the use of very large numbers of subjects, long-term observations, the recording of a series of parameters not directly related to the radiation disease, and so on. For this purpose, large amounts of time and resources were needed, but not always available. Nevertheless, a knowledge of the "classical effects" of radiation made it possible to determine those consequences which were not covered by the classical scheme and could be called "nonclassical." During the studies of the nonclassical effects, it was found that the biological effects of small doses possess a number of previously unknown and virtually unstudied characteristics.

During the last decade, it was established that even a single irradiation of tissues with a small dose increases the frequency of incidence of nonsurviving descendants. This was observed in all kinds of cells studied, on hundreds of cell divisions, and was accompanied by the increase in sensitivity of these cells to various kinds of damaging influences. It was also observed that in many living cells, after irradiation, genetic anomalies could occur again with very high frequency, during hundreds of cell divisions. In higher plants, a single irradiation of the seeds also leads to long-term development of genetic anomalies, often observed "without inhibition" for a minimum of three generations.[5] It is also known that the frequency of chromosome mutations in human lymphocytes, and the frequency of carcinogenic transformations of cells under the action of small irradiation doses are significantly larger than one would expect by linear extrapolation from high doses. Further, irradiated animals and their offspring are more sensitive to chemical carcinogens than nonirradiated animals.[6] As the tragic case of the Chernobyl incident showed, the humans who received small doses became ill more often than those who received no radiation, which indicates directly that irradiation suppresses the immune system. These facts suggest that the low dose approach underestimated the risk of small doses by a factor of ten.[7] Although the results of such studies have not yet been summarized, even those data that are known lead to the conclusion that the nonthreshold concept on which Sakharov based his arguments represents a particularly valid approach to the evaluation of the possible hazardous effects of small dose irradiation.

In this regard, it is appropriate to compare the nonthreshold concept with the currently generally accepted concept of a threshold. According to the official radiation safety rules, the threshold dose for category B people (i.e., those who do not work continuously with radiation sources) is 0.5 rem per year. It is considered that such a dose of radiation does not induce radiation sickness, and is thus not hazardous. If one adopts the approach developed by Sakharov, it appears that in those who receive a small dose, the probability of incidence of various nonthreshold effects may reach 0.1, i.e., up to 10 percent of the irradiated people and their offspring may experience various anomalies. This is probably a problem humanity will have to deal with, not only due to the testing of nuclear weapons, but also as a result of nuclear reactor accidents, leaking of radioactive wastes, etc.

The problem of threshold radiation doses becomes even more complicated for the following two reasons. First, major nuclear accidents like that at Chernobyl result in exposure to the environment and to humans of radio-active isotopes of various elements, in particular, of sources of alpha radiation and "hot particles" (microscopic residuals of various isotopes), whose effect on healthy organisms has been studied very little. Second, we know even less about the individual sensitivity of humans to the action of low doses, especially of isotopes of various kinds. It is, however, known that in animals (for example, in mice) under external irradiation, the radiation sensitivity of the representatives of a heterogeneous population may differ by a factor of ten; some animals feel as bad after irradiation with doses of 50 rad as others irradiated with doses of 500 rad. Particularly sensitive to radiation are embryos during the period of implantation and formation of various organ tissues. The analysis of the data from Hiroshima and Nagasaki shows that irradiation of women in the eighth through fifteenth weeks of pregnancy with doses of even 1–2 rem doubles the frequency of the birth of children with severe mental impairment.[8] If the individual differences in the sensitivity to radiation in humans are as large as in animals, then the damage due to radioexposure for various population groups may be significantly higher than the average for the entire population. Evidently, low doses should be established on the basis of the data provided by the most sensitive representatives of the population.

One more important point. Regarding the Chernobyl catastrophe, we proved to be ignorant in a problem as important as the effect of irradiation of a large territory on the population in general. Even such irradiation doses, which some authors[9] call "stimulative," and which are certainly of nonthreshold type, can lead to severe consequences, causing deformations of the composition of biocenoses and decreasing their sensitivity to various additional interactions. Thus the approach to evaluating hazards of radioactive contamination in humans and the biosphere is still of great importance.

Counting Victims

The second characteristic feature of the ideas promoted by Sakharov is the evaluation of radiation dangers to humans, not in terms of the increased percentage of expected anomalies (e.g., cancer incidences), but in absolute value. This is very important. Regarding the population of an extended region, the republic, the country, or the entire world, the effects of atomic tests or radioactive contamination may represent only small percentages, as it is sometimes said, "within the error limits of the experimental measurements." "However," wrote Sakharov, "this argument does not annul the fact that, to the already existing suffering and death in the world, the suffering and death of hundreds of thousands of more victims are added, even from neutral countries, and also from future generations. Two world wars contributed less than 10 percent of the deaths in the twentieth century, but this does not qualify the two world wars as normal phenomena."[10]

The moral aspect of the problem of nuclear weapons testing particularly disturbed Sakharov. As he noted, a widely held argument in the literature "is that the progress of civilization and the development of new technology in many other cases also lead to human victims. Often one cites traffic victims. But the analogy here is not correct and not fair. Transportation by automobile improves the quality of life, and accidents in some cases are caused only by the negligence of people who bear criminal responsibility for this. On the contrary, the accidents caused by the tests are the unavoidable result of each explosion." According to the author, the unique characteristic of the moral aspect of this problem "is the total impunity of the crime, since in each particular case of the death of a person, one cannot demonstrate that this was the result of irradiation, and also the total defenseless state of the offspring in regard to our actions."[11]

This ethical principle is fully applicable also to the results of the widespread injuries which occurred in 1957 in the Chelyabinsk region and in 1986 in Chernobyl, after which hundreds of thousands of people found themselves to be participants in an "experiment" performed without their knowledge or approval. This principle should also be acknowledged by those who so far have sanctioned the testing of nuclear weapons; those who support the construction of "cheap" atomic power plants; those who were called to assure the radiation safety of the population of our country; those who are responsible for dealing with the effects of this type of damage, and for such recommendations as the "deactivation" of contaminated agricultural products by adding them to "clean products" and dispersing them through various regions of the country;[12] and by those responsible for the voluntary increase of the human radiation dose limits.

The recent publication titled "Declaration of the Group of Scientists Working in the Field of Radiation Safety and Radiation Medicine Regarding the Situation Created as a Result of the Disruption at the Chernobyl Atomic Power Plant," discusses the "basis" for a new limiting dose (or "the concept of the life tolerance dose") for category B, equal to 35 rem, proposed by the National Committee on Radiation Protection of the Soviet Ministry of Health.[13] This figure was obtained by multiplying the "old" limiting dose of 0.5 rem per year by seventy years, which is assumed to be the average lifespan of humans. The Committee does not indicate over what period this dose could be absorbed, as a result of a single exposure, or through random irradiation over the entire life, including old age. They also ignore the following two circumstances: first, 35 rem under a one-time irradiation (or over two to three years) is significantly larger than the tolerance dose for category A (5 rem per year) which has severe pathological consequences in the irradiated people, especially in children. Secondly, a dose of 35 rem is close to the dose which causes doubling of the frequency of mutations in man, which results in doubling the genetic anomalies in offspring whose parents received such a dose.

The methods of evaluation of the effects of atomic weapons tests developed by Sakharov give an understanding of his uncompromising position with regard to the development and testing of these weapons: "The cutoff of testing will directly lead to saving the lives of hundreds of thousands of people. It will have an even greater indirect value by diminishing international tension and diminishing the danger of a nuclear war, which is a basic danger of our time."[14] Moreover, his work contains a series of basic statements that have very important methodological significance for the entire problem of evaluating radiation hazards related to the use of nuclear technologies, even those with strictly peaceful purposes.

Notes and References

1. *Proceedings of the International Conference on the Peaceful Uses of Atomic Energy*, Geneva, August 8–20, 1955; *Biological Effects of Radiation* 11, Moscow (1958).

2. *The Hazard of Ionizing Radiation on Man*, Moscow, 1958.

3. A. D. Sakharov in *Soviet Scientists on the Danger of Nuclear Tests*, ed. by A. V. Lebedinsky, Moscow: Foreign Languages Publishing House, 1959, pp. 36–45.

4. *The Standards of Radiation—Safety and Major Health Rules*, Moscow, 1981, p. 11.

5. I. B. Bychkovskaya, *The Problem of Remote Radiation Death of the Cell*, Moscow, 1986; V. I. Korogodin *et al.*, *Radiobiology* 17:4 (1977): pp. 492–499; G. S. Olimpienko *et al.*, *Plant Biology* 3 (1989): pp. 136–138.

6. N. V. Luchnik and A. V. Sevankaev, *Mut. Res.* 36:3 (1976): pp. 363–378; C. K. Hill, A. Han, M. M. Elkind, *Int. J. Rad. Biol.* 46:1 (1984): pp. 11–15; J. E. Vorobtsova, *Perinatal and Multigenerational Carcinogenesis*, IARC, 1989, pp. 389–401.

7. B. B. Baliga, *Science and Culture* 47:1 (1981): pp. 30–34.

8. R. W. Miller, *Health Physics* 55:2 (1988): pp. 295–298.

9. A. M. Kuzin, *The Peculiarities of the Action Mechanism of Atomic Radiation on the Biosphere in Small, Favorable Doses*, Pushino, 1989.

10. A. D. Sakharov, op. cit., p. 45.

11. A. D. Sakharov, op. cit., pp. 43–44.

12. *Izvestia*, September 3, 1989; *The Socialist Industry*, November 25, 1989.

13. *Medical Radiology* 1 (1990): pp. 7–9.

14. A. D. Sakharov, op. cit., p. 44.

Magnetic Cumulation

A. I. PAVLOVSKI

All-Union Research Institute of Experimental Physics

Birth of the Idea

ANDREI SAKHAROV writes in his *Memoirs*: "In 1951-52 I proposed two designs to produce superstrong pulse magnetic fields and electric currents by using the energy of explosion."[1] In the first of these designs, an axial magnetic flux in a cylindrical conducting shell is compressed toward the center by an explosive force. Such devices were called MK-1 based on the Russian acronym for "magnetic cumulation."

"Imagine a hollow metallic cylinder placed in a solenoid," he explained in *Izvestia*. "The cylinder envelopes, as it were, the bundle of magnetic lines of force produced by the solenoid of the initial field. Outside the cylinder is an explosive charge. At a certain moment, it explodes along the entire external surface. The hollow cylinder is compressed by the explosion and, in turn, like a gigantic fist, it compresses the bundle of magnetic lines of force, increasing the strength and the energy of the magnetic field."[2] The conversion of the kinetic energy of the cylinder into the energy of the magnetic field is the result of the deceleration of the shell's collapse by the magnetic pressure. As a result of the magnetic cumulation, the energy of the explosive substance (chemical or nuclear), initially distributed over a significant volume, becomes concentrated within a small region of space in the form of the magnetic field energy. The high density of the magnetic energy in principle makes it possible to heat a mixture of deuterium and tritium up to temperatures of 10^8 K (10 keV), as is necessary for the ignition of the fusion reaction. Sakharov proposed a design for heating the plasma by a powerful gas discharge induced by a rapidly varying field. Although the detailed analysis subsequently done by him revealed the difficulties in the realization of this design (it was one of the first approaches to inertial thermonuclear fusion), the basic idea appeared to be fruitful. The magnetic cumulation of the energy of such a powerful source as an explosion allowed one to achieve the strongest magnetic fields on Earth.

At the end of 1952, Sakharov considered the possibility of using the magnetic pressure to compress a small mass of fissionable substance (approximately 100 g) into the supercritical state, and to achieve a nuclear explosion of small intensity. Since the critical mass depends on the density of the fissioning substance, it is possible in principle to bring very small masses to a supercritical state, but for this purpose they must be compressed to a high density, which means that they must be concentrated into a small volume of large energy. Magnetic cumulation appeared to be more advantageous than the gas-dynamic method of energy concentration achieved by the direct use of the energy of the explosion. Sakharov accordingly proposed a second type of magnetic cumulator—MK-2. In this design, the electromagnetic pulses are generated by the direct conversion of the energy of the explosion into the field energy through the process of compressing and forcing out the magnetic flux into a load. The MK-2 generators are compact and powerful pulse sources of electromagnetic energy, with performance parameters that represent the limits of modern technology.

Sakharov suggested several other possible uses of magnetic cumulation. "The study of the electric, magnetic, optical, and elastic properties of various substances in such fields, which earlier could not be attained, is of great scientific interest. These studies may prove to be important for the physics of semiconductors, metals, and polymers."[3] He foresaw the promise of using compact, powerful, pulsed energy sources for long-range communications in the radio and optical ranges, in the study of the physics of plasmas, for simulation of astrophysical phenomena, for achievement of superhigh pressures, and so on. Sakharov considered that one of the basic scientific applications was the use of magnetic-cumulation generators as energy sources for superhigh-energy charged particle accelerators. The energy of particles in cyclic accelerators is determined by the radius of their orbit and the strength of the magnetic field. The use of superstrong magnetic fields makes it possible to construct compact, high-energy accelerators.

In 1952 Ya. B. Zel'dovich and Sakharov showed that a 10-GeV proton accelerator could be built with magnetic-cumulation generators using

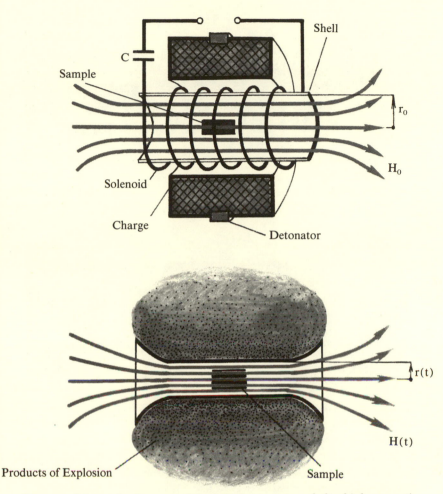

FIGURE 1. *Schematic diagram of the MK-1 generator of ultrahigh magnetic fields. When a capacitor bank C discharges into a solenoid, diffusion of the field through the shell of radius r_0 induces a magnetic flux Φ inside the shell. The detonation of the explosive charge is synchronized in such a way that the products of the explosion cause the shell to move when the initial magnetic field H_0 reaches its maximum. As it converges on the center, the shell compresses the magnetic flux. Since this flux remains approximately constant, the strength H(t) and the energy W(t) of the magnetic field increases: $H(t) = H_0 r_0^2/r^2(t)$; $W(t) = W_0 r_0^2/r^2(t)$.*

chemical explosions. A few years later, Sakharov proposed a facility for the acceleration of 10^{18} protons per pulse up to an energy of 10^3 GeV, through the use of a thermonuclear explosion with an energy release of about a megaton of TNT equivalent.[4] In such an accelerator, the magnetic

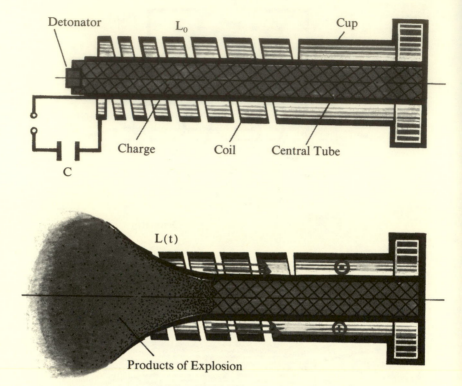

FIGURE 2. *Schematic diagram of the MK-2 energy generator. The deformable current-carrying loop with initial inductance L_0 consists of a coil, which transforms into a cup, and a central tube. Under the pressure of the explosion products, the walls of the tube extend in the shape of a cone and fly toward the beginning of the coil at the time of the maximum current, I_0. As the detonation front expands, the cone in a sense slides into the coil. Acting as a piston, it displaces the magnetic flux Φ into the cup. The inductance $L(t)$ of the current-carrying loop decreases, while the current $I(t)$ and the energy $W(t)$ of the electromagnetic field increase:*
$$\Phi = L(t)I(t) \approx L_0 I_0; \quad I(t) = \Phi/L(t); \quad W(t) = \Phi^2/2L(t).$$

field varies in space and time, and the particle is accelerated on an orbit with a decreasing radius. To obtain a magnetic field of intensity 10^8 Oe on the final 30-cm radius orbit, it was necessary to compress the magnetic flux of the shell by a weight of about one ton, at a speed of more than 10^7 cm/s. The energy of the beam was about 10^{11} J. Another "rather fantastic" (as Sakharov called it) possibility involves the use of pulsed magnetic lenses (which could be produced in explosions with energies on the order of hundreds of kilotons of TNT equivalent) to focus a beam of 10^{23} proton/s intensity on an area of 1 mm^2. With two colliding beams from two accelerators, it would be possible, in his view, to record interaction processes with cross sections on the order of 10^{-30} cm^2.

The Principle of Magnetic Cumulation

Magnetic cumulation is based on the law of electromagnetic induction and is similar in principle to the usual method of generating electrical energy. A current is induced in a conducting loop by varying the area of the loop. This current holds constant the magnetic flux within the loop.

Let us consider an ideal magnetic cumulation—the compression of the axial magnetic flux by a cylindrical shell made of a superconducting non-deformable material whose density remains constant. In this case the magnetic flux $\Phi = \int_s \vec{H} \, d\vec{s}$ is conserved at any compression velocity. When the cross section of the shell S decreases, the strength H, the pressure $P \sim H^2$, and the energy of the magnetic field $W \sim SH^2$ increase as $H(t) \sim S^{-1}(t)$, $P(t) \sim S^{-2}(t)$, and $W(t) \sim S^{-1}(t)$. When the shell implodes, the velocity of its inner wall also increases, $u(t) \sim r^{-1}(t)$; i.e., the kinetic energy of the shell, W_k, concentrates on its inner wall. The strength, energy, and pressure of the magnetic field reach maximum values at the time when the pressure of the magnetic field stops the shell and its kinetic energy is totally converted into the energy of the magnetic field.

In the case of a real loop with resistance different from zero, and which is compressible, conservation of the magnetic flux depends on the velocity of deformation of the loop. The magnetic flux decreases due to losses from the diffusion of the field into the walls of the conductor. Fields larger than 4×10^5 Oe cause intense heating of the conductor and consequently increase its resistance, and for $H > 3 \times 10^6$ Oe, the surface layer at the "matter-field" boundary starts to evaporate, and the region of conductivity loss propagates rapidly toward the interior of the material. Under these conditions, the magnetic flux is conserved if the velocity of its compression by the more remote conductive layers is larger than the velocity of the front of conductivity loss. At the same time, at the boundary surface, formation of a plasma layer is possible, which for fields larger than 2×10^7 Oe may have rather high conductivity and participate in the compression of the magnetic flux.

While compressing the magnetic flux, the conductor itself undergoes compression. When the magnetic pressure at the "matter-field" boundary increases, a compression wave is formed. This wave subsequently changes to a shock wave, which increases the density of the shell material and its

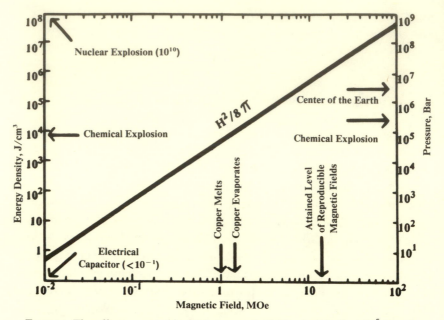

FIGURE 3. *The effects created by high magnetic fields. At $H > 8 \times 10^5$ Oe, the surface layer of the conductor starts to melt. At $H > 1.5 \times 10^6$ Oe, the material evaporates and the energy density reaches the density of the chemical energy of the explosion. The intensity $H = 1.6 \times 10^7$ Oe corresponds to the level of reproducible magnetic fields, for which the energy density (10^6 J/cm^3) exceeds the binding energy of most solids, and the field pressure exceeds the pressure at the Earth's center by a factor of more than two.*

internal energy (elastic energy, thermal energy, ionization energy, and the energy of electromagnetic radiation). When the shell of compressive material implodes, $u(t)$ varies as $r^{-n}(t)$, where $0 < n < 1$; i.e., in this case, the kinetic energy of the shell is concentrated at its inner wall. Thus at high-energy densities, the hydrodynamic processes in the layer of material at the border with the magnetic field become decisive. Based on qualitative arguments, one can derive the criteria for efficient magnetic cumulation $\rho u^2 > H^2/8\pi$ (ρ is the density of the shell material). It thus follows that, by taking into account the final conductivity and compressibility of real conductors, the magnitude of the generated magnetic field is determined by the limitations on the kinetic energy density of the shell accelerated by the explosion. In 1952 Sakharov and M. P. Shumaev derived the analytic solution in the case of constant conductivity σ, and demonstrated that the magnetic flux is conserved if $\eta = (4\pi\sigma r u/c^2)^{1/2} \gg 1$. In general, one must use numerical methods to solve the system of magnetohydrodynamic equations, which is supplemented by the conducting material's equation-of-state and the law of variation of its conductivity.

The magnetic cumulation may be severely limited by instabilities of the shrinking cylindrical shell (loss of symmetry) due to the unlimited increase of small initial perturbations. Therefore, it is very important to assure good initial cylindrical symmetry of the compression, i.e., a good quality detonation wave formation, and precise fabrication and assembly of the charge and the shell.

The First Experiments

In the USSR, the beginning of the work on magnetic cumulation is marked by the experiment with the MK-1 generator performed during the first half of 1952 at Sakharov's initiative.[5] In this experiment, a twenty-five-fold increase of the magnetic field was recorded (maximum value of 10^6 Oe).

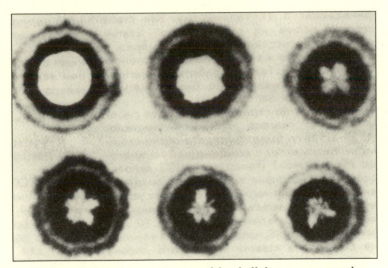

FIGURE 4. *Reduced x-ray pictures of the shell that compresses the magnetic field. The pictures were taken along the axis at a sequence of times after the compression. When the intensity of the magnetic field exceeds 3.5×10^6 Oe, an unlimited increase of perturbations occurs on the internal surface of the shell. These perturbations have catastrophic consequences: the energy cumulation stops at $H = 6 \times 10^6$ Oe. At this time, the shell slows down and has a shape far from its initial shape. Inside it, the evaporated material becomes mixed with the field.*

Unfortunately, at that time this result and Sakharov's idea were not published. This happened only in 1965.[6] The first publication, a brief note devoted to the explosion as a possible source of superstrong magnetic fields, appeared in 1957 and was authored by Ya. P. Terletskii. Later on, it was learned that American scientists at the Los Alamos Laboratory independently began work on magnetic cumulation at about the same time.

From 1952 until the middle of 1960, the work in the USSR was intensive. In 1955–56, a series of very complex experiments was conducted, using a combination of MK-1 and MK-2 generators. (The MK-2 generator was used for the generation of the initial magnetic field.) In these experiments, fields of approximately 5×10^6 Oe were recorded in a cavity of 10 mm diameter. The series of experiments on improving the symmetry of the magnetic flux compression and increasing the kinetic energy density of the shell was completed in 1964 with an experiment in which a record value of the magnetic field of 2.5×10^7 Oe was recorded in a cavity of 4 mm diameter. This experiment used a stainless-steel shell, prepared with high precision and coated on the inside with a thin (20 micron) layer of copper. The compression velocity of the magnetic flux over the first third of the initial diameter was about 10^6 cm/s. The magnetic field was recorded with an induction transducer with a massive insulating screen, and the induced signals were controlled by background sensors. The coefficient of conservation of the magnetic flux obtained in the experiment ($\Phi/\Phi_0 = 0.3$) was close to the expected value. In a number of very difficult experiments the attempt to achieve a record-high result failed. It was observed that the operation of the coil of the initial field (the insulation breakdown) was unstable. However, subsequent research showed that the cause of the failure of these experiments was the instability of the magnetic cumulation, which does not exclude the possibility of obtaining large fields in isolated experiments.

A 1960 publication, which reported on the generation at Los Alamos of a field with strength approximately equal to 1.5×10^7 Oe, triggered an intensive development of the work in the U.S., Italy, France, and other countries. The results of the initial research period were reported in 1965 at the first international conference at Frascati, Italy. It was noted that, although American and Soviet scientists achieved record values of the field in isolated experiments, in the majority of experiments the field intensities did not exceed 5×10^6 Oe. This fact could not be explained. It became clear that the problem of stable generation of superstrong magnetic fields was much more difficult than had been anticipated, and the intensity of the produced fields was lower than that expected. Possibly for this reason the work on the generation of superstrong magnetic fields by the explosive method was stopped in most laboratories immediately after the conference.

A Critical Limitation

In the USSR, the research on cumulation of superstrong magnetic fields was continued by a small group of scientists, whose aim was to enhance the level of reproducibility of the fields.[7] The reproducibility was extremely important for the individual explosion experiments. Without any certainty that the announced value of the magnetic field could be reproduced with high probability in any experiment, the studies performed in such fields would be meaningless.

During that period, nearly all the possible methods of increasing the values of the stable generated magnetic fields were studied. A single possibility remained, namely, to increase the initial magnetic field, in order to limit the variations of the radius of the shell as much as possible, and thus attempt to avoid the deterioration of the stability of its compression due to the evolution of these initial perturbations. It was accordingly necessary to develop an explosive device which could assure reproducibility of the initial conditions, to expand the diagnostic capability, and to develop mathematical methods of simulating the processes occurring in the actual construction of the generator.

Generation of an initial magnetic field with intensities up to 2×10^5 Oe inside a shell with good conductivity, with a cavity of 5×10^3 cm^3, and without significant perturbations in the magnetic flux compression system, proved to be very difficult. Lengthy research led to a fundamentally new solution, namely, combining the functions of the solenoid which generated the initial magnetic field, and the shell, which compressed the magnetic flux, in a single solenoid-shell device. Such a device begins as a cylindrical solenoid with a special winding made of thin (0.25 mm) insulated copper conductors. The solenoid is placed inside a cylindrical charge of explosive material. After the explosion, the shock wave travels through the material of the solenoid with a pressure of 1.5×10^5 bar at the wave front, destroying the insulation. The conductors become welded to each other, and the solenoid is transformed into a solid shell with uniform conductivity, which effectively traps and compresses the magnetic flux.

It is not a simple matter to collect reliable information about magnetic fields—which last a fraction of a microsecond under the conditions of an explosion—by using transducers subjected to high temperature, a magnetic pressure similar to the pressure at the Earth's center, and intensive beams of evaporated material, plasma, and electromagnetic radiation. The most developed methods are the optical methods using lasers to measure magnetic fields with the Faraday effect (rotation of the plane of polarization) and the pulsed radiography methods to probe the inner cavity. The

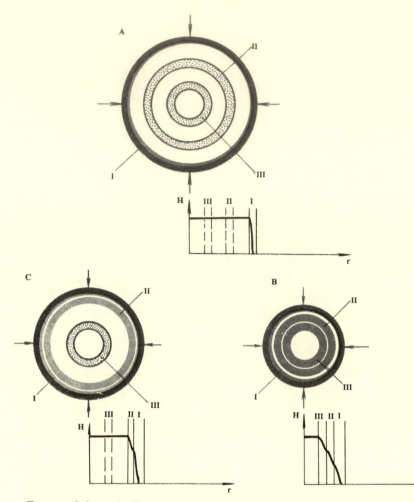

FIGURE 5. *Schematic diagram of the magnetic flux compression by a system of coaxial shells. (a) Compression of the magnetic flux is done by shell I, while shells II and III are at rest and are transparent to the magnetic field; i.e., they don't affect the compression process. (b) Generation of the magnetic field continues in shell II; after its collision with shell I the internal boundary of the skin-layer (shown in lighter shading) moves to the inner surface of shell II. (c) Generation of the magnetic field in shell III. During each collision of the shells, the field generation is transferred from one shell to the other and part of the magnetic flux is lost in the material surrounding the shell. However, stabilization of the matter-field boundary is achieved and makes it possible to obtain higher magnetic fields.*

instrumentation was placed inside a protective building and, except for the field sensor, could be used many times. The experimental data, together

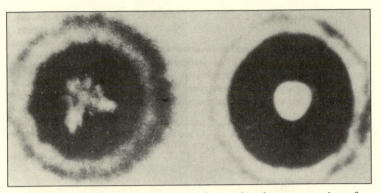

FIGURE 6. *Reduced x-ray pictures obtained in the compression of the magnetic flux by one shell (left) and by a system of three shells (right). In the first case, the picture was taken when the magnetic compression was stopped at $H = 6 \times 10^6$ Oe. In the second case, the picture was taken when the field intensity reached 10^7 Oe; the compression process continues.*

with the numerical calculations, provided a rather complete picture of the processes being studied.

The results of the first experiments were discouraging. The maximum value of the recorded magnetic field did not exceed 3×10^6 Oe, and recording of the magnetic field was interrupted before the moment of maximum compression. When the field sensor was surrounded by a massive insulating screen that occupied the entire volume of the cavity at the time of maximum compression, it was possible to extend the recording time of the field and to stabilize the field strength to $(5-6) \times 10^6$ Oe. An investigation of the state of the cavity by the pulsed x-ray radiography method made it possible to determine the cause of deterioration of the stability of the magnetic cumulation, namely, the development of perturbations at the matter-field boundary. Already at magnetic fields of 3×10^6 Oe, the compression symmetry of the internal boundary of the shell is significantly deformed, the material evaporates rapidly, and jets are formed. The temperature of the material reaches 10^4 K, and the pressure of the magnetic field is 3.6×10^5 bar. Such conditions rapidly give rise to instabilities of the Rayleigh-Taylor type, which are characteristic for the boundary between a heavy layer (matter) and a light layer (field), for an acceleration directed toward the heavy layer (precisely the situation when the shell is slowed down by the magnetic field pressure). At the end of compression ($H \sim 5 \times 10^6$ Oe), the deformation of the internal surface of the shell is so large that it is difficult to consider its boundaries. A faster way of losing the kinetic energy of the shell than through the compression of the magnetic field appears: direct conversion into heat. The magnetic cumulation process then stops.

Thus the attempt to increase the value of the reproducible magnetic field by increasing the initial field ended in failure. Moreover, a basic limitation of cumulation was determined. In light of this limitation, the prospects did not seem to be very promising. For the scientists involved in magnetic cumulation, the situation became rather serious.

Compression of the Magnetic Flux by a System of Shells

The solution of this problem was found to be the stabilization of the magnetic cumulation process.[8] This turned out to be amazingly simple: the compression of the magnetic flux could be accomplished not by a single shell, but by a system of coaxial shells. Whenever there is a danger of losing stability at the inner wall of a shell, that shell is replaced by a new shell, which takes over the compression of the flux. By using such a system of coaxial shells it is possible to stabilize the magnetic flux compression for larger variations of the radius and thus increase the strength of the final field. Part of the kinetic energy is transferred from one shell to the other by the collision of the moving shell with the shell at rest. In this way, the inner wall of the skin-field is transferred to the inner surface of the coupled shell, and its outer wall remains inside the material of the previous shell. At the matter-field boundary, the hot material is replaced each time by fresh, cold material. In this compression method, the load on the inner layer of each shell is significantly diminished, which slows down the formation of instabilities. The criterion of efficient cumulation is satisfied at small velocities, suggesting that magnetic cumulation has a promising future.

For the compression of magnetic flux by a system of shells to work, it is necessary that they each let the magnetic flux pass freely through them when at rest, and trap it when moving. Shells with such properties were built on the same principle as the solenoid shell. The transformation of the transparent (with respect to the axial magnetic flux) fixed shell made of insulated copper conductors into a solid copper shell, which traps and compresses the magnetic field, is caused by the shock compression wave formed by the collision of the moving shell with the shell at rest.

Experiments with Superstrong Fields

Stabilization of magnetic flux compression at high-energy densities made the continuation of research on magnetic energy cumulation meaningful. The devices in which magnetic flux was compressed by a system of coaxial shells became known as "cascade generators of superstrong magnetic fields." Two models of such generators were built, each with a system of three cascade shells for flux compression (the solenoid shell was considered to be the first shell), but differing by the amount of explosive material used.

The first, with an external charge diameter of 300 mm, made it possible to obtain reliable magnetic fields up to 1.3×10^7 Oe in a volume of about 4 cm^3. For the first time anywhere, this rather simple and compact device was produced at a commercial level with the final experimental operating parameters. With this device the magnitude and volume of the final field could be varied without additional tests of its performance. Its stability and the high reproducibility of the generated fields were confirmed by hundreds of experiments.

The second model of the cascade generator had an external charge diameter of 650 mm, a final volume of 5 cm^3, and produced stable fields of up to 1.6×10^7 Oe. It should be mentioned that the capabilities of this upgraded version of the cascade generator are not yet fully known. The fields obtained in cascade generators have now reached record levels. Stabilization of the magnetic cumulation has made it possible to reach magnetic field energy densities up to 10^6 J/cm^3, which is a hundred times higher than the density of the chemical energy of explosive materials. In this case the pressure of the magnetic field amounts to 10^7 bar.

What are the future prospects? With regard to *reliable* superstrong magnetic fields, which are the only ones of interest to scientists, there is no known alternative to the explosive method of generation. It is believed that in the next few years, by using chemical explosion energies, it will be possible to obtain fields of intensity 3×10^7 Oe in a volume of 1–5 cm^3. Today there seem to be no basic limitations on the magnitude of magnetic fields obtainable by the explosive method. Fields of 10^8–10^9 Oe can be produced by using the energy of nuclear explosions. In this case the initial magnetic field must amount to at least a few megaoersted, which is not difficult to obtain by using chemical explosions. Calculations have shown that magnetic fields up to 10^9 Oe could be generated with rather small nuclear explosions with energy release no higher than 100 tons TNT equivalent. Apparently, even such fields are not the limit under terrestrial conditions.

Generation of stable magnetic fields in the range of tens of megaoersteds opened great opportunities for physicists. Experiments have been performed on the optical and magneto-optical properties of many materials in magnetic fields of up to 1.1×10^7 Oe, even at low temperatures. Based on analysis of experimental data in which the absorption coefficient and the Faraday effect were measured, one can draw conclusions about the influence the external field has on the energy spectrum, the band structure, and other quantum-mechanical characteristics of solids. In strong magnetic fields, the paramagnetic and cyclotron resonance frequencies were observed to shift toward the optical region. For the first time, a puzzling effect was observed in a GaAs semiconductor: in fields above 4.3×10^6 Oe, the sample became transparent to radiation with a wavelength $\lambda = 0.633$ microns, and in reflected light it changed color from red to yellow in a field of 10^7 Oe.

Experiments are currently being carried out in fields of about 3×10^6 Oe, at $T = 4\,\mathrm{K}$, with bulk and thin-film superconductors of the Y-Ba-Cu-O type, in which H_{c2}, the magnetic field at which the superconductivity vanishes, is measured directly.

An interesting area of research makes use of pulsed magnetic fields in order to obtain high pressures. If a metallic tube filled with a certain material is placed in a magnetic field whose strength is increased, then the walls of the tube will experience a gradually increasing magnetic pressure $H^2/8\pi$, while the pressure of the material will be determined by its compressibility. Such a compression regime results in minimal heating of the sample even at high values of the generated pressures. In this way scientists studied the equations-of-state of several materials at pressures up to 5×10^6 bar, and the spectrum and the shift of the R-line of luminescence of compressed ruby. The compression of solid hydrogen and deuterium ($T \sim 4\text{--}6$ K) has been studied for several years over a range of pressures $(3\text{--}5) \times 10^6$ bar. An important feature of these experiments is that they can directly measure the conductivity of the compressed materials. All these experiments are, in fact, the first steps in mastering the topic of superstrong magnetic fields. The strength of the magnetic fields obtained so far and the promise that they can soon be increased further, are grounds for returning to Sakharov's idea: the realization of pulsed thermonuclear fusion in MK-1 generators.

MK-2 Generators

Another direction of research was related to the development of MK-2 magnetic-compression generators.[9] In these generators, the conversion of the explosion energy by slowing down an accelerated conductor occurs in moderately strong fields of $(0.25\text{--}1.0) \times 10^6$ Oe. By deforming such a contour at a rate of 2×10^5 cm/s, the magnetic flux losses, which are associated with the diffusion of the field through the conductor during its compressibility, are small. Basically, the losses are determined by the

FIGURE 7. *Cascade generator, which generates magnetic fields at reproducible intensities up to 1.3×10^7 Oe, set up for an explosion experiment. At the left of the generator is a bundle of coaxial cables. Energy from a capacitor bank in a protective enclosure is dumped through these cables to create the initial field.*

deterioration of the regularity of the induction of the deforming contour, by the cutoff of the magnetic flux in the insulators, and by electrical breakdown inside the generator. All these losses can be reduced by choosing an optimum design of the generator.

The basic design of the MK-2 generator proposed by Sakharov was thoroughly studied by 1956. In the experiments with such generators, currents of up to 10^8 A and energies on the order of 10^7–10^8 J were recorded in a load with inductance up to 10 nH. Later, MK-2 generators were developed with a modified geometry of the deforming current-carrying contours. The power of the generators was increased by increasing the area of the current-carrying surface that is deformed at the same time, by using a multipoint system of setting off the explosive material. The agreement between the laws governing the energy released by the explosion and the generation of magnetic energy makes it possible to increase the energy conversion efficiency. The modern MK-2 generators are characterized by an energy density of $(6-7) \times 10^2$ J/cm^3, a power density of $10^7 - 10^8$ W/cm^3, and an energy conversion coefficient up to 20 percent.

One version of the MK-2 generator with an expanded deformable loop is the disk-type generator, in which the loop has the shape of a toroid with a large external to internal diameter ratio. In 1967, during its testing, a record current greater than 3×10^8 A and an energy of about 10^8 J were achieved, in a load with an inductance of 3 nH. The conversion efficiency was 20 percent.

The MK-2 type generators operate efficiently with a low inductance connected to the output circuit. With loads having a large inductance, the generator is tuned by using devices which increase the magnetic flux in the load.

The characteristic operating time of MK-2 generators is $10^{-4} - 10^{-5}$ s. Modern methods make it possible to modify the law governing the increase of the current pulse, and to form pulses on the order of 10^{-7}–10^{-2} s inside the material. The energy can be transferred from the generator to a shielded area that protects the experimental facility. In such an experiment an energy of 3×10^7 J (power of 10^{12} W) was transported from an MK-2 generator to an experimental setup situated a distance of 30 m. Several MK-2 generators connected in series have characteristics that considerably exceed those of a single generator.

FIGURE 8. *The MK-2 cascade generator manufactured by the Leningrad Science and Engineering Society "Elektrofizika". The apparatus consists of three generators coupled by transformers. Each generator serves as an energy source for the next generator. In this way, a high energy gain (10^4) and an efficient conversion of explosive energy (up to 10 percent) are achieved. The output energy of the generator is 1.5×10^7 J.*

MK-2 generators have now been studied thoroughly. Numerical methods make it possible to predict their characteristics with a satisfactory accuracy. The fabrication technology of cascade MK-2 generators has been developed. These generators deliver an energy of 1.5×10^7 J, and operate with a wide range of loads.

MK-2 generators are the most powerful pulsed sources of electromagnetic energy. They are widely used in research as power sources for pulsed charged-particle accelerators, in high-velocity mass accelerators, gas lasers, and microwave generators, and for generation of high-voltage pulses. The cycle of work on the study of magnetic cumulation and the development of magnetic-cumulation generators, which extended over many years, was performed by a group of scientists at the institute, led by Yu. B. Khariton. His active support was very important for the development of this field of research.

The gigantic projects on superpowerful particle accelerators, considered by Sakharov twenty-five years ago, remain "rather fantastic" even today. However, up to his last years Sakharov continued to hope that such projects might be realized. "It seemed to me," he wrote in his *Memoirs*, "that one-time systems with record characteristics might also provide very valuable scientific information; in fact, I still wouldn't rule out the possibility that at some point it might become necessary to return to the impulse MK accelerator."[10] One such possibility, which is of considerable scientific interest, is magnetic cumulation by nuclear explosions. Such experiments could be performed in ecologically safe underground nuclear explosions with a relatively small energy release. In Sakharov's opinion, such work should be conducted under international cooperation.

Notes and References

1. A. D. Sakharov, *Memoirs*, New York: Knopf, 1990, p. 149.

2. A. D. Sakharov, "Record-high Magnetic Fields," *Izvestia*, April 29, 1966, p. 3.

3. Op. cit.

4. A. D. Sakharov, "Explosive-Driven Magnetic Generators," *Soviet Physics Uspekhi (Uspekhi Fizicheskikh Nauk)* 88 (1966): p. 725.

5. The experiment was performed by R. Z. Lyudaev, E. A. Feoktistov, G. A. Tcyrkov, and A. A. Chivileva.

6. A. D. Sakharov, R. Z. Lyudaev, E. N. Smirnov, Ju. I. Plyshev, A. I. Pavlovski, V. K. Chernyshev, E. A. Feoktistova, E. I. Zharinov, and Ju. A. Zysin, *Soviet Physics Doklady (Doklady Akademii Nauk)* 196 (1965): p. 65

7. A. I. Pavlovski, N. P. Kolokolchikov, M. I. Dolotenko et al., in *Megagauss Physics and Technology*, ed. by P. J. Turchi. New York: Plenum Press, 1980, p. 627.

8. A. I. Pavlovski, M. I. Dolotenko, N. P. Kolokolchikov et al. *JETP Letters (Pis'ma v Zhurnal Eksperimental'noi i Teoretischeskoi Fiziki)* 38 (1983): p. 437.

9. A. I. Pavlovski, R. Z. Lyudaev. "Magnetic Cumulation," in *The Questions of Modern Experimental and Theoretical Physics*, ed. by A. P. Alexandrov, Leningrad: Nauka, 1984, p. 206.

10. *Memoirs*, pp. 152–153.

Sakharov and Induced Gravitation

Stephen L. Adler

Institute for Advanced Study, Princeton

Commentary by D. A. Kirzhnits

Lebedev Physical Institute, Moscow

In the standard model of the fundamental forces of physics, gravitation appears on a quite different footing from the electromagnetic, weak, and strong forces which govern the small-scale physics of atoms and nuclei. All four forces are described by so-called gauge fields, in which the physically measurable field-strengths (like the familiar electric and magnetic fields) are represented by potentials in a non-unique way; the potentials can be altered in different regions of space and time by gauge transformations without affecting the field-strengths or the physically measurable results. Also, for all four forces the equations-of-motion are obtained by variation of an action which is constructed from the gauge potentials. In the case of the electromagnetic, weak, and strong forces, this action principle involves only dimensionless coupling constants linking the various matter fields and gauge potentials When such theories with dimensionless couplings are quantized—modified to take quantum mechanical effects into account—they are renormalizable; that is, the infinities encountered when doing calculations in perturbation theory can all be absorbed by rescalings of a finite number of mass and charge parameters.

Einstein's general theory of relativity, on the other hand, arises from an action principle in which the fundamental coupling has the dimensionality of a mass squared. Such theories with dimensional coupling constants have long been known to be non-renormalizable, that is, when quantized and developed in a perturbation expansion in powers of the coupling constant, as one calculates to higher orders one encounters an ever-increasing number of different infinite quantities which must be rescaled away, requiring the adjustment of an infinite number of parameters. This difficulty has been known since the 1930s, and has prompted a great deal of research and speculation aimed at solving the problem of successfully quantizing general relativity.

This statement of the problem of "quantizing gravitation" assumes, however, that the conventional Einstein-Hilbert gravitational action (which is proportional to the curvature scalar R, the simplest Lorentz-invariant measure of spacetime curvature) is in fact the fundamental quantum action for gravitation. Since all gravitational experiments done to date involve macroscopic wavelengths greater than about ten centimeters, there is in fact no experimental evidence for this assumption. Thus before proceeding to study quantum gravity, we must first address the question: is the Einstein theory a fundamental theory, or is it a long-wavelength effective field theory, describing the long-wavelength limit of physics which looks qualitatively quite different at very short distances?

A familiar example of a long-wavelength effective field theory is provided by the Fermi theory of weak interactions, as extended by investigations in particle physics over the last twenty years. For energies well below 80 GeV (i.e., for wavelengths much longer than 10^{-16} centimeters), the weak interactions are described by the four-fermion effective action originally proposed by Fermi, which has a dimensional coupling constant called the Fermi constant. As expected for a theory with a dimensional coupling constant, the Fermi theory is non-renormalizable, and repeated attempts to quantize the weak interactions starting from the Fermi theory as the fundamental quantum action met with frustration. It is now known that the Fermi theory is only a long-wavelength effective theory. The fundamental quantum theory for the weak interactions is the renormalizable gauge theory of Glashow, Salam, and Weinberg, in which the weak interactions are mediated by the exchange of massive intermediate vector bosons, which obtain their masses (in the neighborhood of 80 GeV) from a symmetry-breaking mechanism involving Higgs scalar bosons. The fundamental interaction in this theory consists of the coupling, by a dimensionless coupling constant, of an intermediate boson to a fermion pair, and leads to a renormalizable quantum theory. At low energies or long wavelengths, where the intermediate bosons cannot be directly observed, the only relevant physical processes are those in which an intermediate boson is emitted from a fermion pair and then absorbed into another fermion pair. Thus at low energies, one observes an effective pair–pair interaction, which is just the four-fermion coupling introduced by Fermi. In the formal, mathematical language of quantum field theory, the Fermi effective action is obtained from the Glashow-Salam-Weinberg action when the intermediate boson (and Higgs scalar) degrees of freedom, which cannot be observed in low energy experiments, are integrated out. When the Fermi action is derived in this way, the Fermi constant is no longer an *ad hoc* coupling constant, but instead is related in a specific way to parameters of the fundamental theory, such as the intermediate boson couplings and masses. This prediction of the Fermi constant has of course been brilliantly confirmed by high-energy weak interaction experiments.

WITH THIS BACKGROUND in mind, let us now return to the problem of quantizing gravitation. In a very interesting paper published in 1967 (before the advent of the modern understanding of the Fermi interaction), Andrei Sakharov proposed the idea that gravitation is not a fundamental interaction, and suggested a specific mechanism for producing the Einstein-Hilbert gravitational action as a low-energy effective theory.[1] Briefly, the reasoning in Sakharov's article runs as follows. He begins by making the observation that the phenomenon of gravitation consists not in the existence of spacetime curvature, but in the existence of a large "metrical elasticity" which opposes the curving of spacetime, except near very large concentrations of matter. This statement has the following quantitative basis: as we have already noted, the equations of general relativity arise from an action principle, obtained by adding to the action of the matter fields (quarks, leptons, photons, gluons, intermediate weak bosons, etc.) the Einstein-Hilbert gravitational action, which has an action density proportional to the scalar spacetime curvature R multiplied by the inverse of Newton's constant. Since Newton's constant is a very small number (reflecting the weakness of gravitational forces) the inverse of Newton's constant is a very large number; in the so-called atomic units used by particle physicists, the inverse of Newton's constant is the square of a large mass called the Planck mass, which is equal to 1.3×10^{19} proton masses. Because the Einstein-Hilbert action equals the local spacetime curvature times a very large number, a very large action penalty is paid when appreciable curvatures develop—or in Sakharov's terms, there is a large elastic stiffness opposing the development of curvature. The practical consequences of this are familiar to all of us. Because of the large elastic stiffness of spacetime, even as massive an object as the earth produces very little local spacetime curvature. Light rays traveling near the Earth obey the laws of Euclidean geometry, which is what a surveyor assumes when sighting a plumb bob with his transit.

To explain the origin of this elastic stiffness, Sakharov proposes that it arises from the quantum fluctuations of the matter fields (following a line of investigation originated by Ya. B. Zel'dovich in the context of studies of the cosmological constant, which for the purposes of our discussion here we assume to be strictly zero). In flat spacetime, the quantum fluctuations of the matter fields lead to an infinite action density which is removed by the renormalization procedure mentioned earlier. When spacetime is curved, the action density arising from quantum fluctuations is altered, and is only partially canceled by the renormalization constant computed in flat spacetime. The residual effect is a Lorentz scalar that (in the absence of a cosmological constant) vanishes when the spacetime curvature vanishes; hence, in leading order, it must be proportional to the scalar curvature R, and so has just the form of the Einstein-Hilbert gravitational action! Thus Sakharov gives a natural way for obtaining the Einstein-Hilbert action as an effective action. In formal field-theoretic language, if a matter theory is quantized in a curved spacetime, and the matter quantum fluctuations are integrated out, one obtains an effective action for the spacetime curvature itself which has just the form assumed in the general theory of relativity.

Continuing with this line of reasoning, Sakharov shows (with details in subsequent papers) that in naive models of the matter fields, the proportionality constant in the effective action is given by an infinite sum over masses of the fluctuation quanta (so-called virtual quanta) which are present. He then postulates (following a suggestion of M. A. Markov) that in the true unified theory of the matter fields, there is in fact a maximum virtual quantum mass of the order of the Planck mass. The infinite sum then becomes a finite sum, with a cutoff at the Planck mass, and yields an inverse Newton's constant of the correct magnitude. Note that here there is a significant difference from the Fermi theory: In the case of the Fermi theory, the proportionality constant in the effective action (the Fermi constant) has the dimensionality of mass to the power negative two, and so the dominant contributions to the Fermi constant come from the smallest mass intermediate states with the relevant quantum numbers, which are the intermediate bosons. By contrast, the proportionality constant in the gravitational effective action (the inverse of Newton's constant) has the dimensionality of mass to the power positive two, and so the dominant contributions to Newton's constant will come from the largest characteristic mass scale appearing.

SAKHAROV'S PROPOSAL attracted the attention of physicists from the outset,[2] but it is only recently that our theoretical understanding of matter fields has advanced to the point where one can begin to see how his ideas can be realized. We now believe that the electromagnetic, weak, and strong interactions become part of a grand unified field theory at masses near the Planck mass, giving the maximum mass postulate a credibility which it did not have in 1967. However, the existence of a maximum mass is not in itself enough to make Sakharov's residual action a well-defined quantity; this requires that the mass scale be introduced into the physics of the matter fields through spontaneous breakdown of scale invariance symmetry. This concept is also a natural outgrowth of recent progress in electroweak unified theories, where renormalizability is achieved only when the intermediate bosons are given their masses by spontaneous symmetry breaking, which occurs in the Higgs scalar sector of the theory. By analogy with Higgs models, a number of authors constructed models of scalar matter fields in a curved background spacetime, and showed that when all naturally occurring couplings are present, including a coupling of the scalar

In February 1971 Sakharov was invited to a small but elite conference on gravitation and field theory to be held at the International Center for Theoretical Physics, Trieste. He could not, of course, attend, but the invitation was kept because this puzzling drawing by Sakharov was found on the back of the page bearing the list of anticipated world-famous participants.

field to the spacetime curvature, spontaneous symmetry breaking in the scalar field sector induces a gravitational effective action, just as envisioned by Sakharov.

Further progress stemmed from the observation which I made in 1980 that in scalar-free theories with dynamical breaking of scale invariance, an Einstein-Hilbert action is induced with a calculable Newton's constant. The simplest example of a field theory satisfying these calculability criteria is a pure non-Abelian (i.e., Yang-Mills) gauge theory, in which the dimensionless coupling constant of the bare action gets replaced, by a process called dimensional transmutation, by a dimensional scale mass which serves as the coupling constant for the renormalized quantized theory. This is by now familiar in the theory of the strong interactions, quantum chromodynamics, where the coupling parameter measured by experimentalists is a scale mass, and not a dimensionless number like the electric charge. Thus the simplest model of induced gravity is a non-Abelian gauge theory quantized on a classical curved background manifold; when one formally integrates out the gauge theory degrees of freedom, one is left with an Einstein-Hilbert effective action for the curvature, with an induced Newton's constant which can be explicitly related to the gauge-field scale mass.

To go beyond a background field model, one must take into account the fact that in a realistic theory, gravity (i.e., the spacetime geometry) is itself quantized. Using the effective action formalism developed by field theorists, one can make a self-consistent splitting of the gravitational potential or metric into background metric and quantum fluctuation parts, and derive a formal expression for the induced gravitational constant including quantum gravity effects. A detailed review of spontaneous symmetry breaking and its applications in induced gravity is given in an article I wrote which appeared in 1982.[3]

In order for the induced gravity idea to fully resolve the problems of quantum gravity, one of course must address the question of what is the correct fundamental gravitational action. If only metrical degrees of freedom are involved, the natural candidate actions which have only dimensionless couplings (and hence are renormalizable) are actions which are quadratic in the curvature tensor. Such actions lead to fourth-order equations-of-motion, which have the classic problem that in a small-fluctuation analysis, they lead to an energy spectrum which is unbounded from below. However, there is some evidence that when nonlinearities are taken into account this problem is eliminated; the issue is one on which research continues. My own view, however, is that if induced gravity is the correct route (and I still consider it an enormously appealing idea), the fundamental gravitational action is likely to involve new, non-metrical degrees of freedom; at the Planck scale, there may be no clear separation between matter and geometry, but rather, new pregeometric degrees of freedom may be the ones in terms of which a completely unified theory should be constructed.

In closing, I should note that most of the recent work on quantum gravity has been along a different avenue from induced gravity, namely the Kaluza-Klein idea that there are hidden compact dimensions of order 10^{-33} centimeters (corresponding to the inverse of the Planck mass), whose existence is observed by us only through the small size of Newton's constant. The modern version of the Kaluza-Klein idea is contained in string theory, which is a finite theory of gravitation in which a fundamental Einstein-Hilbert action is present, with the scale of the compact dimensions providing a natural cutoff and thus preventing the usual non-renormalizability problems from arising. In theories of this type, Sakharov's observation is still relevant in the sense that quantum fluctuations provide a calculable and in some cases important correction to the Newton's constant appearing in the original action, but Einstein gravity is no longer an effect induced entirely by the quantum corrections. Which route to the construction of a satisfactory quantum theory of gravitation (and of everything else) will prove to be the correct one? Only time will decide.

COMMENTARY BY D. A. KIRZHNITS

IN HIS PAPER, S. L. Adler emphasizes that Sakharov's approach allows one to consider the standard gravitation theory as being the effective low-energy limit of a more general theory. The latter, one might hope, is renormalizable; i.e., after quantization it does not contain infinite quantities. There is no doubting the importance of this property of the theory of induced gravitation for the construction of a noncontradictory and workable quantum gravitation theory.

However, on a more general plane, I see the value of Sakharov's ideas in a different way. Any field theory has two aspects: an active one (the effect of the field on physical processes, in particular, on the particles moving through it), and a passive one (generation of the field by external sources). In the general theory of relativity (GTR), the physical content of the active aspect was disclosed in the most profound way by Einstein: based on the principle of equivalence, he correlated the effect of the gravitational field on physical processes with the change in metric (curvature) of spacetime. At the same time, the passive aspect of GTR is treated much more formally: the equation that describes the variation of the metric under the influence of matter is obtained by generalizing the Poisson equation for the Newtonian potential, using conditions of general covariance, the absence of higher derivatives, etc. The arguments presented above apply to the conclusion based on the expression for the gravitational field.

The thrust of Sakharov's approach consists, in my opinion, of expanding the physics of the passive aspect of GTR by correlating the "metric elasticity of the vacuum" (in other words, the energetics of the metric field) with the quantum fluctuations of matter in curved spacetime. This is exactly the action that determines how the metric changes under the influence of matter. In fact, Sakharov correlated the passive effect of GTR with the active effect: In order to determine the metric elasticity, it is sufficient to describe the effect of the gravitational field (the curved metric) on the quantum fluctuations of matter.

Gravitational forces, considered from the point of view of induced gravitation, have a direct analog known as "Casimir forces" in condensed-matter physics. Let us imagine two metallic bodies separated by a narrow empty gap. The less the distance between them, the more such bodies will attract each other. The Casimir force can be described as follows: In the absence of the bodies, the vacuum contains electromagnetic waves (called zero-point oscillations) which, however, are not observable. The metallic bodies distort these oscillations since the electric field must vanish near the bodies. This deformation depends on the width of the gap and alters the energy in the zero-point oscillations. Because the energy depends on the gap, the deformation manifests itself as the Casimir attraction between the two bodies. All these arguments also apply to induced gravitation: The heavy bodies deform the quantum fluctuations of matter, which manifests itself in the appearance of gravity. It can be said (with all due reservations) that the gravitational attraction between the Earth and the Moon is not so different in nature from the force that attracts highly polished steel plates — the Johanson plates.

Regardless of whether the hopes mentioned above will be realized, Sakharov's idea about induced gravity (possibly his most profound idea) should be considered as the next step, beyond GTR, toward understanding the nature of gravitation.

Notes and References

1. A. D. Sakharov, *Soviet Physics Doklady (Doklady Akademii Nauk SSR)* 177 (1967): pp. 70–71.

2. This is described in careful, pedagogical detail in: C. W. Misner, K. S. Thorne, and J. A. Wheeler, *Gravitation*, New York: W. H. Freeman, 1970, pp. 426–428.

3. S. L. Adler, *Reviews of Modern Physics* 54:3 (1982): pp. 729–766.

Inappropriate Questions: Courage or Insanity?

A. D. Linde

Lebedev Physical Institute, Moscow

IN EVERY CULTURE, country, or science there are some questions which should not be discussed during certain times: the existence of God, the truthfulness of a political party, the four-dimensionality of space and time, etc. One of Sakharov's principal characteristics, which manifested itself with equal clarity in his political activity and his scientific work, was the absence of fear in asking questions that were "inappropriate."

At the end of 1960, the main structure of cosmology seemed to be nearly complete. The theory of the hot universe reigned supreme. All believed that the universe, like a fiery globe, formed from a singularity about 10–15 billion years ago and then began to expand, gradually cooling. Only a few questions slightly disturbed the tranquility of cosmologists: What preceded the birth of the universe? Why does it not contain antimatter? Why is it so uniform on large scales? How did its various parts begin to expand simultaneously, since there was no physical mechanism to synchronize this process? However, all these questions appeared to be metaphysical in nature, with patent answers which, like an analgesic, reduced the pain but did not treat the disease. It was said that Einstein's equation cannot be extended beyond the singularity, and therefore, any attempt to understand what happened before the creation of the universe is meaningless. The discussion of other questions was considered equally inappropriate, since they were related to the initial conditions of the universe. For example, in order to explain the existing excess of matter over antimatter (baryons over antibaryons), it would be sufficient that the relative excess amount to only 10^{-9} at temperatures higher than the mass of a proton (~ 1 GeV), i.e., at the earliest stages of evolution of the universe. As the universe cooled, the baryons annihilated with the antibaryons, and the initial slight asymmetry between them supplied all the matter remaining in the universe today.

What could be wrong with such an idea? Of course, it seemed slightly strange that the original asymmetry was not equal to 0.5 or, say, 0.1, but 10^{-9}. But that is how it was at the very beginning, the cosmologists calmed themselves. There is only one universe, and it would be pointless to discuss why this excess was so small. That's how the universe is. It is also pointless to determine why it is uniform and isotropic, why parallel lines never intersect each other, why the total entropy of the universe exceeds 10^{87}.

The first sign of interest of physicists in such "metaphysical" problems is traceable to Sakharov's paper of 1967.[1] In that paper he showed that the asymmetry of matter and antimatter could be explained by assuming that some nonequilibrium processes took place in the early stages of evolution of the universe, with violation of CP invariance, (and C invariance) and also the law of baryon number conservation.

In 1967, the idea that baryon number is not conserved seemed unlikely, and to promote such an idea to get rid of a "small imperfection" in the world was pointless. For many years, the only sequel to Sakharov's paper was the interesting paper by B. A. Kuzmin, which was written three years later.[2] Only in 1976, when unified theories of the weak, strong, and electromagnetic interactions were proposed,[3] did it become clear that baryon number may indeed not be conserved, and that our previous conviction about the stability of the proton did not have a sufficiently strong foundation.

That year, Andrei Dmitrievich presented a paper at a seminar of the theoretical physics department of FIAN (the Lebedev Physical Institute) on the work of J. C. Pati and A. Salam, which formulated the first version of the unified theory of the weak, strong, and electromagnetic interactions. During the presentation, he pointed out that such theories made it possible to generate baryons in the manner proposed in his 1967 paper. This remark seemed interesting, but nobody dropped his work to pursue this direction.

A sudden change in physicists' attitudes occurred in 1978–79, when scores of papers on this topic were published. Most of the authors didn't know about Sakharov's paper and it was later shown that many of these papers were erroneous: their authors didn't know that in the processes with nonconservation of baryon number, CP invariance is also not conserved, as well as that these must be nonequilibrium processes.

At the end of 1979, after the publication of a landmark paper by
S. Weinberg,[4] the main features of the mechanism for the baryon asymmetry of the universe were clarified, and many physicists understood that the
discovery of this mechanism was the most important achievement of the
theory of evolution of the universe in the last fifteen years.

Specific models for the baryon asymmetry generation were rather complex, and the initial enthusiasm began to wane under the burden of doubts.
The true value of the discovery of the mechanism for baryon production
was recognized only a few years later, when it was shown that without it, it
would be impossible to construct the self-consistent theory of the evolution
of the universe.

In 1978–79, it was found that the standard theory of the hot universe ran
into difficulties when attempts were made to reconcile it with the present-
day theory of elementary particles (problems involving monopoles,
domain walls, gravitinos, etc.). In the beginning of the 1980s, the so-
called inflationary universe theory was proposed. This theory not only
eliminated these difficulties, but also solved several other problems. It
explained why the universe is homogeneous and isotropic on a grand scale,
why its various parts began to expand almost at the same time, why its
three-dimensional geometry is close to being Euclidian, and why the total
entropy is so large. The main feature of the inflationary theory is the
extremely rapid (exponential in many models) expansion of the universe
during the earliest stages of its evolution. During the inflationary stage,
however, the baryon density decreases to a negligible value—many orders
of magnitude below its present value. The only way to obtain a sufficient
number of baryons in the inflationary cosmology was to use the mechanism
for baryon generation after the inflationary stage.

Today, it appears to be very difficult, if not impossible, to construct a
systematic cosmological theory without including some form of inflation.
If this is so, then the mechanism for generating the baryon asymmetry of
the universe is no longer just an interesting theoretical possibility but is a
key part of modern cosmology.

It thus took eleven years (from 1967 to 1978) to see the importance of
Sakharov's ideas concerning the baryon asymmetry of the universe and the
possible nonconservation of baryon number. Almost an equal amount of
time was required to fully understand its value in the development of cosmology. Many other ideas of Sakharov had a similar fate.

A large part of his subsequent work on cosmology involved study of the
singularity and time. We now know that time "runs" only forward, that
entropy increases, and that the universe is expanding. Might these facts be
related to each other? Isn't it possible for time to reverse itself at the point

of maximum expansion of the universe or (which is more probable) at the singularity, where spacetime vanishes and the basic laws of physics no longer work? Why do we think that our spacetime has three spatial dimensions (or even more, if some of them are "hidden" by compactification, as multidimensional theories predict) and only one time dimension? And what would happen to a universe without time directions or one with two or three time directions? It is possible that we live in such a universe, but are not aware of it because some of the time directions are "hidden" and we cannot move along them? And what if our universe consists of many regions that differ from each other by the direction of time, by the compactification of spacetime, and by the number of time coordinates?

Is it courage or insanity to raise such questions and hope to be able to answer them? For Andrei Dmitrievich Sakharov, it was neither one nor the other. He simply understood that such problems exist, and he could not disregard them or avoid searching for an answer. This is how he was in science and in all aspects of life.

Notes and References

1. A. D. Sakharov, *Pis'ma v Zhurnal Eksperimental'noi i Teoreticheskoi Fiziki (JETP Letters)* 5 (1967): p. 32.

2. B. A. Kuzmin, *Pis'ma v Zhurnal Eksperimental'noi i Teoreticheskoi Fiziki (JETP Letters)* 12 (1970): p. 335.

3. For details, see e.g., A. A. Anselm, "In the Search for a Unified Theory of Fundamental Interactions," *Priroda* 6 (1980): p. 9; 7 (1980): p. 63. V. S. Berezinski, "The Unified Gauge Theories and the Unstable Proton," *Priroda* 11 (1984): p. 24.

4. S. Weinberg, *Physical Review Letters* 42 (1979): p. 850.

The Symmetry of the Universe

Andrei D. Sakharov

Introduction by I. G. Virko

Publishing House Znanie, Moscow

It all began in 1966, with the publication in *Uspekhi Fizicheskikh Nauk* of a short article[1] by A. D. Sakharov, entitled "Magnetoimplosive Generators" (the generation of superstrong magnetic fields by explosions). With the permission of my supervisor E. B. Ettinhoff (the executive editor of the annual *Future of Science*, where I was working) I obtained (through some physicists whom I knew) Sakharov's telephone number and called him, asking him to write an article elaborating on this topic. He said that he had studied this topic exhaustively, and no longer had interest in it, but that he was ready to write an article on cosmology.

Some time later he wrote the article that is reprinted below.[2] I should say at the outset that this article was very difficult to read. A few times I went to his home (the old apartment, next to the Kurchatov Institute), where we tried to make the article understandable to the average reader. My attempt was not very successful: I could not grasp more than half of what he tried to explain to me, although I humbly shook my head, as if to say that now everything was clear to me.

One day, when I arrived at the editorial office later than usual, I was told that Sakharov's driver had brought the final draft of the article. From the description of the "driver" I knew that it was Sakharov himself—my colleagues imagined the father of the Soviet hydrogen bomb differently.

Those who saved that issue of the *Future of Science*, which today is a collector's item, probably noticed that of the twenty-four articles included in it, twenty-two were prefaced by a picture and a brief biography of their authors. Sakharov and I. V. Bestuzhev-Lada, the now famous futurist, had no such luck. When I asked Sakharov for a picture, he replied that this request probably needed higher approval from the personnel office called the "Second Division" and that he had no pictures of himself, except possibly a photograph taken at the Plenary meeting of the Soviet Academy of Sciences.

But how can one find the telephone number of the second division of the USSR Ministry of Medium Machine Building, whose address and telephone number are not listed in any directory? With the supervisor's participation in the search, the telephone number was quickly found. The reply he received, however, was short: not recommended. Ettinhoff's recollection of this conversation is as follows: "But you have given the green light for the article! We have twenty-three photographs but not the twenty-fourth!" "That is your problem," was the answer, "but we do not recommend it." To get out of this situation, it was decided to "depersonalize" another author, too. This author turned out to be I. V. Bestuzhev-Lada.

I. G. Virko

THE SYMMETRY OF THE UNIVERSE

MODERN PHYSICS HAS LAID DOWN a series of "conservation laws" for baryons (a collective name for protons, neutrons, and their "excited states"), leptons (electrons, positrons, and neutrinos from the beta decay), and the μ-leptons (μ-mesons and μ-neutrinos). In all the transformations of elementary particles, the number of baryons minus the number of antibaryons (the so called baryon charge n_b) is conserved. The lepton charge, n_l, and the muon charge, n_μ are determined in a similar way. In their "additive" nature, all these "charges" are similar to the electric charge n_e (the number of positively charged particles minus the number of negatively charged particles).

The universe as a whole is undoubtedly neutral with respect to the electric charge. But what about the baryon and lepton charges? If the baryon charge of the universe is zero, this means that half of the galaxies consist of antimatter—antiprotons, antineutrons, and positrons. At present, there are no observational data either to confirm or refute this hypothesis. Antimatter is identical to matter in its gravitational properties (its energy is positive!) and in the nature of its emissions of electromagnetic radiation. The solution lies either with the neutrinos that are emitted by thermonuclear reactions occurring in stars, or with a direct contact between matter and antimatter (the annihilation of 0.3 g of matter and 0.3 g of antimatter has the effect of an atomic-bomb blast).[3]

In the Big Bang model, the total number of "heavy" particles, the baryons, is 10^8 times smaller than the number of photons. At the superhigh temperatures of the initial moment (zero time), all types of particles were represented in equal amounts. There may have been some processes that led to the spatial separation of matter and antimatter, so that a one-hundred-millionth part of all heavy particles avoided annihilation as the temperature decreased. The Swedish scientists Alfvèn and Klein assumed that such separation processes are possible in the presence of very high gravitational and magnetic fields in the initial stage of development of the universe. In their opinion, particles and antiparticles are separated, and move without collisions in nonuniform magnetic and gravitational fields. This hypothesis cannot be reconciled with the gigantic densities of matter occurring in the past in the expanding universe model. Motion without collisions is possible only when matter is sufficiently rarefied.

In our view there is no evidence to suggest the existence of antigalaxies or other macroscopic masses consisting of antimatter. In other words, we assume that n_b is not equal to zero. The explanation of this baryon asymmetry should be sought in a deeper analysis of the internal symmetry properties of elementary particles and their conservation laws.

The starting point of the author's arguments is the quark hypothesis and the violation of some symmetry properties in elementary particle reactions.

According to Gell-Mann and Zweig, baryons consist of three quarks, and antibaryons consist of three antiquarks. The author of this paper assigns the composite baryon-meson charge $n_c = +1$ (introduced by him) to the quarks, the μ^+-meson and the μ-antineutrino $(\bar{\nu}_\mu)$, and he assigns the charge $n_c = -1$ to the antiquarks, the μ^--meson and the μ-neutrino (ν_μ). It is assumed that only n_c is strongly conserved, but not n_b and n_μ separately. That is, the quarks could be transformed into antimuons (μ^+ and $\bar{\nu}_\mu$) or, equivalently, one baryon into three antimuons. Let us assume, for example, that a quark q transforms into a μ-antineutrino, $q \rightarrow \bar{\nu}_\mu$. The composite charge in this reaction is conserved—it is unity on each side of the reaction. The baryon number, however, is one-third for the quark (left side) and zero for the μ-antineutrino (right side). It is easy to verify that the muon number is also not conserved.

According to the hypothesis relating conservation laws and force fields, the universe should be neutral with respect to the strongly conserved charge n_c, and the existence of a slightly larger amount of matter over anti-matter is simply the result of the asymmetric distribution of this charge between baryons (quarks) and μ-leptons. In the initial hot "soup," par-ticles and antiparticles were generated from the neutral matter M (photons, neutral pairs, etc.) in reversible reactions:

$$3\bar{q} + \mu^+ + 2\bar{\nu}_\mu \rightleftarrows M \rightleftarrows 3q + \mu^- + 2\nu_\mu.$$

Here 3q are three quarks that form a proton, and $3\bar{q}$ are three antiquarks that form an antiproton. We assume that the equilibrium of these reactions is displaced to the right, in favor of matter. When the universe expands, pairs of baryons–antibaryons annihilate each other, yielding as a result a small excess of baryons. The asymmetry in baryons leads to a similar asymmetry in leptons, with the conservation of the total lepton charge.

Accordingly, the total average composite charge n_c, the lepton charge n_l, and the electrical charge n_e are each equal to zero, but the distribution of these charges is different for particles and antiparticles. A cubic centimeter of the universe might have on the average (the figures are arbitrary): 10^{-5} baryons (of which 80-percent are protons), no antibaryons, $125+3\times10^{-5}$ μ-neutrinos, 125 μ-antineutrinos, 0.8×10^{-5} electrons, no positrons, 75 neutrinos, $75 + 0.8 \times 10^{-5}$ antineutrinos, 500 photons, and no μ^+ or μ^- mesons. The positive electric charge is thus concentrated in the protons, and is equal in absolute value to the negative charge, which is concentrated in the electrons ($n_e = 0$, as it should be). The positive com-posite charge is concentrated in the baryons, and the negative composite charge, which is equal to the positive charge, is concentrated in the excess number of μ neutrinos ($n_c = 0$). The positive lepton charge is concentrated in the electrons, and the negative charge is concentrated in the excess num-ber of antineutrinos ($n_l = 0$).[4]

According to our hypothesis, the violation of the charge distribution symmetry between particles and antiparticles is a gigantic manifestation of the symmetry violations discovered between 1956 and 1964, in the trans-formations of elementary particles. Before 1956, three types of symmetry were identified in the elementary particle theory: (1) P symmetry, which expresses the equivalence of processes observed in nature and in a mirror; (2) C symmetry, which expresses the equivalence of processes involving particles and antiparticles; and (3) the T symmetry, which expresses the time-reversal symmetry of mechanical processes. (That is, if the process $\overrightarrow{A} \rightarrow \overrightarrow{B}$ is possible, then the process $\overleftarrow{B} \rightarrow \overleftarrow{A}$ can also occur with the same probability. In the reversed process the velocity and momentum of each particle is reversed). The theoretical discoveries of Lee, Yang, Landau, and other theorists in 1956, showed that in some processes (for example, in β decay), the P and C symmetries are not observed separately. What is observed is instead the CP symmetry; i.e., the process observed in the mirror can occur only with antiparticles (but not with particles). These theories were confirmed by a series of brilliant experiments.

In the experiment of Garwin, Lederman, and Weinrich, for example, a stopped μ^+ meson decays into a positron and emits it primarily in the direction corresponding to its spin. But in the mirror-reflected experiment (physicists usually have in mind reflection with respect to three mirrors perpendicular to each other), the spin direction remains the same, but the direction of positron emission reverses. However, this latter direction remains the same as the direction of electron emission in the decay of a μ^- meson with the same spin. A similar situation was also observed in the experiment of the American scientist Wu, on the decay of cobalt nuclei polarized in a magnetic field.

This discovery did not break the T symmetry. A blow to this symmetry came as a result of the astonishing discovery of the American scientists Christenson, Cronin, Fitch and Turley, who in 1964 observed the decay of a long-lived, neutral K_2 meson into two π mesons. The probability of this decay is very small, 250 thousand times smaller than the probability of a similar decay of a short-lived K_1 meson, and it took some time to detect it. Why is it that such important implications follow from such a barely noticeable effect?

In optics, the intensity of light is determined by the square of the amplitude of the light wave. When light waves interfere, the amplitudes are added, not their squares. Quantum mechanics extended this superposition principle to mechanical phenomena. A brilliant example of this is the theory of neutral K mesons constructed by Gell-Mann and Pais. The observed states of K mesons are superpositions of a K^0 meson and its antiparticle. If the T symmetry holds, then the phase of this superposition can either be the same or opposite and does not alter over time. A concrete analogy to this is two bicyclists on a circular path riding with the same speed; neither one passes the other. The T symmetry is valid if they remain side by side or at opposite sides of the circle.

According to Gell-Mann and Pais the superposition applies to all types of decay. If in one type of K meson (the K_2 meson) the phases coincide exactly, and in the other type (the K_1 meson) they are exactly opposite, then in the first case the decay into two π mesons is completely forbidden, and in the second case it is completely allowed, due to the subtraction and addition of amplitudes in each case.

The experimentally observed decay of the K_2 meson into two π mesons demonstrated that the amplitudes are not subtracted exactly; i.e., the phases do not coincide exactly. This means that the states of the particle and the antiparticle shift relative to each other as time passes. In other words, the T and C symmetries are violated, and only the composite TC symmetry is valid. (One of the bicyclists overtakes the other. If we change the direction of motion, then the relative configuration of the bicyclists is conserved only if they simultaneously exchange places—the TC symmetry). Linking this fact with the violation of the C and P symmetries, physicists assumed that the universal symmetry, which applies to all processes, is CPT symmetry.

The theory of the expanding universe gives a natural explanation of CPT symmetry. We could assume that the state of the universe up to the moment

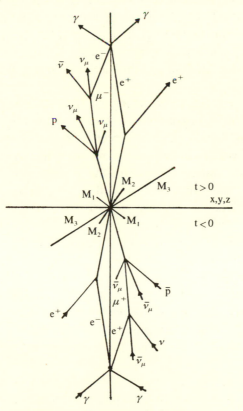

Schematic diagram of elementary-particle transformations.

of infinite density exactly copies the state that exists after this moment, with exchange of particles for antiparticles and all the spatial configurations of particles for their mirror image. Such a model gives a consistent answer to the first question posed in this paper—the state of the universe at the moment of maximum density. The state at $t = 0$ should be assumed neutral. This is the basic hypothesis about the cosmic CPT symmetry of the universe.

The transformations of elementary particles is shown schematically in the figure. The letter M represents hypothetical neutral particles (introduced by the Russian physicist Markov), with a mass of the order of the Planck mass, $m_0 = 2 \times 10^{-5}$ g. Markov called these particles "maximons." The figure shows how the antiparticles which exist up to the moment of infinite density, upon contraction of the universe, fuse into neutral maximons (for example, the antiproton fuses with three antimuons: $\bar{p} + \mu^+ + \bar{\nu}_\mu + \bar{\nu}_\mu \rightarrow M$), and after the moment of maximum density, the maximons decay into protons and muons: $M \rightarrow p + \mu^- + \nu_\mu + \nu_\mu$. What happens at the moment of maximum density is shown in the figure only conditionally. Strictly speaking, we do not understand much about these processes. According to the English scientist Milne, we can assume that at this moment the maximons somehow pass through each other without interaction (like the Martian and the Earthling in Ray Bradbury's science fiction story).

The reflection considered by Milne did not exchange particles for antiparticles, but after the experiments showing symmetry violation due to simple reflection, it was evident that such an exchange (the C reflection) is necessary. The spatial arrangement of the particles, as can be seen in the figure, undergoes mirror reflection—the P reflection. In the reflected world, at $t < 0$, all processes proceed in reverse in comparison with $t > 0$—the T reflection. CPT symmetry is conserved. It is assumed here that this reversal of physical processes is exact and absolute, that it extends to all processes: the decay of particles corresponds to the reverse process of fusion, the heat flows from the colder body to the warmer one, the elderly become younger, etc. However, the inhabitants of the reflected world (who consist of antimatter, and have a heart on the right side), do not notice this difference. In fact, *they* are *we* (or *we* are *they*), since up to the arbitrary definition of time, the arbitrary definition of right and left, and the arbitrary definition of matter and antimatter, the reflected world is the same as our world.

This doubling of physical reality should frighten us no more than the doubling of people in a room when a mirror is brought into it.

How does the observed distribution of particles and antiparticles occur during the expansion of the universe? I cannot give a precise, concrete answer to this question, but I believe that it involves the violation of the T symmetry and the CP symmetry in the transformation of particles with a large mass. According to the current theory, violation of the T and CP symmetries in the decay and interaction of elementary particles results in different probabilities for the production of particles and antiparticles from initially neutral material. But this fact alone would not account for the asymmetry of the baryon and antibaryon number if another repository of baryon number (in our terminology, the composite charge) is not introduced in the form of muons, thus allowing the baryon number conservation law to be violated.

Our hypothesis can thus be stated as follows: It is assumed that until the moment of maximum density, all phenomena and objects are exact mirror images of the phenomena and objects after this moment, with the exchange of the particles for antiparticles and the reversal of the direction of the processes ("the CPT symmetry of the universe"). At the maximum density all the particles are thus exactly neutral, and the baryon asymmetry of the universe is attributed to the fact that the decay of particles is slightly different from that of antiparticles (violation of the CP invariance). In addition, baryon number is, according to the author's hypothesis, not an exactly conserved quantity (one baryon can decay into three muons).

The title of this article, "The Symmetry of the Universe," reveals the natural partiality of this author to this hypothesis. But even if this hypothesis is not correct, this title will call the reader's attention to the importance of determining the explicit and the secret symmetry laws of the world around us.

Notes and References

1. A. D. Sakharov, *Soviet Physics Uspekhi: (Uspekhi Fizicheskikh Nauk)* 88 (1966): p. 725.

2. *The Future of Science,* Moscow, Znanie, 1968, p. 74. We call the attention of the reader to the section of this article titled "Symmetry and the Conservation Laws" [editor's note].

3. By receiving signals from the inhabitants of another galaxy, we could determine the sign of its baryon charge if they gave us the decay reactions which are different for particles and antiparticles (for example, the decay of the K meson differs from the decay of the antiparticle K. This difference is a manifestation of CP violation).

4. It is ironic that because of the recently discovered background thermal radiation we now know more about the number of neutrinos and μ-neutrinos than we do about the number of "ordinary" protons and neutrons. If the basic mass of the universe consists of μ-neutrinos, then the total number of baryons would be ten times smaller.

A Scientific Report by Sakharov

G. I. Barenblatt

Shirshov Institute of Oceanography, Moscow

A Soviet-American seminar titled "Nonlinear Systems in Earthquake Prediction" was held October 10–14, 1988, in the historic building of the Soviet Academy of Sciences in Leningrad. The seminar was arranged by the U. S. National Academy of Sciences and the Soviet Academy. The idea of the seminar as envisaged by its primary organizers — V. I. Keilis-Borok (USSR) and L. Knopov (U.S.) — was to assemble leading figures in a field known now as "nonlinear science" to brainstorm on the problem. The organizers expected that this brainstorming might suggest some fundamentally new ideas and important progress in the difficult and important field of earthquake prediction.

It seems that the primary difficulty in the prediction of earthquakes stems from the circumstance that the occurrence of earthquakes depends on a very large number of diverse factors. Many years earlier, I. M. Gel'fand (who also participated in the seminar) had expressed the opinion that no mathematics adequate for dealing with biological problems existed. The difficulty lay in the multifactorial nature of these problems. It may be that in this regard the earthquake problem has something in common with biological problems.

On Friday, October 14, the last working day of the seminar, participants who had ridden over to the Academy building from the hotel saw A. D. Sakharov in the corridor in front of the session room. The schedule of reports was changed: Sakharov had expressed the desire to present a report but said he was very pressed for time by other matters.

Sakharov expressed the opinion that earthquakes could be triggered artificially, through the use of nuclear explosions deep underground. He pointed out that the earthquake prediction problem remains unresolved, and the purpose of an explosion would be to release the energy which was building up in rocks before it reached a critical level. Major losses could thus be avoided. Sakharov stressed that he did not consider himself an expert on seismology—simply an outsider—but that he did know the problem of large explosions, and he wished to discuss this proposal at the seminar.

In Sakharov's words, nuclear explosions could be used in specific because equivalent explosions from conventional TNT would be far more costly, and the technical difficulties in achieving them would be substantially more serious. A hundred-megaton device had been tested back in 1961, and arranging larger explosions would be a relatively simple matter. The explosions should be carried out deep underground, for safety and also because of considerations concerning the explosion's effectiveness as a trigger of the earthquake mechanism. Depths of many kilometers are realistic, but 5 km seemed sufficient. One should drill a mine shaft on the order of a meter in diameter (to do so is technically feasible and relatively inexpensive) and stack the charges on top of each other. The shaft should then be sealed off reliably. The flow of liquids in porous strata is a rather slow process, so the radioactivity of the products of the thermonuclear explosion would have decayed over the time scale of these processes. Another advantage here is that the cavity arising in the course of the explosion would be covered with a glassy crust. A serious problem (Sakharov made a point of stressing the seriousness of this problem, in answering a question from W. Newman of the U.S.) would be presented by the cracks which could be expected to form as a result of an underground explosion. The transport of radioactive products along these cracks would be far more rapid, but the difficulty seemed to be surmountable.

To determine the safe explosion energy E (in megatons) at a depth h (in kilometers), Sakharov proposed the formula

$$E = Ah^4 + Bh^3,$$

where he estimated the coefficient A to be 0.1–0.01. Sakharov estimated the cost of the project to be 10^7–10^8 rubles, under the assumption that an equal distribution of this sum between the cost of the explosion and the cost of the mine shaft was the optimum. Sakharov estimated the total energy of the explosion to be 10^{23}–10^{24} erg (10–100 megatons) At the end of his report, he sketched a rough plot of the ratio of the energy which would be released in the course of the earthquake, E_1, to the energy of the original explosion, E_0, versus the time, putting the origin of the time scale at the time of a spontaneous earthquake, t_0. The time interval of greatest interest, in Sakharov's opinion, would be from a year to a month before a spontaneous earthquake.

After the report there was an interesting discussion. Some of the Americans grumbled: Who was going to let him and his bomb into California, to go to the San Andreas fault, the location of major earthquake foci? I collected the transparencies Sakharov used for illustration, and with the complete approval of the other participants I asked him to autograph one of them (see figures).

I knew Sakharov for many years and grew to understand that any of his thoughts, no matter how paradoxical and unrealistic they might seem at first, warranted careful study and preservation. The present paper is intended to serve that purpose.

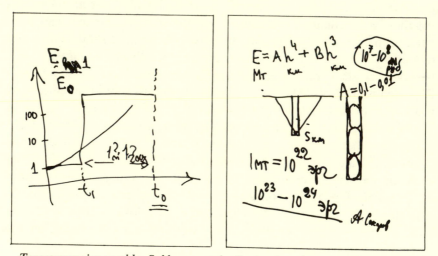

Transparencies used by Sakharov at the Soviet-American seminar on Non-linear Systems in Earthquake Prediction in October 1988. Sakharov's signature is at the lower right.

"They Expect a Good Program From Us"

M. Yu. Khlopov

Keldysh Institute of Applied Mathematics, Moscow

I WOULD LIKE to relate an undertaking in which Andrei Dmitrievich Sakharov was forced into playing the role of scientific organizer that he found so repugnant.

Recognizing that as circumstances would have it he was the only person capable of doing so, he took over the Scientific Council on the Complex Problem of Cosmoparticle Physics under the presidium of the Soviet Academy of Sciences in the last two years of his life.[1] My close contacts with Sakharov in this matter make is possible to add a few brush strokes to his portrait.

In the second half of the 1980s it became progressively more obvious that the interpenetration of cosmology and particle physics should lead to the establishment of a unified science combining physicists and astronomers. Accordingly, Sakharov, who was one of the pioneers in this scientific field from the outset, was the only figure capable of doing the organizing and fostering the development required here. When the question of the creation of this council arose, in the spring of 1987, however, Sakharov had just returned from his exile. He declined the suggestion that he head the council, citing the fact (among others) that Ya. B. Zel'dovich was considerably more active than he in this field. In addition, Sakharov asserted that he was more inclined to be simply an "individual theoretician" studying questions at the border between cosmology and elementary particle theory than to be an organizer of scientific research in this direction. When Zel'dovich died in December 1987, however, before the council had been formed, it became clear that only Sakharov's authority would make it possible to overcome the interdisciplinary barriers and to combine the efforts of scientists in very different directions. This became progressively more obvious to Sakharov also, who painfully reached the conclusion that "this particular thicket was not going to let him through."

In a sense, Zel'dovich compared our scientists with a runner who had been tied hand and foot and then ordered to set an olympic record in the hurdles. The ossification which had occurred in science placed barriers in the path of any reasonable project.

To many people, Sakharov's consent to continue what had been begun by Zel'dovich appeared at first to be nothing more than a symbolic gesture of good will. "To develop a program which combines laboratory, cosmic, and astronomical studies is a very difficult task, requiring time and effort," he was warned. "However, this has to be done," he answered. Although he was very busy, he tried to reach an understanding of both the essence of the individual projects and the specifics of the problems involved in implementing them. Quite quickly, it became clear that his role in the development of the council could not be simply a nominal one. Making one's way through the debris of official corridors required special knowledge and skills (when this debris was penetrable at all!). However, the history of the development of the cosmoparticle council is a small piece of mirror reflecting the course of the process of which Sakharov was the living embodiment. In late 1988, a general meeting of the Soviet Academy of Sciences chose him a member of the presidium—and suddenly all the obstacles disintegrated.

As Sakharov related to me, the first words to him as a member of the presidium from the president of the Academy were as follows: "Andrei Dmitrievich, you are heading our most important scientific council. We expect of you a large and good program." Sakharov thought it was not a good time to bring up the organizational difficulties: They expect a good program from us. We must prepare it. And work began.

Sakharov immediately sent to the journal *Vestnik Akademii Nauk SSSR* an analysis, prepared by a group of strong supporters, of the reasons for the appearance of this new science of cosmoparticle physics and of the circumstances under which it was developing. The goals of this science and the prospects for its development in the USSR were discussed.[2] This paper was preceded by an introduction written by Sakharov himself, which reflected his attitude toward the problem. I should point out that Sakharov was very cautious about the authorship of various ideas and projects, and he did not feel that he could put himself even slightly above the immediate authors or the people actually carrying out these projects. He was equally as attentive to Zel'dovich's legacy in shaping the scientific council. He made organizational changes in the structure and composition of the council only where clearly necessary.

On September 12, 1988, after Sakharov's report, the presidium of the Soviet Academy of Sciences ratified the structure and composition of the Scientific Council on the Complex Problem of Cosmoparticle Physics. A goal was also formulated for the council: to develop a nationwide program of research at the border between elementary particle theory and cosmology.

In preparing for the first session of the council, Sakharov thought it necessary to distinguish between large, expensive projects and small ones which could be carried out soon. "We must begin with small projects: those which will involve a minimum in cost and which will yield a maximum in terms of results. Things can proceed from there," he said, determining the agenda for the session and examining in an extremely meticulous way the basic ideas of each report listed.

On November 29, 1989, the council met for its first session. For the most part, the astronomers, physicists, engineers, and mathematicians who filled the conference room of the P. K. Shternberg State Astronomical Institute were only slightly acquainted with each other. You could count on your fingers the people who personally knew all the other scientists on the council. This situation was one of the complications in its future work. The chair of the council not only had to know each person but also had to be able to grasp the specifics of their work. Understanding this point, Sakharov actively filled the void in both senses, literally in front of everyone's eyes. Declining on principle the raised position reserved for the chair, he took a seat in the first row and listened tirelessly to the alternating physics and astronomy papers. Most of the project proposals concerned fields which did not fall within the sphere of Sakharov's direct scientific interests, but it was necessary to deal with them. He asked questions, catching the general idea in mid-flight and discussing the details of the proposed realizations.

After standing up to the long session (which lasted more than four hours), Sakharov was still not completely satisfied with it. Much of the material seemed to him to be still undeveloped and raw.

He had little more than two and a half weeks to live and, in the context of everything that he left unfinished, his work on the cosmoparticle council might look like a digression from what was most important. However, his sense of responsibility and his simple ethical norms—those norms which do not come easily at all to us—were reflected in this undertaking, which was far from being the most important one for him.

Notes and References

1. In Russian, the council's name refers to "Cosmology and Microphysics," since there is no short term for "particles" in Russian. In English, the term "cosmoparticle physics" is appropriate. Andrei Sakharov admired this term greatly and confirmed the English name for the council "on Cosmoparticle Physics." The Presidium of the Soviet Academy of Sciences has since established Keldysh Institute of Applied Mathematics as one of the basic institutions of the Council.

2. A. D. Sakharov, "Cosmomicrophysics: An Interdisciplinary Problem," *Vestn. Akad. Nauk SSSR* 4 (1989): p. 39.

Misunderstanding Sakharov

B. L. ALTSHULER

Lebedev Physical Institute, Moscow

THE REVOLUTIONS in our views of reality are marked by the appearance of geniuses whose ideas change the entire system of generally accepted concepts, although at the beginning these ideas usually are not understood or are even attacked. We have been the contemporaries of a man who achieved such revolutions in knowledge, and who caused a transformation not only of ideas but also of reality itself. This is the "the miracle of Sakharov." This is the way I saw the activity of Andrei Dmitrievich in the last twenty years, and I will try to explain my impressions.

In science, as in social activism, Sakharov's way of thinking was the same, but in science everything occurred "without bloodshed." Starting with a general and rather clear idea, he drew concrete conclusions. And this transition—from the general to the particular, and through details to the solution of the entire problem—only a few understood. Only later did it become clear that this progression followed from the general premise.

THERE IS AN old idea, a cosmological idea, probably Sakharov's favorite: the hypothesis of the CPT symmetry of the universe. It states that under the simultaneous transformation of particles into antiparticles—this transformation is denoted by C, mirror reflection P, and time reversal T—nothing should change. This idea is very general, but it leads to the conclusion that in the history of the universe there was a moment when all charges, in particular the baryon number, were equal to zero. But why, then, do we observe today a world consisting only of matter; i.e., with a gigantic excess of baryons over antibaryons? This cannot be understood if one does not reject the law of conservation of baryon number, which was considered an absolute; i.e., if one does not reject the idea of the absolute stability of the proton. The entire chain of arguments was clear to Sakharov as early as 1967, but this idea received general acceptance only twelve years later.

Curiously, this coincided with his exile to Gorki, and may have saved his life. During the first few weeks following January 22, 1980, the newspapers wrote (among other insults) that Sakharov had degraded himself as a scientist. The thrust of this fierce attack implied that the deportation was only the first step. During those days, the theoreticians at FIAN, the Physical Institute of the Academy of Sciences, attempted to bring to the high administration's attention the wide international recognition of Sakharov's contribution to the solution of the problem of baryon asymmetry of the universe. The same idea was independently included in the open letter to the United Nations by a group of Soviet human rights activists. Who knows what finally helped, but at the beginning of March, after the U.S. Academy of Sciences declared a boycott against the Soviet Academy of Sciences, an order from the top kept Sakharov within FIAN and allowed his collaborators from the theoretical department to visit him in Gorki. The propagandistic slander also became more moderate.

In addition to baryon nonconservation, one further conclusion necessarily follows from the hypothesis of the *CPT* symmetry of the universe: the existence of a point on the time axis when the "arrow of time" reverses. This idea has so far been in the incubation stage. However, for Andrei Dmitrievich, the arguments were sufficiently unambiguous. These arguments basically follow from the idea (which Sakharov persistently supported) that the arrow of time (i.e., the direction of flow of time) is uniquely determined by the increase of entropy, and by nothing else.

During his last years, I had many opportunities to discuss the time-arrow problem with Andrei Dmitrievich, and in all my assaults—"And what about the small, nonstatistical systems in which the concept of entropy does not exist?" "And the retarded potentials in electrodynamics?" And so on—he invariably answered roughly as follows:

> The laws of microphysics are invariant with respect to the reversal of time, and this means that they cannot determine a given direction on the time axis. The second law of thermodynamics is the only law of physics that contains irreversibility (increase of chaos, of entropy) and, therefore, only this law determines the arrow of time. A broken cup cannot be put back together from its fragments; a dead man, alas, does not come back to life only

because these processes have low probability. And if such irreversible processes didn't exist in nature, then the very idea of time flowing in a given direction wouldn't have been born.

All this seems rather simple, but from this simplicity Sakharov formulated far-reaching conclusions. As in the case where the observed baryon asymmetry of the universe could be reconciled with the general hypothesis of the *CPT* symmetry of the universe only by rejecting conservation of baryonic number, so also the agreement of this hypothesis with the observed irreversible flow of time requires the introduction of the moment of reversal of time's arrow. This is exactly the moment of minimum (zero) entropy of the universe, the moment at which the concept of "earlier" does not exist and time flows ahead "in both directions."[1]

IN THIS WAY Sakharov went from the most general ideas to specific, nontrivial conclusions and actions. And in everything he did, the same high professionalism was evident. In science, in his struggle in defense of human rights, or in his activity as a deputy, everywhere Andrei Dmitrievich worked honestly. He needed the problems to be solved, and thoroughly solved. The concept had to work, be it the bomb, a package of propositions on disarmament and human rights, or a series of declarations in the defense of particular individuals.

On December 18, 1989, the day of Sakharov's burial, I got to know Z. Romaszewski, an activist in the Polish opposition, who that year became a senator of the Polish Parliament. He is a physicist, worked in the 1970s at FIAN, and in 1979 visited Sakharov at home, on Chkalov Street, to establish contact between Polish and Soviet human rights activists. He came "from the street" without any recommendation, so that Andrei Dmitrievich did not know what kind of person stood before him. How did Sakharov handle this situation? He gave Romaszewski a one-hour lesson in physics. Romaszewski told me that before that moment he had never met a physicist of Sakharov's caliber. As a result of their conversation, everything became clear; Romaszewski could not be a "provocateur." This was an example of professionalism.

Another proof of professionalism was Andrei Dmitrievich's sense of responsibility. After my speech at the Sakharov lectures at Gorki, in January 1990, Academician A. V. Gaponov-Grekhov told me about another episode from earlier years. During the period of the attempted Kosygin "reform of the economy" in the 1960s, the presidium of the Soviet Academy of Sciences held an informal meeting on these problems. Basically, everybody went there simply to chat, but Sakharov came with a well-prepared, detailed plan of economic changes for the country, based on statistics. His proposal, of course, got nowhere; Sakharov understood well how difficult it is to reach the top, and even more difficult to persuade them to change anything. But he could not act in any other way.

This most difficult task—to reach the top and to succeed—he also approached with professionalism, always seeking a constructive solution. A clear example is his victory in banning nuclear tests in three media. Sakharov's idea to exclude underground explosions from the treaty was presented to Khrushchev at the right time during his visit to the United Nations in 1962. "For Sakharov, it was unbearable to know that an additional number of people, in the thousands or tens of thousands, would become ill with cancer. He was very sensitive," remembers Yu. B. Khariton.[2] But for others this thought was "bearable," and not because they were insensitive people, but because it is the nature of mankind: one's emotional, moral sphere responds basically only to what directly involves oneself. Besides, they were creating a bomb, an affair of enormous importance. And all these unknown victims of the nuclear tests? After all, many more die in car accidents every day. Should we ban automobiles, too? This is a typical example of the disagreement of two "obvious" points of view: one adopted by Sakharov and one by everyone else. Andrei Dmitrievich was unique indeed in his ability to react with acuity to rather abstract concepts, and also in feeling personally responsible for everything that happened.

His activity in the defense of human rights, his obsession in the struggle for each individual person—was this also an excessive sensitivity? And this was all about not thousands of people, but individuals.

In the opinion of many, very many, the distinguished academician did "strange" things: he stood for hours in front of court buildings, traveled throughout the country to attend trials, and went on hunger strikes. Sakharov did all these things and much more with a kind of pedagogical perseverance. But the political "re-education" was difficult.

Like the revolutionary theories of Copernicus or Einstein, which emerged from "simple" initial ideas, so also Sakharov's social activity (or, more correctly, his life) was based on two principles:

1. The absolute moral justification of every action; justification with the most simple, humanitarian point of view, unbiased by any prejudices.

2. The necessity to win, even on a small scale; to reach a positive result by concentrating a maximum of effort on a minimum objective.

In essence, these principles appear to be very simple. Their consequences, however, are nontrivial. Conclusions and especially actions that were absolutely clear and necessary to Sakharov struck others as naive and ridiculous and often irritating.

EVEN DURING the most difficult times, Andrei Dmitrievich continued to work on physics; evidently he could focus on a number of problems at the same time. In 1980 Sakharov published three articles in *JETP*, the Soviet *Journal of Experimental and Theoretical Physics*, entitled "Cosmological Models of the Universe with Reversal of Time's Arrow," "Mass Formula for Mesons and Baryons," and "An Estimate of the Coupling Constant between Quarks and the Gluon Field." In his report of 1981, submitted to the physics department of FIAN from Gorki, he outlined in detail the basic ideas of a new article, later published in *JETP* in 1982, entitled "Multisheet Cosmological Models of the Universe." It deals with models of an oscillating universe, whose cycles Sakharov calls "sheets". The paper ends with the words:

> The work is not yet formulated and not yet fully completed. I intend to complete it in the near future. I also hope that the positive solution regarding the fate of my daughter-in-law will give me the opportunity in the near future to renew my scientific association with my colleagues in the theoretical department of FIAN. Respectfully, A. D. Sakharov.[3]

The report is dated November 16, 1981, immediately before the start of his and Elena Bonner's seventeen-day hunger strike to obtain an exit visa for Liza Alekseyeva, Bonner's son's fiancée. Everything, as usual, was well calculated: the report is written; now I can move to the solution of another problem. The fact that the hunger strike threatened his life, that these days might be his last ones—this was another matter. The positive final result was crucial. "It is important to go in the right direction, and when you fall—this is not important." To understand this thought is to fundamentally understand Andrei Dmitrievich Sakharov.[4]

In May 1982, Sakharov's wife, Elena Georgievna Bonner, brought me a letter from him. That spring my family also encountered a number of unpleasant problems which, in principle, could have occurred much earlier. And Andrei Dmitrievich responded to our plight. Skipping the private part of the letter, I reproduce here the second, scientific part:

> As for science, the present (as, I suppose, always) is an unusually exciting time. "Blissful is one who has visited this world . . ." [a quotation from Tutchev]. The unification of supergravity and GUT, the composite quark,

lepton, and gluon models, sensational discoveries in cosmology . . . As regards the cosmological ideas of the exponential initial phase (with or without Linde's refinements), so far I regard them with guarded caution (perhaps it's old age?). I do not understand how, starting with the giant cosmological constant, one could obtain zero in the present-day vacuum. And most importantly, I do not want to reject the multisheet model. But that's enough, let's wait. The future will show who was right; it will also show us all much more. Fortunately, the future is unpredictable and (because of quantum-mechanical effects) indeterminate.

With best regards, A.S.
May 10, 1982

Let me comment on a few of the concepts in this letter. Supergravity is the generalization of the theory of gravity based on the group of supersymmetry transformations. These transformations mix particles with integer and half-integer spins; i.e., particles that obey the Bose-Einstein and the Fermi-Dirac statistics.[5]

Grand Unification Theory (GUT) is the theory of grand unification of the weak, electromagnetic, and strong interactions, in the framework of which the instability of the proton results in a natural way. This means that Sakharov's hypothesis of 1967, about the decay of baryons, received support.

"The cosmological ideas of the exponential initial phase"—these are the so-called inflationary models about which much has been written in the popular literature. That the present day vacuum energy vanishes (i.e. the cosmological constant is now practically zero), is one of the central unsolved problems of modern theoretical physics.

"Fortunately, the future is unpredictable and (because of quantum-mechanical effects) indeterminate." I think that these words are much more than a statement of the probabilistic nature of the laws of quantum theory. The future, both history as a whole and individual personal lives, is not only unpredictable, but at each instant of time simply does not exist; various scenarios are possible, even those with opposite results. And the result may depend on personal activity (or nonactivity) right now. Sakharov lived with this feeling of responsibility and inability to "let things go."

"The future will show who was right; it will also show us all much more." Of course, one would like to know what Andrei Dmitrievich had in mind. But, in general, he did not like to guess. In 1977, after the arrest of most of the members of the Moscow division of the Helsinki group, I met Sakharov at FIAN and asked him, "What will happen?" To this he answered, "What is important has already happened." Andrei Dmitrievich was a realist, and in his decision making he tried to rely on facts. And that which is about to happen depends on these decisions. And God forbid one should make a mistake. This complex problem of choices is incomprehensible to those who were not confronted with the problems Sakharov was. Decisions had to be made under the most difficult, internally contradictory, circumstances. In order not to be led astray, one had to have an intuition, a few intuitively felt, indisputable, general principles.

THE TRAGEDY OF AN INDIVIDUAL. From a simple, everyday point of view, it triggers compassion and the desire to help much more than knowledge of millions of victims of terror. The entire human-rights movement began as a result of such an aspiration of the soul, and it set for itself helping individuals as the basic practical task. But why does the salvation of one individual have such global political, ideological, and geostrategic consequences? Why has human-rights activity proved to be so effective? Again an admirably simple answer: a system that destroys millions of its citizens, which is based on prohibitions and self-sustaining mechanisms of oppression, is not capable of making concessions. Achieving even the smallest concession is possible only by including the highest political mechanism, maybe even the top man in the government, in the solution of highly personal problems. Under the conditions of our centralized structure, such nonstandard behavior by the highest administration influences in a nearly irrational way the system in general, destroying its firm ideological and organizational structure.

Very recently, an elderly scientist who knew Andrei Dmitrievich well, told me that he didn't understand what the human-rights movement in the USSR (and Sakharov, in particular) had achieved. Look, it saved a few men, but the global problems are still not solved. In expressing this view (which is rather widespread), he showed his total lack of understanding of Sakharov and of his social and especially moral position. The old philosophy "By killing one man, one kills the universe; by saving one man, one saves the universe" simply did not exist for my interlocutor, just as it did not exist for the great majority of people who grew up during the post-revolution years. And how many times did I hear from Andrei Dmitrievich, in a low voice and seemingly without conviction, but at the same time as if putting in a corner-stone: "Perhaps I saved his life after all."?

He also understood the possibility of the reverse situation: the small influencing the big. He worked in this direction during all of the last twenty years. You see, each such nonstandard case is like a "small cloud" that predicts a new reality, similar to the two famous "small clouds" in the clear sky of classical physics—the Michelson experiment and the problem of blackbody radiation—from which the theory of relativity and quantum mechanics emerged. "The existence of Sakharov and Solzhenitsyn is a violation of the law of conservation of energy," said some Moscow physicists in the beginning of the 1970s. Dissident activity was considered as something absolutely impossible, incomprehensible, even meaningless. This attitude remained typical until *perestroika*.

However, for the great majority of people, revolutions in physics remain outside their field of vision. Specialists talk about these revolutions with enthusiasm; at times they manifest themselves as wonderful (or terrible) technical achievements, but without a certain base of special knowledge these grandiose changes cannot be understood. The situation is different for moral and interhuman relationships, in which almost everyone understands what they are all about, and in general assumes that everyone else understands. Even in politics, everybody considers himself a specialist. And in these areas, accessible to everyone, Sakharov and a small group of other human-rights activists continually do something revolutionary, and at the same time absolutely obvious.

Kaysyn Kuliev wrote: "It is easy to love all mankind, but try to love your neighbor." Andrei Dmitrievich recalled that Elena Georgievna quoted these words to him many times. Sakharov wrote much about the influence that Elena Georgievna had on him in this respect. But his motivation was his own from the beginning.

Sakharov's family included several generations of rural priests. His grandfather Ivan Nikolaevich Sakharov (1852–1918), a famous Moscow lawyer, was at the beginning of this century the editor of a collection titled *Against the Death Penalty*. His great-grandfather Nikolai Ivanovich Sakharov (1837–1911) served as archpriest for twenty years in Vyezdnoe (now the Arzamasa district), and then for about ten years in Nizhni-Novgorod. This is how his daughter, Nadezhda Nikolaevna Raikovskaya, the younger sister of Ivan Nikolaevich—she was the fourth child, Sakharov's grandfather was the second, and altogether there were ten children in the family—remembers Nikolai Ivanovich:

> He was, and remained until the end of his days, a very gentle and modest man. In his prayer book, which he always carried in his pocket, there was a note on the first page: "Do not hurt anybody." As I remember, this meant not to bring suffering and pain to anybody. He himself was simple and preferred simplicity. They buried him with a moving ceremony. This simple old man had many spiritual children; a few years before his death, the city clergy chose him as their "father confessor."[6]

I read these lines and recognize Andrei Dmitrievich with his strong immunity against pride, and ideas that are set above the human rights and needs, in fact, above life. He never had any self-pride, not even a glimmer of vanity, knowing the exceptional position he had in this world. But he had a feeling of responsibility and a knowledge of the importance of his words and actions. "It happens that my name does not belong only to me, and I must take this into account," he once said in the mid 1970s, simply acknowledging the objective reality.

ON JULY 2, 1983, on the eve of publication of a letter in *Izvestiya* (written by four academicians in response to Sakharov's letter to Sidney Drell), I received a letter from Sakharov. Here is a part of it:

> Regarding "compactification," this hope has now become foolishly fashionable . . . It occurred to me that the compactification radius seems to approach a constant value, taking into account quantum effects, similar to the radius of the hydrogen atom. How to solve the problem of the Λ-term I certainly do not know (supersymmetry?) . . .

This letter is about the unique geometric models in which spacetime has more than four dimensions. But the extra dimensions are not observed. There is no contradiction with experiment if the space in these additional directions is compactified inside spheres of very small radius. What determines the compactification radius? The theory does not answer this question yet. Andrei Dmitrievich proposed the interesting idea (to the best of my knowledge, not realized by anyone yet) of using the laws of quantum theory in the problem; i.e., to consider everything in terms of quantum cosmology. The letter closed with a remark about his health, and about the endless situation: "And it possibly could have been different." But it all turned out so terribly. Especially after the publication in *Smena* of the chapter from the book by N. N. Yakovlev. And then things got worse and worse . . .

From the moment Sakharov became more involved in social activities, attempts were made to silence him. But why didn't they put him and the entire human-rights group "up against the wall"? This apparently constitutes the "violation of the law of conservation of energy" that the physicists whispered of, not understanding what Sakharov understood: that the government monolith had shown some signs of decay, and that the entire process can also depend on the action of individual people.

ON THE FACE OF A callous power
That moves ahead without a hitch

On a steep road of proud glory
There are some imperceptible cuts.

A. D. Sakharov, Gorki, Shcherbinka[7]

From May 25 to May 27 the most excruciating, degrading and barbarous method was used. I was again pushed down onto the bed without a pillow and my hands and feet were tied. A tight clamp was placed on my nose so that I could breathe only through my mouth . . . They would hold my mouth shut until I swallowed so that I could not spit out the food. When I managed to do so, it only prolonged the agony.[8]

Is this an absurd obsession, or an intelligent struggle with a quite real and not fantastical evil force? In such matters it is not the intellect that makes decisions, but a sixth sense, a higher conscience.

There is also this interpretation: look, he went on hunger strikes, bashed his head against the wall, and then came Gorbachev, *perestroika* started, and everything was solved on its own. The psychological motive of such arguments is fully understood. This is the position of the little man, convinced that nothing depends on him; future historians will explain what initiated all these incredible and redeeming transformations called *perestroika*. I am trying to demonstrate that Sakharov not only anticipated the events but also created the new reality. Certainly, this is why the first reaction to his declarations or activities was often, "Sakharov does not relate to reality." Even sympathizers and free-thinking people frequently thought that it was too early. Such was the view, for example, regarding his proposal to reduce military forces by 50 percent (at the Forum for a Nuclear-Free World in February 1987), his call for the modification of the sixth article of the Constitution (June 1989), his call for a political strike (December 1989), and so on. But Sakharov knew that it was not too early and shattered the prevailing view, forcing the mind to struggle against stereotypes.

Incidentally, he knew how to measure time. I do not remember him ever being in a hurry, or worrying that he would be late. He simply, at the right moment, interrupted the conversation and, excusing himself, started to leave. He knew how to forecast the outcomes of situations, both in everyday life and in more serious matters. He could easily evaluate the whole situation, all the concurrent circumstances and the multiple factors, and this explains his highly efficient activity. This was the case with science, too. He could solve problems in his head very quickly. His colleagues recall that after thinking for a few minutes, he could draw a diagram, which they would study for a few months, or that he could suddenly tell the results of very lengthy calculations.

In April 1984, on the eve of the tragic hunger strike in May, Sakharov sent to *JETP* a fundamental paper titled "Cosmological Transitions with a Change in Metric Signature." It was published in August of the same year, a terrible time when he was still in the hospital. This paper deserves special discussion. Its basic idea was the possible existence of regions in spacetime with additional dimensions (not only spatial, but also temporal). In the 1980s, a few new directions emerged in physics that Sakharov considered truly revolutionary. One example was superstring theory, the unified theory of all interactions, including gravity. This also revived the old idea of Kaluza and Klein that very small additional dimensions might exist. The authors of the many papers on unified geometric models of this type only introduced extra spatial dimensions, leaving time as only one dimension, as we are accustomed to. Sakharov proposed that the additional, compactified dimensions may also be temporal ones. In the following years, models of this type have been considered with increasing frequency, and the number of references citing Sakharov's article has been increasing.

In his article, Sakharov calls the number of time coordinates the "signature," and labels it σ. In the universe observed by us $\sigma = 1$, but he also proposed the existence of purely spatial regions, in which time simply does not exist: $\sigma = 0$; for them, Sakharov introduced special notations:

"We label conventionally the region of spacetime with $\sigma = 1$ by the letter U, from the word *universe*; the purely spatial regions with $\sigma = 0$ are labeled P from the name of the Greek philosopher of antiquity, Parmenides, who thought of a world without motion (As Pushkin wrote: 'There is no motion, said the bearded philosopher.')". Andrei Dmitrievich liked to quote poems.

Quantum transitions are possible between regions with different signatures. These are tunneling transitions that change the number of temporal coordinates, and are not described by the classical equations of the gravitational field. In quantum theory, any dynamic quantity fluctuates. In quantum gravitation, one such quantity is the metric tensor which describes, according to Einstein, both a gravitational field and the geometry of spacetime. If the fluctuations of the metric are small, we have a rather well-defined spacetime, namely, the one in which we live. If, on the other hand, the fluctuations are not small, then changes of both the signature and the topology of the Riemannian manifold (spacetime) are possible. Also possible is the existence of a multitude of other universes, in general, different from our universe. Imagine a room full of soap bubbles ("universes"), some of which are connected by thin connecting tubes, while others have "handles," i.e., tubes which begin and end in the same bubble. This is a two-dimensional analogy to quantum cosmology in four and more dimen-

sions. In quantum gravitation, one should consider all the possible configurations of this type. Andrei Dmitrievich proposed to consider tunneling
transitions with a change in the signature; i.e., with a change in the number
of time coordinates.

One of the basic parameters of the universe is the energy of the vacuum,
or the cosmological constant. In our universe, this constant is very small
(or equal to zero). The theory is not yet capable of explaining why this is
so. There are also other important parameters, whose numerical values
need to be explained. In this matter, Sakharov holds to the anthropic principle; he clearly explains its essence in the introduction to the article:

> In 1950–70, a few authors independently formulated the hypothesis that, in
> addition to the observed universe, there exist an infinite number of "other"
> universes; many of them possessing essentially different characteristics and
> properties than "our" universe. Our universe and the universes similar to it
> are characterized by such parameters that allow some structures (atoms,
> molecules, stars, planetary systems, etc.) to arise, which could sustain life
> and intelligence. This hypothesis removes many questions such as 'why is
> the world built exactly as it is and not in a different way?' by using the
> assumption that there are some differently built worlds, but their observation
> is impossible, at least for the time being. Some authors consider the
> anthropic principle unsuccessful and even inconsistent with the scientific
> method. I note, in particular, that the requirement to use the fundamental
> laws of nature in other universes which are essentially different from ours,
> may have a heuristic significance in determining our laws. As early as 1917,
> P. Ehrenfest noted that the observed number of spatial dimensions, namely
> three, may be explained by noting that for a different number of dimensions
> the exponent in the Coulomb law changes, and the existence of atoms
> becomes impossible. This, of course, is an argument in the spirit of the
> anthropic principle.

Sakharov insisted on the validity of the anthropic principle, although,
trying as always to be accurate and objective, he remarked that not all physicists agreed with him in this respect. In an alternative approach formulated
at the end of 1988, and still being developed and considered very popular
(the so-called Big Fix, i.e., the determination of all universal fundamental
constants), all the worlds (like soap bubbles) are connected by an infinite
number of wormholes (tubes).[9] Because of this circumstance, the values of
Λ and of other fundamental constants in all the universes are the same. This
approach is traceable to quantum cosmology and is based on the existence
of some exact solutions of the equations of gravitation theory. Despite its
attraction, this approach encounters great difficulties, the most important
of which is the absence of a definite result. So far, a numerical value has not

been derived for any fundamental constant. (The initial excitement occurred because of the "prediction" that the cosmological constant vanishes, but in subsequent works this result was contested.) And so, until now, the "Big Fix" remains a hope. Andrei Dmitrievich, although he was incredibly busy, was well-informed and interested in this topic.

But let us return to his paper of 1984. I quote several final paragraphs:

As is known, the cosmological constant Λ is either zero, or anomalously small. What is more amazing, this is not in the internal symmetry state of a virtual vacuum, but in the state of a real vacuum with symmetry violation. The small size or vanishing of Λ is one of the basic factors which determines whether the lifetime of the universe is long enough for the development of life and intelligence. It would seem reasonable, therefore, to invoke the anthropic principle in order to solve the problem of the cosmological constant.

If the small value of the cosmological constant is determined by the "anthropic choice," then this value is determined by discrete parameters. In this case, Λ is either exactly equal to zero, in some version, or is extremely small. In the latter case, it should be assumed that the number of possible choices of the discrete parameters is sufficiently large, so that the spectrum of values of Λ in the neighborhood of the point $\Lambda = 0$ is sufficiently dense. This obviously requires a large value of the dimensionality K of the compactified space and/or the existence of a complex topological structure (such as a large number of "handles") in some topological factors.

We note in conclusion that, in the space P (remember Parmenides), one should consider an infinite number of U inclusions (for the entire set of trajectories or even for a single trajectory); in this case, the parameters of an infinite number of these trajectories may be arbitrarily close to the parameters of the observed universe. It should be assumed, therefore, that the number of universes similar to our universe, in which matter, life, and intelligence are possible, is infinite. This does not rule out the fact that life and intelligence are also possible in an infinite number of significantly different universes, which form a finite or infinite number of classes of "similar" universes, including universes that have a signature different from our universe.

This paper was submitted to *JETP* in April 1984, and on May 11 Sakharov was forcefully administered a drug that induced a microstroke. Apparently he was given psychotropic drugs during the entire summer. Almost one month after he was released from the hospital (September 8) he could not (and did not want to) work, did not sit at his desk, and did not read new preprints. He then recovered, but he again went on a hunger strike from April 16 until October 1985.

THAT YEAR was a period during which almost nothing was known about Sakharov. During this period, theoreticians went to Gorki twice—in November 1984 and in February 1985—but unfortunately the visits hardly changed this "black hole" situation. In the summer of 1985, the United Nations declared Sakharov "to be missing." At the end of October 1985, the blockade was lifted and Elena Georgievna was allowed, at last, to travel to the U.S. for medical treatment. For half a year Andrei Dmitrievich lived alone. In June 1986, Elena Georgievna returned to Gorki, and they were again together, in almost total isolation. And so the situation lasted until the famous December.

But this was not the same isolation as before. It became possible to write (although Andrei Dmitrievich later mentioned that in the summer of 1986 part of his private correspondence, in which he wrote about the Chernobyl disaster, never reached the addressee). During this period, Sakharov's colleagues traveled to him four times: in December 1985, and in January, April, and May 1986. Andrei Dmitrievich started to work on physics again, and in 1986 he published a paper in *JETP Letters* titled "Evaporation of Mini–Black Holes; High-Energy Physics," and in January and March I received two long letters from him:

> . . . I am very glad that you are in the mainstream of great events of our time—Kaluza-Klein superstrings, etc. I try with great difficulty to grasp the meaning of these things—the edge is gone, and the gaps in knowledge and acquired education are terrible; and the authors in a hurry to "put an idea across" write for those readers who themselves work in this field and know everything but the given article. Earlier they did not write like this (I would like to say "in our time," but what does it mean, "our time"?). I think that the work of Polyakov on strings and the subsequent work of Fradkin and Tseytlin are very important, but much is not clear to me due to my setbacks. Witten's work is too difficult for me to read at this time. *Soviet Physics— Uspekhi* has a good selection of articles in the August issue. But even in these articles not everything is clear to me, and, alas, I cannot read them easily.

Then he wrote some special formulas—Andrei Dmitrievich presented the idea of using a purely geometric method to write the action functional for a superstring. I immediately showed this letter to E. S. Fradkin and A. A. Tseitlin and, to the best of my knowledge, some discussions took place during the visits of the theoreticians to Gorki.

At the end of the letter he, in a purely "Sakharovian" style, shows *ab initio* that a two-dimensional surface of arbitrary topology (a sphere with handles) can be described by using rectangular polygons on the Lobachevski surface, whose opposite sides are the mirror images of each other: "It seems to me that such surfaces may appear in the compactification . . . and confirm (given a large number of handles) my idea of an 'anthropic' vanishing of the cosmological constant . . .''

The second letter (dated March 9, 1986) was written after Elena Georgievna had undergone heart surgery. This letter dealt largely with the discussion of the spontaneous violation of CP invariance and T invariance in a model of three complex scalar fields. Sakharov talked about this model in his lecture titled "The Baryon Asymmetry of the Universe," presented in June 1988 in Leningrad at the international conference on the hundredth anniversary of the birth of A. A. Friedmann.

AFTER HIS RETURN to Moscow, Sakharov's life became very stormy, which was difficult to endure even purely physically. I remember in February 1987 he came to a seminar in FIAN looking extremely pale. I asked what

Part of the text of the paper "The Baryonnic Asymmetry of the Universe," presented by Sakharov at the International Conference on Cosmology, on the one-hundredth anniversary of the birth of A. A. Friedman: "In 1965 (as I recall), I read a paper by S. Okubo, in which it was shown that, in principle, CP violation might lead to an inequality of the partial widths of particles and antiparticles in multichannel processes; in this case, the total probabilities would be equal. I later wrote the following on a copy of my paper as a gift to E. L. Feinberg:

"The effect of S. Okubo
At a temp so very high
Gave the Universe a shape that
Was quite puzzling to the eye."

A drawing from the same report: While discussing the equivalence of gravitational mass and intertial mass, Sakharov mentioned Galileo's experiments involving the dropping of objects from the leaning tower of Pisa.

happened. "Nothing, I simply didn't sleep last night, I was writing my speech for the Forum. The night offers quiet, solitude. During the day, it is impossible to work."[10] Roughly, this is how Sakharov explained the situation. "And now, I'll have no time at all," concluded Andrei Dmitrievich in March 1989, when he was elected deputy of the people. And he was right. But Andrei Dmitrievich did not renounce his responsibility, and did not try to make life easier for himself. He continued to attend scientific conferences and seminars, was interested until the last day in the fundamental problems of physics, and didn't want his social responsibilities to remove him to the periphery of science.

These are simply notes, not a chronicle. I write about how they didn't understand Sakharov, how his actions and declarations changed the climate, taking it out of a dangerous stagnation, destroying myths and (as often happens in such cases) causing perplexity or indignation. At the risk of repeating myself, I list a few such known declarations, dating from 1989: the declaration published in *Moscow News*, entitled "At the Academy of Sciences, or Nowhere" (February); the interview in Canada about "The Means to Prevent the Capture of Afghanistan by the Soviet Military Command" (February); the series of declarations during the summer tour of the West-European countries about the danger of subsidizing the bankrupt Soviet economy, about the fact that it was too early to fall into euphoria, and that the USSR was at the brink of a civil war; the declaration at the second session of the Supreme Soviet of the USSR of the necessity of a multi-party system (October); and finally, the appeal for a two-hour political strike (December).

And one more example of how they didn't understand, and continue not to understand Sakharov, and the great perseverance with which he tried to bring to life what he believed was necessary. The key phrases here are: Chernobyl, atomic energy, underground siting of nuclear reactors. Still in Gorki, in the summer of 1986, Andrei Dmitrievich wrote a long letter to G. I. Marchuk, the president of the Soviet Academy of Sciences, in which he insisted in particular on the radical re-evaluation of the nuclear power plant construction program, in order to reprofile it toward underground siting of the nuclear reactors. Sakharov's main arguments were that the probability of large-scale nuclear accidents cannot be calculated by using the theory of probability; they always occur in an unpredictable way. The largest catastrophes, like that at Chernobyl, should never occur again, anywhere in the world. Realization of this idea is the most important lesson we can learn from the Chernobyl accident. The only hopeful guarantee against "idiots" or terrorists, against destruction by earthquakes or war, is the underground placement of reactors. Andrei Dmitrievich thoroughly studied the special literature on this topic, knew all the concomitant financial and technological difficulties, and continued to persevere. They continued to ignore his appeals, and he understood well why they ignored him: too many billions had already been invested, and a modification of the whole program clearly would be against the entrenched interests. "The problem of underground construction of nuclear power plants can be solved only on a political level. Specialized institutes or departments cannot, in principle, resolve it." — that's how he explained the core of the problem, and I heard this from him continually.

Sakharov did not take a position against nuclear energy. Renouncing it today would cause an even more dangerous pollution of the atmosphere by the wastes of conventional power plants, increasing the greenhouse effect, and so on. He proposed a unique possible solution. The time still available to solve the energy "dilemma" is very short:

> The five-year plan on nuclear energy should be scrapped; this, I admit, would be a blow to all those people who are connected with the work on the construction of nuclear power plants. A walled-up building was constructed for the future, a multibillion dollar expense . . . I think that there should be an international law which forbids any above-the-ground construction of nuclear reactors . . .[11]

And again the re-education, as in countless times before, encounters great difficulties. In general, the revolutions of conscience encounter great difficulties.

And so, what is "Sakharov's miracle"? How did Andrei Dmitrievich himself evaluate this matter?

> My fate was, in a sense, exceptional. It is not false modesty but the desire to be precise that prompts me to say that my fate proved to be greater than my personality. I only tried to keep up with it.

But do you believe in fate in general?

> I believe virtually nothing in this regard, except some sort of general idea of the intrinsic meaning of the course of events. The course of events, not only in the life of a man, but also in the world at large. In fate as a destiny, I do not believe. I believe that the future is unpredictable and indeterminate; it is created by all of us, step by step, in our endless, complex interactions. But freedom of choice is our inherent right. This is why the role of an individual whom fate has singled out at some crucial moment in history is so important.[12]

Notes and References

1. See: "The 'Hot Points' of Cosmology", *Priroda* 7 (1989): p. 17.
2. The "L.G." File, January 1990.
3. He interrupted contacts with his colleagues for a year and a half, understanding the simple fact that their visits were used against him by the authorities.
4. Sakharov's health reached a critical state during the hunger strike. On December 4, 1981, P. L. Kapitza wrote to Brezhnev: "Dear Leonid Il'itch: I am already a very old man and life has taught me that magnanimous acts will not be forgotten. Save Sakharov's life. Yes, he has faults and a heavy temperament, but he is a great scientist

of our country." Kapitza's assistant P. E. Rubinov brought the letter to the office of the Communist Party Central Committee and it was received by Brezhnev the same day.

5. Yu. A. Golfand, professor of physico-mathematical sciences, a pioneer in this field, was reinstated at FIAN in March 1980, by the same decision that allowed Sakharov to remain at this institute. This happened as a result of a strong protest campaign by scientists abroad.

6. From the weekly archives of E. R. and A. R. Gaginski.

7. The poem contains a pun. "Shcherbinka," the area of Gorki in which Sakharov lived, also means "imperceptible cuts."

8. From the letter to the president of the Soviet Academy of Sciences, A. P. Aleksandrov, dated October 15, 1984, *Znamya* 2 (1990): p. 5. (See also Elena Bonner's *Alone Together* and Sakharov's *Memoirs*, page 703.)

9. See: "The 'Hot Points' of Cosmology", p. 15.

10. At this meeting of the Forum for a Nuclear-Free World, Sakharov insisted that the controversy over the American SDI or "Star Wars" program not block further nuclear arms reductions. Several months later, Sakharov's idea was accepted by the Soviet government and the dismantlement of the missiles began.

11. *The Art of Cinematography (Iskustvo Kino)* 8 (1989).

12. *The Youth of Estonia (Molodezh Estonii)*, October 11, 1988.

Photographs:
After the Return

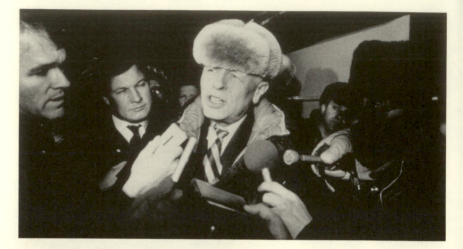

Overleaf: *Sakharov campaigning in the election campaign of R. I. Pimenov in Syktyvkar, 1989.* **Top:** *Sakharov returns to Moscow on December 23, 1986, after nearly seven years exile in Gorki. (AP/Wide World photo.)* **Bottom:** *Sakharov with Ya. B. Zel'dovich at the International Conference on Quantum Gravity in Moscow in 1987, the year Zel'dovich died.*

Top: *In the courtyard of the house on Chkalov Street in Moscow, late 1980s.* ***Bottom:*** *At the I. V. Kurchatov Institute of Atomic Energy, 1988. B. B. Kadomtsev (left), S. Yu. Luk'yanov (right), and Sakharov (center).*

Above: *At a session of the presidium of the Soviet Academy of Sciences.*
Opposite top: *With N. N. Bogolyubov at the Academy of Sciences.* ***Bottom:***
Also at the Academy, with A. B. Migdal (center) and V. I. Goldanskii
(right).

Opposite top left: Sakharov signs the official members' book on November 13, 1988 in the Great Hall of the National Academy of Sciences in Washington, D.C. His stepdaughter, Tatyana Yankelevich, looks on. (Photo by Audey Bradtke.) **Top right:** *Sakharov with volume co-editor Sidney Drell at the Lepton Photon Symposium, 1989. (Photo by Harvey L. Lynch.)* **Bottom:** *During his visit to the U.S. in 1988, Sakharov insisted on meeting Edward Teller, who also bore the appellation "Father of the H-bomb." They met just before a gala banquet in Washington, D.C., where Teller was honored on his 80th birthday. In his remarks to an elegantly dressed audience, Sakharov praised Teller as a man of unswerving principle and patriotism. (Photo by Susan Steinkamp.)* **Above:** *Sakharov receives an honorary doctorate from the University of Bologna, 1988.*

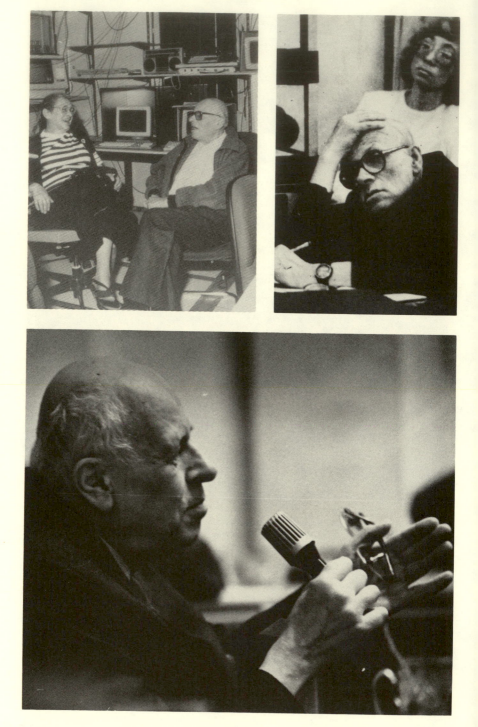

*Opposite top left: Sakharov and Bonner as guests of J. Steinberger at CERN, the European acclerator laboratory. **Top right:** During a session of the Scientific Council on the Complex Problem of Cosmology and Microphysics, Moscow, 1989. (See chapter by Khlopov in this volume.) **Opposite bottom and above:** Sakharov during the election of People's Deputies of the Soviet Union from the Academy of Sciences, Moscow, House of Scientists, 1989. Lenin's bust broods over the deliberations (above).*

Opposite top: *Sakharov with A. P. Aleksandrov during the election of People's Deputies from the Academy.* ***Bottom:*** *Sakharov speaking at the same occasion.* ***Above:*** *Outside the Congress hall in Moscow. The sign in the background reads "Congress of People's Deputies of the USSR." (AP/Wide World photo.)*

Sakharov's funeral, Moscow, December 18, 1989. **Top left:** *Arrival of the funeral procession at the site of the ceremony in Luzhniki.* **Top right:** *Mikhail S. Gorbachev, N. I. Ryzhkov, and V. A. Medvedev (right to left).* **Bottom:** *Funeral ceremony in Luzhniki. On the speaker's platform are (first row, left to right) I. Zaslavskii, Yu. Afanas'ev, G. Kh. Popov, A. A. Sobchak. B. N. Yeltsin, and A. Shabat.*

Top: Bonner and Sakharov. Sakharov wrote five days before in the epilogue to his Memoirs: *"The main thing is that my dear, beloved Lusia and I are united . . . Life goes on. We are together."* **Bottom:** *Farewell in the Soviet Academy of Sciences. First row, left to right: V. I. Goldanskii, R. Z. Sagdeev, I. M. Makarov, and G. I. Marchuk.*

Without Sakharov. Pro-democracy rally in Moscow, February 25, 1990.

On Free Thought

Overleaf: At the Congress of People's Deputies, 1989.

On Free Thought

A Panel Discussion
Organized and Moderated by

I. N. Arutyunyan
G. M. L'Vovskii

Only a few years ago, it became possible to talk about Andrei Dmitrievich Sakharov out loud and, more important, to be able to speak to him himself, but his influence began to be felt much earlier. Even those who were not familiar with his scientific work, and had not read his studies on humanitarian problems, knew that here was a man who always said what he thought. Only this changed people—more or less; it was not always realized, but it changed them. Andrei Dmitrievich's death compelled many to start thinking and to attempt to interpret the part which he played in our lives. However, since history will be the final judge of his role, today we can speak only of our own understanding of Sakharov's social and political activity.

This is the subject of a panel discussion organized by *Priroda*, whose participants were: V. V. Zhurkin, corresponding member of the Soviet Academy of Sciences and director of the Academy's Institute of Europe; S. A. Kovalev, candidate of biological sciences and people's deputy of the Russian Republic; M. K. Mamardashvili, doctor of philosophical sciences and section head of the Institute of Philosophy of the Academy of Sciences of the Georgian Republic; B. N. Topornin, corresponding member of the Soviet Academy of Sciences and director of the Academy's Institute of Government and Law; L. A. Shelepin, doctor of physical and mathematical sciences and chief of the scientific staff of the Lebedev Physical Institute.

Politician or Prophet?

Moderator. Speaking at the funeral of Andrei Dmitrievich, D. S. Likhachev said that Sakharov was a prophet in the ancient, primordial sense of this word. A very high evaluation, it would appear. However, many people draw from it a certain negative meaning. Even among people who were closely associated with him, there was the following opinion: Sakharov was a very honest and sincere person, but he was not a politician, and the suggestions which he made cannot be carried out in real life. These views have persisted to some degree until the present time. According to the point of view that represents the other extreme, Sakharov was a magnificent politician and very accurately calculated all possibilities of the development of events, and for this reason, it is necessary to pay careful attention to every word which he said.

Which of these two positions is closer to the truth? Reducing the question to its basic form, we could ask: Was he a politician or a prophet?

V. V. Zhurkin. I do not know if it is possible to say unambiguously that Andrei Dmitrievich was a politician, but in addition to the scientific approach, there appeared in his thinking also the political approach—of this there is no doubt. I shall give one example—an excerpt from an open letter to the American physicist Sidney Drell:

> Of course I realize that in attempting not to lag behind a potential enemy in any way, we condemn ourselves to an arms race that is tragic in a world with so many critical problems admitting of no delay . . . *If* the probability of such an outcome could be reduced at the cost of another ten or fifteen years of the arms race, then perhaps that price must be paid while, at the same time, diplomatic, economic, ideological, political, cultural, and social efforts are made to prevent a war.[1]

This course is not the reasoning of a preacher who calls on the world only to disarm, to reduce stress, and to solve problems by discussion. The political ideas of Academician Sakharov are characterized by humanism and the value of all mankind. Nevertheless, what distinguishes a politician? To me, it is the ability to associate high and noble goals with realism in the choice of the means of reaching them. And if, for example, we take his analysis of the strategic situation or of the approach to various scenarios of the use of nuclear weapons, then here we see a constructively thinking politician, in the highest sense of this word.

S. A. Kovalev. Andrei Dmitrievich constantly felt personal responsibility for what had occurred and tried to look into problems that he considered important, as professionally as he could. He then did not retreat from his conclusions, not worrying about what people thought. He applied himself with the same responsibility and fundamentalism to the present discussion on disarmament. In fact, calculations show that too rapid and complete disarmament will not reduce the risk of military confrontation and use of nuclear weapons, but will rather increase it. In the first approximation, this is easy to show. Imagine that complete nuclear disarmament has occurred. However, the technology of nuclear weapons production is already well-known and in the presence of general nuclear disarmament the risk that some country or even a small criminal group will be able to use this weaponry will increase. This is a crude model, but there is logic in it. He, of course, in contrast with many peace movements, did not call for rapid and complete disarmament, but looked at matters considering all aspects.

L. A. Shelepin. In my opinion, Andrei Dmitrievich was neither a politician nor a prophet—he was first of all a scientist. His "Reflections on Progress, Peaceful Coexistence, and Intellectual Freedom" begins with the premise that the scientific method must be introduced into politics and the social sciences. However, this was very difficult to do. Since Stalin's era, there had been a strict separation: Physics had its own laws, biology had its own, and social sciences had their own. The various disciplines were separated by a unique Chinese Wall. Therefore, the social sciences did not have available those methods used in the exact sciences. Actually, the social sciences were no longer sciences; they became dogmas. Even today we encounter this difficulty. Not only among us but also in the West, in the social sciences to a significant degree the very structure of the sciences does not exist. For no purpose they usually use the word "teachings": the teachings of Marx, teachings of Galbraith, and so forth. Instead a unified science of society is needed, a science to which some contribution was made by Marx, some by other scholars, where the limits of applicability of each postulate are known, the dynamics of social processes are studied, and the hierarchy of characteristic times is taken into account. In other words, in order for the science of society to become a full-fledged science, it is necessary to bring into it the entire set of methods developed in other disciplines—cybernetic methods and synergistic methods. The world is not divided into cells; everything in it is interrelated, and therefore social scientists cannot be considered by themselves.

If scientific methods are introduced, it will be possible to predict the development of society scientifically, and this has a fundamental significance. Of course, we are not discussing a mathematical prediction; mathematics is an ideal. Mendeleev once said that a field of study cannot be called a science if quantitative relations are not introduced in it. This means that our problem, possibly, is to introduce quantitative relations into the social sciences, even for the characteristics of social consciousness. However, the important thing now is to look into the structure of these sciences. How are they constructed? What we call dialectic and historical materialism is essentially a metascience. It must be treated as such. We must get rid of this or that teaching.

In addition, as far as I can judge, an important feature of Andrei Dmitrievich's approach was dialogue. It was possible to argue with him and not to agree with him. He never imposed his views, and during discussions they could change, and could be perfected. Such was his method of analysis, and such is the scientific method. He was not afraid to reconsider his opinions, and in this he differed greatly from many politicians who, once they had expressed an opinion, would not change it for anything. In this respect, his approach was scientific.

V. V. Zhurkin. If we nevertheless talk about Andrei Dmitrievich's social and political views, they are set forth not so much in scientific papers as in the statements of a politician, or, let us say, a scientist-politician. What characterizes his approach? First of all, professionalism of the highest order. It is seen in the very logic of reflections on subjects which determine the fate of mankind at the end of the twentieth century and the beginning of the twenty-first century, such as global nuclear war, local nuclear war, conventional war, disarmament . . . His professionalism manifests itself even in small things, in the clarity and subtle nature of his formulations. These are rarely correct formulas, although the most complicated problems were discussed in very simple and clear language. I shall give only one example. Academician Sakharov is speaking of the nuclear arsenals in the USSR and the U.S. and is analyzing their specific natures. Then he compares rockets and bombers, which actually differ greatly from each other in their capabilities, and he suddenly points out: "Massive penetration of aircraft into the interior of the USSR is doubtful—this last remark should be modified to take into account the possibilities of winged rockets [cruise missiles]—they probably can overcome the antiaircraft defenses of the enemy."[2]

This sentence, outwardly so simple, implies a thorough knowledge of the particular features of the antiaircraft defenses of the Soviet Union and of the U.S. Probably this professionalism is explained primarily by an incredible honesty. Nevertheless, in my opinion, the mind of a scientist in principle is such that it grasps such nuances from the sphere of strategic thinking and social sciences as a whole very rapidly. It seems to me that this ability manifested itself very strongly in Andrei Dmitrievich Sakharov.

The second point which characterizes Sakharov's approach is his completely clear political position, based on solid ethical and moral principles. The third point is his realism. Many people in our society have formed an opinion of Academician Sakharov as one with the greatest number of good intentions, an idealist. However, his work on questions of nuclear strategy or military-political problems is not the work of an idealist, but is exceptionally realistic work. Proceeding from humanistic priorities, he almost always obtains the most constructive solution possible of the problem in hand, but he does not, as a rule, cross the boundary beyond which the solution becomes unrealistic. It seems to me that this is the greatest advantage of a politician, an extraordinary and outstanding politician.

S. A. Kovalev. It seems to me that Andrei Dmitrievich himself was never occupied with the question of whether he was a scientist, a politician, or a social worker. For him the beginning of any social effort was determined by a moral impulse. That is, we must speak of the relation of morality and science, because in his genes and in all of his biases he was a scientist and he remained one to the end of his life.

In general, natural science has no relation to morality. In any case, it is customary to think so, because no moral evaluations are applicable to the results of, say, physics. However, if we pose the problem of what relation in principle exists between science and morality, we can find a deeper connection. In my opinion, the only moral basis of science is an unbiased, disinterested, and fearless search for truth (and this applies not only to science, but to creative thought in general). But since it is disinterested and fearless, this means that it is also highly responsible. This was his initial position. When he understood the entire extent of his responsibility (his own, that is; he never shared it with anyone else; for him, his own responsibility was always higher than any collective responsibility), all of his further actions were determined by the structure of his personality as a thinker and a scientist. Here, it would appear, are two mutually inconsistent traits: on the one hand, constructivism and realism and, on the other, an inclination to pointed and far-reaching formulations of problems.

Consider this: He did not hesitate to put into his publications such a far-reaching and nonpragmatic question as the question of world government. The question is not new, but everyone now prefers not to talk about it. Andrei Dmitrievich did not talk about it, but wrote about it in his Constitution Project. At the same time, the feeling of responsibility resulting from the psychology of a scientist made other projects extremely pragmatic, and therefore of no fundamental importance. For example, when we developed a bill relating to an extraordinary situation, then in accordance with current international law, we very bluntly pointed out that no kind of extraordinary

circumstances can be considered a justification of such a measure as intern-
ment. Andrei Dmitrievich for the most part approved the plan, but made
the following remark in connection with this point: "You see, the circumstances may be entirely different. It is necessary to think further about
this." "But, how?" I said to him, "The United States Congress discussed
this problem actively for two years and finally apologized to the Japanese
who were interned during the war." To which Andrei Dmitrievich replied:
"Yes, they apologized, but thirty years after the war, and not just after two
years of discussion. And would Congress have made this apology if a Japanese landing on the United States territory had taken place or had been realistically feared?"

It appears to me that here we have fearlessness of thought and a lack of
prejudice which follow from the moral basis of science, and that his professionalism, of which we were just now speaking, is of the same origin. If
you defend independence of thought, and if you are occupied with some
problem, then be so kind as to study it thoroughly. I well remember how in
the beginning of the 1970s, when the Sakharov committee was formed—it
initially contained Sakharov, Chalidze, and Tverdokhlebov, and subsequently increased in size and changed its composition—the theoretical and
legal directions of this committee's actions disturbed Andrei Dmitrievich.
The point is that the committee undertook to consult everyone, including
the government, on legal questions. Sakharov held Chalidze's legal
knowledge in high regard, but he nevertheless doubted whether the committee had the right to play the role it took upon itself. This was not at all
modesty—when well thought out matters were involved, Andrei Dmitrievich was not distinguished by any special modesty—he simply said what he
thought. But this was the uneasiness of a professional and the manifestation of a deep feeling of responsibility. He understood that it was necessary
for amateurs to occupy themselves with these problems, because it could
not be left to professionals alone, especially to Soviet professionals of that
time in the field of law. On the other hand, there was an extensive
literature—many well-educated and clever people had thought and written
about these problems before us—and it was impossible to ignore their
experience.

M. K. Mamardashvili. I cannot accept the basic formulation of this question. I cannot understand at all what politics is, or, more precisely, what it is
that politicians call politics and how they themselves perceive it, and how
they persuade us to perceive it. Politicians believe that they make politics. I
think that the entire life and activity of Sakharov proves that they are mistaken. The fact is that politics exists wherever open and articulated social

opinion exists, or, more precisely, wherever social understanding exists, i.e., an understanding of society which is not borrowed from the departments of the sciences but which lives and is developed in the heads of the members of society—an understanding of science, economics, or something else. This understanding by itself is already political. Professional politicians can only be credited with it if they are clever, or not be credited if they are stupid.

Sakharov lays claim to thought, and not to science. When he says that science alone cannot provide the means of guiding politics, economics, art, education, and military affairs, we must understand that he did not actually have in mind the methods of science as they are represented in academic departments (modeling, mathematical analysis, or something of this sort). He had in mind one fundamental question: Can reason and common sense prevail in social, political, military, and other affairs? The reality of the twentieth century and, in particular, the reality of the Soviet Union have shown him that the involvement of reason in these affairs is minimal.

If we say that society must be guided by means of science, we are simply repeating the great blunders of an earlier age. Say that some system-controlling theory is possible (we have a persistent dream that it can be produced either in an individual head or in a collection of different heads) and that this theory will control politics, economics, art, education, and military affairs. First of all, this assumption radically contradicts the scientific style of the twentieth century. Such ideas were possible in the eighteenth and nineteenth centuries, but not in the twentieth, when everywhere, including in the most exact sciences—mathematics and physics—the properties of self-regulation and self-organization of living processes are explicitly taken into account (politics is a living process, like economics, education, and art). Shall we forget the entire experience of contemporary physics, cosmology, quantum mechanics, and economics and again begin to dream of a well-arranged ordering, of a unified technical system of scientific control (which is insufficient)? Thought and reason are also insufficient, because the system of science itself is contaminated with an irrational force, so that all models and all calculations may turn out to be an unstoppable flow of nonsense. And then the talk about scientific planning is a completely Kafkaesque delirium. Our economic plan is a noneconomic mechanism of forced labor. In such conversations it seems to me I see people who gather on a staircase landing and talk about inviting each other into their apartments, without noticing that the staircase has accidentally been built outside the building.

A good example is the activity of the former Ministry of Reclamation and Water. All hydroelectric power station projects and all irrigation projects are complex scientific projects which were clearly calculated on the basis of models. Is it really possible to correct them by using the same methods that were used to build them—to improve the models and to make the calculations more accurate? Did Sakharov really have this in mind? No, he had in mind that the mass behavior of people, who individually appear reasonable, is characterized by the greatest irrationality and incomprehensibility. However, thought (a scientist understands this) is always connected with a root which resides in the personal integrity of a man, in his intellectual honesty. The very act of thinking is based on a certain measure of validity.

I believe that Sakharov's impetuosity was a collection of these qualities, which had been forced into a hidden "underground," and which are an integral part of thought itself, regardless of whether it appears in the garb of natural science or in a freer social and humanitarian attire. I would say that it has helped us to understand two basic things. First: politics cannot be entrusted entirely to politicians, just as military affairs cannot be entrusted entirely to military persons. And therefore, to discuss to what extent Sakharov was a politician and to what extent a scientist, means to proceed from the representation which politicians suggest to us—that politics is actually made just by them. I assert that this is not so, in any case, in cultured European society. Politics becomes a professional field of activity only when it is recognizably present in the civil life of all members of society. Second: the illegality of the brutal professional separation of people, their registration. Let us say that you are occupied with politics. What does this mean in Russia? You are prescribed to be occupied with politics. Are you a scientist? Then do science, you are prescribed to be occupied with it. It is not hard to imagine that a man who perceives himself to be a thinker will be able one fine day to rise against this situation. Not against some specific political decision (although against that, too), but against this determinism.

Moderator. But this division is the result, in part, of education and professionalization.

M. K. Mamardashvili. That is quite true. However, when we are talking about civil thought—and in it there are implicitly present scientific thought, art, and much more—we are speaking of a means of orientation of modern man in the world. And then, of course, we understand that any "prescription" is an archaic residue of serfdom in Russia. There is no need to disguise this in terms of other problems—say, professionalization. The question is very simple. Since the time of the Gospel and the time of the Word, there is nothing which would not have a relation to me, there is no delegation of thought, and no delegation of responsibility. This is the primary, evangelical meaning of Christianity. And for this reason a scientist is not *planted* in a laboratory. He is occupied with science, since it is interesting to him. For a society the thoughts of any of its members are valuable, including the thoughts of the man in the laboratory, about what is happening. He is a person and it is important that he thinks about what is happening, including what people are attempting to explain by their monopoly of politics. Such a monopoly does not exist in the contemporary interrelated world.

V. V. Zhurkin. I agree with the evaluations of Merab Konstantinovich. However, in each specific field, in particular, the military-political field or disarmament, there is some global level of the accumulated complexes of ideas and professional approaches with which, whether politicians wish it or not, they are compelled to deal. Very frequently, it is true, they do not deal with these ideas, but objective reality nevertheless compels them constantly to make corrections and realignments. The statements of Academician Sakharov did not simply correspond to this level, but unavoidably raised it. Most of his papers were written at a time when we were dominated by monolithic thinking, and only one line existed in the approach to great strategic questions. If there were discussions at all, they were so closed that, on the surface, in real politics everything followed this one line. In view of this monostructure, conditions did not allow alternative variants to be discussed in social polemics on the most urgent questions concerning all of mankind and each individual. However, at present, under the conditions of pluralism we understand that much of what Sakharov wrote were magnificent, alternative variants which are necessary for development of a realistic politics. For this reason, I still remain of the same opinion. I am not prepared to judge whether Sakharov was a prophet, but since his work is permeated by political thinking in the best sense of this word—dynamic, realistic, directed to the search for solutions which are not only constructive but also ethically and morally justified—I still think that we can speak of Academician Sakharov as a politician. Of course, he was not among those politicians whom Merab Konstantinovich was discussing.

M. K. Mamardashvili. As to being a prophet, I would give the following answer. Sakharov was a man who did not wish to be a prophet. This is because a prophet has an archaic status, completely inconsistent with contemporary society. Even in the Gospel this status was subjected to doubt. Unfortunately, in Russia it is associated with Christianity. In the New Testament it is said (and this thought is given twice): "The law and the prophets were until John; since that time the kingdom of God is preached, and every man presseth into it." (Luke 16:16.) It means that the law and the prophets are the archaic status of spirituality and thought in a world where there is a law which can function completely automatically and there is only one opposition to it—the outcry of a prophet. The Gospel says: Nothing is foretold either by the Law or by a prophet—things come from your own effort, and your own effort is responsible for everything.

S. A. Kovalev. I would like to support Merab Konstantinovich in his, if we may so call them, evangelical analogies. It seems to me that Christianity, moving away from the idea that everything up to the last fine details can and must be regulated, imposed on people a terrible and sometimes excessive task—to make a choice at each step. Some basic principles are set forth, but no formulas are given as to how to proceed in a particular case. My opinion is that Andrei Dmitrievich realized the full measure of his responsibility and this determined many things in his life.

M. K. Mamardashvili. When people in Russia discuss prophets and the respect or lack of respect for them, the subject is immediately converted to the question of who is master of his own affairs and who is a serf of the state. A man can be occupied with his own affairs, dress for the ballet, make scientific discoveries (which will belong to the government, just like himself), but at any moment when he causes trouble for his master (i.e., those same politicians), they can punish him in the stable. Here is a problem of any man of free thought in our country, which completely inherited the structure of serfdom from the Russian society of the nineteenth century. Yet this structure itself leads such people as Sakharov to social and political activity, because the dignity of a scientist cannot be subdued. This is a continuation of a tradition, which I call the tradition of V. I. Vernadskii.

Vernadskii said that if there is no freedom of thought, this is the coffin and candles of contemporary society. By freedom of thought he meant not simply freedom from censorship, but the presence of thought in all matters—the victory of intelligent force, as he expressed it. It was lacking in the control of economics, art, education, and military affairs. Between the mind of the controller and the mind which exists in society, a tremendous gap was formed at that moment. Therefore, in the articles and diaries of Vernadskii, one can hear at all times a sad inner note. After him, Sakharov presented the government—which is not very clever and which had no morals—with an account which can only be characterized as outraged thought.

Sakharov was a phenomenon of self-dignity of thought, who did not require any support, whether from external authority, government, or the collective. His words were addressed to the "department" of free inner thought. No, he is not a prophet, because he denied himself such an appointment—as a prophet. A prophet would bring to the "powers that be" the voice of reality, validity, and moderation. In this way he would speak for all others. Sakharov considered that each person can and must speak.

Dialogue with Mankind

Moderator. That is precisely what he himself did. He spoke, or rather he thought aloud—after all Sakharov was not an orator in the usual sense of this word, though that is exactly how many people remember him, speaking from the speaker's rostrum at the Congress. Before this occurred, however, there was a long process of evolution—from a scientist, whose intellectual power the state needed, to a free-thinking man, whose thoughts were of no use to the government. Even now, talking about the outcome of this evolution, one cannot help but think about its main stages and try to understand his motives. In particular, many people are puzzled by his attitude toward his own participation in the development of nuclear weapons.

S. A. Kovalev. The writer A. Adamovich had a talk with him about just this matter and is still surprised by Sakharov's answers. Adamovich does not agree with them and believes that a few years from now Sakharov might have answered differently. There exists a popular belief that Sakharov built the bomb, afterwards he became horrified by his creation, and then his conscience forced him to atone for his past sins. Sakharov himself did not accept this view and he gently but persistently denied such an interpretation. He said that he did not regret his participation in these developments, even though he knew that the results did not end up in clean hands and consequences could be terrifying. But still, if he had to relive this life and face the same choice, he probably would again take part in the development of nuclear weapons and protest against their use. As far as I know, he believed that his actions were necessary then. This was not a simple decision. Nonetheless, thinking about it recently, he concluded that he made the correct choice—not morally irreproachable, but nonetheless correct. History, he believed, vindicated this choice, because in the last few years peace was preserved precisely because of the balance of power. We are balancing on the brink, but we have been balancing for several decades.

V. V. Zhurkin. Sakharov's moral position, as we now know it, of course, evolved over a period of time, but as a matter of principle, as I see it, it was always present. The question of how he morally justified working on the development of nuclear weapons is one which he himself never answers anywhere in his writings. I personally think that hidden in his works is the idea that any nuclear monopoly is dangerous and some balance is necessary. The idea of balance of forces in itself, or parity, appeared later. When the nuclear arms race was in progress, no one thought about it—both sides tried to develop the next new type of weapon as quickly as possible. I am convinced that the idea that nuclear weapons should not be in the hands of one country and that they have irrevocably changed everything in our world could become not only a justification but a normal, logical, and moral reason for participating in the development of nuclear weapons.

Moderator. But once an approximate balance of forces had been achieved, and Andrei Dmitrievich weighed the need for further nuclear weapons tests, Khrushchev silenced him. This is what Andrei Dmitrievich later wrote about this matter:

> I recall a meeting of atomic scientists with Chairman of the Council of Ministers Khrushchev during the summer of 1961. It was apparent that preparations had to be made for a series of tests which was supposed to support the USSR's new policy regarding the German question (the Berlin Wall). I wrote the following memorandum to Khrushchev: "The resumption of tests after a three-year moratorium will undermine the negotiations on banning tests and on disarmament, and it will lead to a new round in the arms race, especially in the realm of intercontinental ballistic missiles and antimissile defenses"—and I passed it up the line to Khrushchev. Khrushchev put the memorandum in his breast pocket and invited those present to dinner. At the dinner table he made an improvised speech, which I remember because of its frankness, reflecting not only his personal position. He said approximately the following. Sakharov is a good scientist, but leave foreign policy to us— the specialists in this intricate business. We cannot proclaim that we are pursuing policy from a position of strength, but that is the way it must be. I would be a ditherer and not the Chairman of the Council of Ministers if I listened to people like Sakharov.[3]

But to what extent are nuclear weapons tests a policy tool? Who, other than scientists, should determine whether or not weapons should be tested?

V. V. Zhurkin. I would disagree with the fact that nuclear weapons tests can be a policy tool. A moratorium on tests or a treaty to stop testing is, of course, a policy; the international community is persistently striving to achieve this end. It seems to me that in the realm of nuclear weapons tests and their technical aspects there is a constant battle between two forces: more and more scientists, who are proving that nuclear weapons tests have not been necessary for a long time, and the military establishment in all countries, who for the most diverse motives insist on regularly checking and improving their arsenal. In this sense Khrushchev's interference was absolutely incorrect. The argument should be between the professionals, some who know all the complexities of the mechanisms of nuclear weapons (by the way, at the Moscow Forum in February 1987, Academician Sakharov described in detail the main features of these mechanisms), and others who, in the case of war, would have to use these weapons. Of course, it is easy to pass judgment in hindsight, and Khrushchev's position in the argument with Sakharov seems to me to be at least lacking logic.

L. A. Shelepin. As I see it, Andrei Dmitrievich's notions about our society and the paths along which it developed underwent a no less interesting and complicated evolution. For example, in "Reflections" he talks about socialism, its moral foundations, and advantages. In the mid- and late 1970s, he no longer returned to this subject, though he harshly criticized the government and its actions. But there are no contradictions here, because in the beginning of the 1970s there occurred, as the physicists say, a phase transition in this country. What did it consist of? Before the 1970s, the economy grew and sober self-assessment was possible (in particular, reliable statistics were available), but later the following happened. Sheer exaggerations replaced statistics—it is not without reason that serious economists use statistical data only up to 1972. Greed and careerism spread to a national scale. Different Mafia-like structures began to form on the same scale. In short, a qualitative change occurred in our country. Andrei Dmitrievich perceived this. For this reason, there are no contradictions in his position. The evolution of his views is linked with the evolution of society. In the 1960s our country could still have followed relatively painlessly the path he indicated. We could have avoided slipping into a crisis. But the warning was not appreciated or understood, it was a voice in the wilderness. And the government did not take the necessary steps.

M. K. Mamardashvili. There began, as I call it, the "age of the smell of beefsteak." Earlier people were gripped with fear. Then fear was replaced by the smell of beefsteak, and this turned out to be a more reliable method for consolidating the social space.

S. A. Kovalev. In regard to Andrei Dmitrievich's first work "Reflections," I must say that he wasn't sure whether he should include it in his book *Alarm and Hope*. He said that much in "Reflections" was the fruit of immature and naive ideas, but he decided, "Oh, well, let it be published without any changes." In any case, I am convinced that his discussions of socialism did not contain any elements of a tactical maneuver. He wrote what he thought at the time.

I wish to state a hypothesis. The idea of socialism, social justice, is a wonderful idea, that played an important role in history: it corrected narrow-minded and selfish capitalism. Alas, as I see it, this idea cannot be realized. It is simply inconsistent with man's nature and certain laws of economics that cannot be circumvented. This idea has made a fruitful contribution, but, unfortunately, not in the country that first declared itself to be socialist. The socialist idea bore fruit exactly in the capitalist West, where it is prescribed, where because of the democratic nature and freedom of society, it could be realized—probably not in an ideal, but close to ideal form. I am thinking about the guaranteed minimum wage, unemployment benefits, and a developed system of social taxation. So my hypothesis is that Andrei Dmitrievich today would draw the same conclusions regarding socialism and capitalism, especially since the beginnings of these thoughts are already present in his first work, where he discusses convergence.

Moderator. In speaking about capitalism one thinks of Sweden, West Germany, and the United States. But there is also Uruguay or India. Does this mean that the capitalist idea is in itself still not enough for prosperity?

L. A. Shelepin. There is a fundamental difference between capitalism in the underdeveloped and advanced countries. In the former the system is reminiscent of early capitalism while in the latter a new formation has appeared—postindustrial society. It has incorporated the characteristics of both early capitalism and socialism. Its fundamental distinction is that surplus value appears thanks to science. Prosperity in such a society is not based on large enterprises and increased exploitation, but rather on the use of the achievements of scientific-technological progress, immediate adoption of advanced technologies, and rapid response to changes in the marketplace. This is a new society. In my opinion, Andrei Dmitrievich proclaimed such a society in our country—his pluralism, freedom of thought, and respect for science. We could have transformed to this new formation, but the tragedy is that our society fundamentally ceased being socialistic. It began to approach the society of early capitalism.

M. K. Mamardashvili. Of course, Sakharov's work contains the same motif as does that of a few statesmen, so-called initiators of *perestroika*. This motif is the profound awareness of the incompatibility of existing economic and social structures with scientific and technical progress, and the comprehension of the fact that in the modern world the weight of a superpower is completely determined by its scientific-technical potential. It is not simply a question of machines, but it is a question of the method of conducting any business, including waging war. Modern war contains the elements of logistics and the highest technologies, and the Soviet Union in the form it was in would have lost such a war. The pressure of reality brought someone to their senses, and forced them to think about what Russia would be like at the beginning of the next century. How would it appear before the face of history?

That is the source of what is called *perestroika*. Naturally, it is necessary to re-examine the teaching about structures and all of the "structural" terminology: feudalism, capitalism, and socialism. One must bear in mind one simple fact. The language in which we formulate these problems—the European language and the "formational" terms—are lone translations of words that arose in Europe. The trouble is that for us all these words are simply linguistic "pseudomorphs," as O. Spengler called words that denote nonexistent phenomena and are constructed on the basis of the formal laws of language instead of arising from experience. None of these terms has an internal equivalent in our reality, and the principle on which these words were formed itself was not a living one. It could be that because of this circumstance, in Russia socialism was indeed constructed in the direct sense of this word. We can use the word "socialism" in this sense, but this is not what the European tradition has in mind. What happened in this country is partially connected with the tragic incorrectness of Marx's thinking, and partially with the fact that Russian socialists transformed the theory of structures from the arena of scientific thought into a tool for manipulating the masses.

There exists a European civic society, which is constructed on the basis of industrial urban democracies. Capitalism—understood as the maximum extraction of profit based on large industry, presupposing the separation of labor and mass production of goods—is one phenomenon of this society and coexists with other phenomena. The other phenomena arose for other reasons and no capitalist principle runs through them, rather they interact with capitalism as with a special phenomenon. If we look at reality in this way, then we shall understand that the European civic society must be described not in terms of a capitalistic formation, but rather in completely different, broader terms. This seems obvious to me. But if capitalism does not exist as a system, then socialism does exist. It can be shown that here socialistic principles are the core of all social institutions.

What, then, happened to capitalism? All other phenomena of a civic society, including such traditional phenomena as religion or parliamentarism, interacted with it and assimilated it. It found a definite place—as a socialistic idea, belonging to the same civic society and having in it a real equivalent. But this did not happen in the Soviet Union. Here, there has yet to arise a civic society that will assimilate socialism and transform it into one of the phenomena together with the others, in particular, scientific-technical progress. For this reason, if we are talking about Uruguay, we must decide how well developed their civic society is. There we shall find archaic layers that do not correspond to any civic society, and we shall have to study the interaction of capitalism with these archaic layers. We immediately make the problem more precise, instead of breaking our heads comparing socialism and capitalism as European ideas with the pseudomorphs "socialism" and "capitalism" in the Soviet Union.

It seems to me that all Sakharov's thoughts and pronouncements were formulated in socially pragmatic terms. Such terms are the products of observation, and the act of observation itself serves to create an internal analogy, the basis for the appearance and use of the words. This is how, for example, Sakharov got the idea of convergence. He did not start from words. And it turned out that when one does not start from words, then one understands something, while if one starts from words, then one does not understand anything.

Moderator. There is an example of seemingly even more different world views: Japan and Western Europe. In Japan the linguistic estrangement is greater and the system of moral values differs substantially from the European system. Two different world views but the results achieved today are close. Isn't there a contradiction here?

M. K. Mamardashvili. The answer is simple: they did not have any pseudomorphs, everything was different for them. An example from the social realm. The absence of rights can be corrected by the idea of rights or by law as such. In other words, cultures in which the idea of rights is absent altogether can assimilate this idea and create legal structures. But can a right correct an "antiright" in the strict sense of the word? In Russia the pseudomorph "right" already exists; i.e., there exists an imitation of rights, and no true right can penetrate into it.

Moderator. Probably this is precisely why Andrei Dmitrievich put so much effort into the defense of rights—the struggle against the imitation of rights. What was characteristic of his approach and what changed in the movement to defend human rights when Academician Sakharov joined it?

S. A. Kovalev. This question usually brings to mind the exclusivity of his position, his prestige, and finally his three Hero awards. In 1970, for example, we traveled to Kaluga, where Pimenov and Vail were being tried, and no one but Andrei Dmitrievich was allowed into the court room. Later, when "a wild outburst of democracy" started, he too was no longer allowed into the trial. All this is important, but not the main point. The main point is that he contributed a constructive approach, he swayed the intuitive aversion of the defenders of human rights to politics. In this sense he really was a politician.

Before Sakharov, the defenders of rights acted simply: say what you think without worrying about the result—there is much to uncover. Andrei Dmitrievich was building an ideal, but in doing so he did not forget constructiveness and realism. He was not afraid to make suggestions, even though they appeared to be fantastic. He extended his hand to the authorities for cooperation, and although his hand was rejected he never tired of extending it.

M. K. Mamardashvili. That is, he suggested something for the authorities to do and proposed that the opposition accept it, in spite of the fact that it would be done by the hands of authorities?

S. A. Kovalev. Yes, exactly so. There is sufficient proof: many of his specific suggestions are now proclaimed from all speakers' rostrums. But at that time they were almost the first, as far as I can judge, examples of lucid suggestions, ready to be materialized. It seems to me that this is a significant contribution.

This approach was quite rapidly adopted by the defenders of human rights. True, Sakharov found among them not only supporters, but also very outspoken opponents. The stridency of the criticism increased right up to his death, and this criticism, alas, was sometimes unscrupulous. He accepted any rebukes calmly and kept his independence; after all, the position "always against" is not true independence. But at first there were no enemies—there were only admirers. The enemies, and very strident ones, appeared much later, when he returned from Gorki. There were publications that were no longer within the limits of decency, where it was said that Sakharov had abandoned his principles.

You see the movement to defend human rights is a quite complicated thing. It appeared to be unified, but it never was. For many who considered themselves (in my opinion, groundlessly) to be politicians, the appeal to rights was simply a method of attacking the authorities. It was clear to everyone that it is more effective to criticize the authorities precisely for breaking a law than to enter into an open political battle with them—if for no other reason than that the breaking of a law can be proved. But the core of the human rights movement consisted of people who reasoned completely differently. For them the observance of legal norms was indeed the goal. They did not hide behind the law as a convenient method of criticism.

So long as the law remained the only core of the problem (the tactical core for some and the true core for others), the movement appeared to be monolithic. When it became noticeably freer, the schisms quickly became evident. Those who continued to stand on their legal rights, and Sakharov was among them, were subjected to criticism. Why talk about rights in this country where there are no rights and there never will be? Why create the impression that improvements in rights are possible? The system has to be replaced rapidly.

Indeed, the system must be changed. Indeed, improving rights is not the only method, and undoubtedly not the most fundamental. But Sakharov was a man of great responsibility. As soon as the result of an action could be somehow foreseen (and such a moment occurred in the 1980s), Andrei Dmitrievich tried very hard to work it out. The simplicity of our position in the 1960s lay in the fact that there was no need to work out the result—there was no point in even thinking about it. Now the result can be predicted, and the responsibility is a hundred times greater. The opponents believe that the worse the situation, so much the better. Since the system must be destroyed, let it collapse as quickly as possible, and as for how and on whom, well, that is of no consequence. In the words of the "Internationale," "We shall force the world to its knees, and then. . . ." The question "and then what?" was always postponed. Andrei Dmitrievich did not reason that way, he always felt responsibility. The last year of his life shows this especially clearly.

Moderator. I'm afraid that someone will see a contradiction in what you say. What does "work out the result" mean in the defense of human rights and is this morally justified? After all, you yourself said that in the 1960s there was no reason to hope for an outcome. But many people, including Andrei Dmitrievich, did not let this stop them.

S. A. Kovalev. When the matter concerned separate trials, the question of the result—what can and cannot be done—was of secondary if not tertiary importance to Andrei Dmitrievich. He could never stand apart. He had to be involved even if he knew that it would not bring a positive result. When he had sufficiently reliable information and was sure that an injustice had occurred, he always tried to do something. He had an amazing ability to personally feel someone else's misfortune and pain. I can testify to this, because I observed him on many occasions when news arrived about someone's arrest, sickness, or painful hunger strike in a camp, sometimes even threatening someone's life.

But if we talk about the choice of the way of reacting, then Sakharov, it seems to me, did calculate it. The question of the justification for his hunger strikes—for example, demanding that Liza Alexeyeva be allowed to leave the country to join her fiancé—is often raised. Andrei Dmitrievich probably figured that he was in a position to obtain Liza's release. On the other hand, his Gorki hunger strikes in connection with medical treatment for Elena Georgievna do not have this calculated and practical character. He probably fully conceded here the possibility that he would die, but he could not act otherwise. Incidentally, Sakharov's very first hunger strike during President Nixon's visit to Moscow in 1974 was like that—a hunger strike with simultaneous appeals to Nixon and Brezhnev. I cannot imagine that Andrei Dmitrievich did not understand its futility in the practical sense of this word. The demands were too general: political amnesty, examination of the question of human rights in the USSR. I think that he did not doubt for one minute that his demands would not be met. However he followed this symbolic path, and as a result world attention was attracted to the problem of human rights in our country. This is what he was seeking, and he achieved it.

But, after all, he often used other methods, too—protest, appeal to the world media, an open letter or participation in such a letter.

Moderator. Undoubtedly extreme forms of protest such as hunger strikes become necessary only when flagrant lawlessness prevails in the country. In a civilized society, the state itself, through the institutions of justice, must be the guarantor of the rights of its citizens. For this reason the creation of a lawful state could be the most fundamental result of action in defense of human rights. And a lawful state requires an absolute and actually operating constitution. We know that Andrei Dmitrievich, in developing a draft of the constitution, was helping to solve this problem also.

S. A. Kovalev. As I see it, the draft of the constitution is a very clear document. Maybe it should also be translated into a special legal language, though, it seems to me, that this will not change much.

The history of its development is very simple. It was done as a piece of normal scientific work. Andrei Dmitrievich sat down and started to write, and wrote for many months in succession. Then he handed out the text for discussions—at first to a very small group of individuals and then to a wider circle. In the small group the text did not arouse any special discussion. It is difficult to judge about the wider circle, because the draft was still not subjected to public discussion. Andrei Dmitrievich only made it quite widely known not long before his death, and understandably Sakharov's death suspended discussions, though he himself did not regard this draft as final.

B. N. Topornin. Sergei Adamovich [Kovalev] had the fortunate opportunity to be a direct witness and even a participant in the work on the

Sakharov draft of the constitution. But I have only the document to work with. True, after the meeting of the constitutional commission, when the ball was already rolling, we met Andrei Dmitrievich and had a very general conversation. At that time we at the Institute of Government and Law at the Soviet Academy of Sciences were preparing the concept of the constitution and in this connection we wanted to familiarize Sakharov with it. I remember that Andrei Dmitrievich spoke about the importance of alternative drafts and comparing them. However the meeting at the institute was not destined to occur.

We have now gone quite far in preparing a constitution. There is a starting concept—it, incidently, was discussed at a meeting of the presidium of the Soviet Academy of Sciences—there are different drafts of the articles, and so on. But that is precisely how Andrei Dmitrievich reasoned. He stressed that even the draft that was distributed to the members of the constitutional commission at the suggestion of M. S. Gorbachev is not final. Andrei Dmitrievich continued to work on it, and he made quite significant changes and additions. In many of its initial ideas and especially in its humanistic approach, Sakharov's draft is up-to-date and significant by the most stringent standards.

Remember, Sakharov's draft is very short—not much more than ten type-written pages. It is more like the exposition of a general platform, a systems of views, a list of fundamental principles. From the viewpoint of the professional jurist it is striking that there are no mechanisms guaranteeing the implementation of the proclaimed positions. But, it seems to me, it is precisely such a draft that best expresses Sakharov's spirit, his temperament. The juridical fabric would be undoubtedly woven in later.

The new constitution must—and of this I am convinced—differ from the current constitution in at least three respects. First, it must start by separating the "civic society" from the state, especially in the realm of economics, societal development, science, and culture. Second, man—his personal freedom, independence, and defense—must be at the center of attention of the constitution. Third, the constitution must become the foundation of a fundamentally new union of republics, a just solution to the acute problem of relations between the different peoples of the union. Sakharov's draft not only devotes serious attention to all these problems, but it also contains bold and decisive innovations, a departure from the usual stereotypes of thinking.

Moderator. We spoke here about Andrei Dmitrievich's work on the defense of legal and human rights. Do you, as a professional lawyer, see a reflection of this work in his draft of the constitution?

B. N. Topornin. We can argue about who Sakharov is—a scientist, politician, or public figure. But one thing is indisputable: he was first and foremost a great humanist. And it is precisely this aspect of his character that comes out most clearly in his draft of the constitution.

At the very beginning of the document, written, as is fitting for any constitution, in a solemn language, the goal of the people and all the instruments of their power are asserted—"happy, meaningful life, material and spiritual freedom, well-being, peace, and safety for the citizens of the country and for all people on Earth irrespective of their race, nationality, sex, age, and social position."[4] And further, in article V: "All people have the right to life, freedom, and happiness."[5] (I do not recall where else the right to happiness was constitutionally guaranteed!) Sakharov placed the principles of pluralism and tolerance at the foundation of the political, cultural, and ideological life of society. In this draft, broad civil rights are guaranteed and discrimination of any kind is forbidden. And this is far from all the theses characterizing Sakharov's humanistic approach in constructing a lawful model of society.

Undoubtedly, lawyers can say that Andrei Dmitrievich is proclaiming the general human precepts of kindness, justice, and personal freedom, which by no means should be written into the constitution; it should only contain strict prescriptions for rights, correspondingly guaranteed by the state. Partly this is so. But at the same time it must be said that the text of the draft shows traces of the battles that Sakharov waged on the human rights front. And here he is specific, proposing legislative guarantees forbidding unlawful arrest and medically unjustified psychiatric hospitalization, or specifying in detail that "no one can be subjected to criminal punishment for actions associated with convictions, if these actions did not involve force, call for the use of force, other restriction of the rights of other people, or treason."[6]

I want to discuss what is, in my opinion, a very important point. In our previous constitutions a paternalistic approach to relations between the state and the citizen became ingrained. What happened was that the state of its own free will takes care of its citizens, generously granting them different benefits. The duties of the state and its responsibilities to society and individual citizens were put on the back burner. One could only ask, but not demand something from the state. In the process, bureaucrats of all ranks, imbued with the feeling of superiority over all other people, had the opportunity to manipulate them freely. All this engendered social passivity and apathy in society.

Now it is not only important to criticize severely the ideas of paternalism, but a decisive turning away from these positions must be achieved in legislation. At the same time, under modern conditions it is easy to lapse into another extreme, preaching extensive rights and freedom of citizens, forgetting about their responsibilities. Meanwhile, this is a necessary component of the constitutional status of man. It was written in the "Universal Declaration of Human Rights" in 1948: "Every person has a responsibility to society, only in which free and full development of his character is possible." The interests of the people conflict with manifestations of lack of discipline and individual selfishness, violations of the law. It must be said that Andrei Dmitrievich saw the full problem of the constitutional status of man, calling attention to the fact that "the realization of individual rights should not conflict with the rights of other people and the interests of society as a whole."[7]

Moderator. But between every individual and society as a whole, at least in our country, there exist communities of people such as nations and nationalities. In our days the problems of the sovereignty of nations and the relations of ethnic groups have become especially acute, and the solutions proposed by the current constitution do not remove the tension. National movements of the most diverse kind are springing up in many republics.

M. K. Mamardashvili. First of all, we must understand what constitutes a national movement in the Soviet Union. In my opinion, this is simply a form of rebirth of civic society — some societal structuralization, independent of the state and coexisting with it as an autonomous force. But national problems are primarily problems of civil rights, of civic society, expressed in a national form.

It is said that private property is inalienable, and this is the foundation of a civic society. Therefore, in such a society power and property are separated. The Soviet structure is a complete blending of power and property, and any attempt to separate them is an attempt to revive the phenomenon of private or civic society. A particular case is the life of a nation. A nation can be defined in terms of the unity of some group of people before fate and history. Then it becomes clear that a nation is the product of a constitutional process. For this reason, in a national movement there are always people who stand on constitutional principles and who understand that a nation is not an ethnic group, but rather the product of the work done by the constitution within the ethnic groups. It seems to me that it is the intellegentsia who must first introduce a constitutional approach based on rights into the national movements.

Any totalitarian state is, by definition, mononational. And the main enemy to whose destruction the totalitarian state devotes its life is civic society, which, of course, is polynational, and for this reason its rebirth or appearance in the world assumes the form of national movements.

B. N. Topornin. All of us today are directing the cutting edges of our critical analysis into the past and the present. And this is understandable. It is impossible to go forward without determining the dimensions of and the reasons for the deformations, errors, and delusions which have brought our Union to a crisis. Illnesses can be successfully treated only if all necessary information is available. But at the same time it is extremely important to understand how the Union should be restructured so that it will answer not to dogmas, schemes, or subjective goals, but rather to the real interests, dictated by life itself, of the Soviet peoples. Andrei Dmitrievich attempted to find the answer to this question, which he regarded as one of the most fundamental questions.

First of all, he supported the ideas of a Union pact, which was already proposed in a number of republics. Today this idea seems obvious and timely, but one must bear in mind that at that time it met with strong resistance. It was believed that the positions of the Union pact of 1922, which were then entered in the text of the constitution of 1924, were copied and developed in subsequent constitutions. Therefore, even today it is possible to make do with a periodic re-examination of the constitutional legislation pertaining to the national-state organization of our country. Sakharov believed that a new Union pact is useful primarily because in some sense our Union is being recreated anew.

Very recently, the Supreme Soviet of the USSR adopted a series of new laws which reflect the idea of differentiation of the relations of the Soviet Republics with the Union. In this connection it is impossible not to mention that Andrei Dmitrievich stipulated in his draft the possibility of the Republics entering into a Union under additional conditions with formalization of a special protocol. As one can see, he foresaw the general trend of development. Undoubtedly, there are many difficult questions that have yet to be resolved, in particular, regarding the relation between the general and additional conditions. It can be suggested that the new Union pact will contain the minimum conditions necessary for the existence of the Union that are common to all republics. Aside from this, every republic will determine for itself what it will do independently, what it will do together with some other republics, and what it will contribute to the Union.

It is still too early to end the discussion of the Sakharov draft of the constitution—we in the professional milieu will take the discussion further, at least for the simple reason that it is directly related with the development of general human civilization and belongs to the arsenal of great scientific ideas and developments.

It is obvious that by no means all of Sakharov's positions are accepted unequivocally. The draft also contains debatable ideas, some of which are very fundamental. For example, it is hardly possible to agree with an interpretation of the separation of powers in which all branches seem to be acknowledged—legislative (Congress of People's Deputies), executive (Council of Ministers), and judicial (Supreme Court)—but in which, first of all, they are unified by the concept of a central government and, second, a head of the government—the president of the USSR—is "appointed." Even the idea of a congress is in itself obsolete. As I have already said, the draft is interesting owing to its general humanitarian concepts, but is not as well developed from the juridical viewpoint. And here one can argue with Andrei Dmitrievich, especially since he, as any modern scientist, readily entered into arguments and discussions, without leaving his opponents with no answers.

The Gift of Freedom

Moderator. When work on this special issue of *Priroda* was already in full swing, the editorial office received a letter from the staff of the Zhitomirskii regional museum. These readers, suggesting that *Priroda* publish a special issue "devoted entirely to the scientific and societal legacy of Andrei Dmitrievich Sakharov," stressed the need for a nonsuperficial and honest appraisal of his ideas. "It's a pity and at times distressing to see and hear Sakharov's name mentioned in vain, at the wrong time and place," they wrote.

We admit this often happens after the death of great people. In 1911 a similar situation was marvelously described in a story by L. Andreev titled "Gulliver's Death":

> News about the death of the man-mountain plunged the entire country of the Lilliputians into deep mourning. His many enemies and envious people, condemning him for excessive height harmful to the country, became silent, satisfied by his death; on the other hand, everyone happily recalled his strength, and gentleness . . . And groups of friends, at first very small, grew noticeably with each passing day, until all of the people of Lilliput were transformed into a sincere, loudly weeping friend of Gulliver.[8]

Maybe the agitation surrounding Sakharov's name is entirely natural, but still, doesn't the impetuous transformation of Andrei Dmitrievich's image into an icon disturb you?

S. A. Kovalev. It is still more disturbing that not one icon but perhaps a hundred icons are being created, and each is created for somebody's own purpose. Many people no longer care what Sakharov was actually like. He must be quickly pinned to one's own banner, so as, heaven forbid, not to be left without the benefit of his name. Everybody is now fighting for his name! Some Russian Orthodox figures say that an icon is wonderful, that Sakharov should become an icon and be carried on a banner, and in support they even give some geometric considerations. In my opinion no one has expressed himself on this subject as well as Leskov. It is said about the dead—either say kind words or nothing at all. But Leskov said: one should speak the truth about the dead just like about the living.

Moderator. But will Andrei Dmitrievich's picture only adorn banners or will people still be able to be imbued with his wisdom, tolerance, and honesty? Are we ready to truly absorb deeply his ideas?

S. A. Kovalev. I am a pessimist in this respect and do not harbor great hopes for deep universal understanding. It is sometimes asked: what would have happened if parliament consisted only of Sakharovs? In my opinion, it would have been wonderful, because these five hundred Sakharovs would not all hold absolutely the same opinions, but they would have been just as extremely conscientious as was Andrei Dmitrievich. Many people are now talking about the new political thinking and stress that it set Sakharov apart. But I do not understand (I think that he did not understand either) what "new" and "political" mean.

M. K. Mamardashvili. There is no new thinking. Either a thought exists or it doesn't exist.

S. A. Kovalev. That's the problem. And if five hundred people like Andrei Dmitrievich had been elected to parliament everything would have been in order because they would have been just as responsible, wise, and tolerant, and they also would not understand what new thinking and specifically political thinking means. But for now there are not enough such people, and this is being felt.

   In the gulag, when a zone is converted entirely in one stroke into an empty camp, everyone passes through a special regimen and here—as experienced prisoners know—a fast race starts. They run to headquarters to sort out the keys to the bread house, the bathhouse, the barber shop, the laundry, and other vitally important points. Something similar is also observed when new people acquire power. It appears that in the present political battle, tactics sometimes prevail. The constitution, the foundations of different laws—these are always postponed. But elections are the main thing. They must be won and then the fundamental questions can be taken up, but in the meantime they are best sacrificed. Some voters are scared by one question, while others are scared by other questions. Right now, it is important for us not to scare anyone—we do not have the right to lose.

There is some logic in this, but there is also a grave danger: the mask is sticking. For example, how does a young and unscrupulous research assistant reason? During his student years he says "I will do a makeshift thesis so that I can start a candidate's dissertation more quickly. Then he says: "OK, I'll do a makeshift candidate's dissertation also, and then I'll do the doctoral dissertation properly." After all one must obtain job offers! But he will never start working, because he will reason the same way about the doctoral dissertation, about elections to the Academy—after all, possibilities for research increase with each new step. And, of course, he assumes that he will advance science mightily as soon as he climbs high enough. Alas, experience shows that scientific potentials run out before all the necessary steps are achieved. Science is done only by those who start to do science as students and are not concerned with their opportunities.

This does not mean that tactical questions should be ignored. I am only very afraid that everything stops there. In my opinion, Andrei Dmitrievich was also afraid of this. S. Stankevich described how a future interregional deputy group assembled before the first Congress of the People's Deputies of the USSR. Young, energetic people spoke very many intelligent words about politics, about how to operate in order to achieve a particular result. Andrei Dmitrievich at first seemed to doze off, but then he stood up and said, "Everything that you say is probably correct. But I don't understand any of it. In my opinion, once we are given the speaker's platform we must speak what we think. In any case that is what I plan to do." You remember the Congress—that is exactly what he did. And you remember the results. At that time it seemed that all was lost, and now it is obvious that in reality that's not the case. You can see that the question of article VI of the constitution has now been resolved. True, the authorship belongs not to Sakharov, well, OK—that is no longer important. Maybe now we must strive to make sure that the correct conclusions are drawn from the repeal of article VI, and we must do this by the same direct method.

Moderator. Many people find it surprising that Andrei Dmitrievich did not throw up his hands even in the most hopeless situation, and was able to find solutions which some day, maybe in the distant future, will give a result. Two years ago you, Merab Konstantinovich, published an article in *Priroda* where you wrote about absurd situations in which "it is always too late" and which cannot be understood and corrected from within.[9] Andrei Dmitrievich initiated active societal-political work in a situation that can be considered as absurd. What helped him to get out of it?

M. K. Mamardashvili. This is truly a fateful question: What can one do in a situation when everything is already too late? Only one thing: change the coordinates of the problem and the soil on which the node "already too late" springs up. And that is precisely what Sakharov did. Marcel Proust said; "The mind does not know of dead-end situations." Does not know in the sense that the phenomenon of the mind is the solution to the dead-end situation—one does not escape from the dead-end situation, but rather one changes all the givens of the problem. Since the situation cannot be resolved from within, one can only take oneself out of it and create a different soil on which similar situations could not spring up—that is the only intelligent thing to do.

S. A. Kovalev. To the question of what one should do when a solution is not in sight, Andrei Dmitrievich responded directly and unequivocally. One must adopt fundamental solutions, because in the existing system of relations one won't be able to do anything anyway. And he held to this conviction. He gave an interesting interview in Gorki. He was asked whether he counted on the general situation changing in the near future. Andrei Dmitrievich answered that he had no such hopes. What then should one do under such conditions? Build an ideal, he said, because that's the only thing the intelligentsia ever did. But he noted there and then: a mole of history digs imperceptibly. Recalling the discussion about the prophet, only here is the element of prophecy present.

M. K. Mamardashvili. In an absurd situation the fact that it is discussed in public is itself important. In the act of discussion, we repeat the elements of the situation—we do not change the situation, but we repeat it. Perhaps this repetition involves some secret work of history. During that time the mole of history, which Sakharov had in mind, can act.

S. A. Kovalev. But not the one that is already at the surface, but rather the one that has yet to appear.

M. K. Mamardashvili. God's millstones mill very slowly, but thoroughly. For this reason, it is necessary to construct some ideal without expecting that it will be realized in your lifetime. Incidentally, this is a very old tune in Russian culture. In his time, Chaadaev proposed abandoning one of the three Christian virtues—love, faith, and hope. He proposed abandoning hope (God forgive us), since when we take any action in the swamp of a situation, we merely sink even deeper into this swamp. But salvation lies only in free, sober thinking.

Sakharov was a modern professional thinker, for whom a thought was subject only to the laws of the thought itself—a matter of personal dignity and honor. This is a special character, not necessarily typical of the Russian intelligentsia, which actually was the crusader of radicalism. Such a character appeared at the beginning of the century, together with the radical intelligentsia—I did not think of Vernadskii accidentally. And Sakharov, I think, continued this tradition. From the portrait that Sergei Adamovich painted, the look of an antinihilist stands out, and this is a very important figure in Russian history. It is a gratifying exception to the rule of universal nihilism, in particular, that pertaining to rights. I would say that Sakharov was an uncomprising advocate of compromise; i.e., a man who was capable of collaborating with the existing regime, but not to widen the rift between it and society. But the striving for cooperation never forced him to distort his thinking so as to accommodate it. This is an excellent example, especially necessary in today's situation, which is remarkably reminiscent of the situation during the 1890s in Russia, and reproduces the same combinations of political forces and platforms, and therefore could lead to the same results.

The abyss of nihilism is once again opening up before us. In society there prevails an attitude that, first of all, the regime is to blame for everything; second, we don't want anything from the regime—good or bad; and, third, if we do want something, then we want it immediately, everything all at once. This is a classical case of nihilism. The abyss between the regime and society is especially dangerous in that a third force always enters such a vacuum. The Bolsheviks once entered such a void. They exploited precisely the nihilistic state of society, which arose when the natural development of the Russian empire was interrupted in 1914 (this is a more accurate date than 1917). The historical description should be made into an act of accusation of some figures—say, the Bolsheviks; in such a form this would be simply ridiculous. In the words of Berdyaev, a catastrophe of cosmic proportions occurred. Is it worthwhile to look for specific culprits?

Unfortunately, today, as in the past, there are very few people who are capable of filling Sakharov's position. And we once again run into the danger of being betrayed by the intelligentsia. Such a betrayal already happened once—in the 1890s. I have in mind the betrayal consisting of the failure of the intelligentsia to carry out its function, which is to think and not to worry about the people, and to sow the reasonable, the kind, and the everlasting. The unsolvable problem of "the people and intelligentsia" does not exist in any developed civic society, and the intellectuals do not argue about what they should do for the people. Thoughts are not produced for anyone, thoughts are produced for their own sake.

S. A. Kovalev. Independence must be preserved, because without it there is no thought. And the Russian people to whom the term "intelligentsia" was initially applied always chose some side of the barricades, and in the end they turned out to be engaged, dependent. What thought can there be here!

A thought is something that is followed by a result. If the solution exists prior to the thought, then no room remains for the thought. The Russian intelligentsia always adopted solutions before thinking, and in the process lofty words about justice, the offended, humiliated, and insulted were uttered. Merab Konstantinovich is completely correct: in so doing the intelligentsia automatically cut itself off from the people. It knew how to declare its guilt before the people, but it was not able to feel itself a part of the people and it did not want to do so. And since it is guilty before the people, it must help the people, and then it is necessary to choose a side of the barricades. Of course, not all of the intelligentsia, but, say, the rights movement of the 1990s, died down again because of choosing sides of the barricades. The rights advocates turned out to be in the minority and were immediately branded by both sides precisely for their attempts to preserve independence.

Moderator. Even preserving independence of thought, at times it is very difficult to find the correct solution. After all, on the one hand, the ideals cannot be rejected, while on the other one must proceed realistically, responsibly. But Andrei Dmitrievich's ability to construct an ideal and to make constructive suggestions at the same time, I'm afraid, cannot be learned. This, like the moral lessons of the gospel, is a principle of life, and is not a collection of recipes.

M. K. Mamardashvili. I cannot agree with that. The existing ideals presuppose a clear awareness of human imperfections and, therefore, help to make politics pragmatic; i.e., politics not constructed on an idealization of mankind. This is realism. For example, the constitution of the United States is based on a simple concept—an understanding of human malice is embedded in it and social checks and balances, compensating one evil with another are developed. Europeans, and especially Americans, know how to dress ideals in the flesh of sober understanding of mankind. But the Russian tradition is to proclaim the ideality of man and to count on it. If we reject it, then we will be able to act in the spirit of Sakharov. This will happen naturally.

The idea of creating a new man and constructing communism on this foundation is no longer popular, but the remnants of this idea have firmly sprouted in us, so that it still sprouts shoots in hiding places and back streets. This is an antichristian idea. Almost all commandments in the gospels belong to the so-called historical part of Christianity. Only two of them are extrahistorical, metaphysical, and they both cater to mankind. Two things are bequeathed us—eternal life and freedom, the unbearable gift of freedom. There are no other bequests.

Moderator. And accepting this gift, we can follow Andrei Dmitrievich and seek support only in independent thought, absolute honesty, responsibility to others and love for real, living people. Maybe this is the principal message in the life and work of Academician Sakharov?

Notes and References

1. A. D. Sakharov, *Memoirs*, New York: Knopf, 1990, p. 667.

2. A. D. Sakharov, *Alarm and Hope*, New York: Knopf, 1978 and Moscow, 1990, p. 213.

3. A. D. Sakharov, *Peace, Progress, and Human Rights: Articles and Statements*, Leningrad 1990, pp. 5–6.

4. A. D. Sakharov, *Anxiety and Hope*, p. 266.

5. Ibid, p. 267.

6. Ibid.

7. Ibid.

8. Cited in: L. Andreev, *Selected Work*, Moscow 1982, pp. 348–350. We are grateful to one of the authors, V. M. Bolotovskii, who directed our attention to this story.

9. M. K. Mamardashvili, "Consciousness and Civilization," *Priroda* 11 (1988): pp. 57–65.

Acknowledgments

GRATEFUL ACKNOWLEDGMENT is made to the following for permission to reprint previously published material:

"Precursor of *Perestroika*" by Vladimir Ya. Fainberg is reprinted from the August 1990 issue of *Physics Today*. Copyright 1990 by the American Institute of Physics. The essay is based on an article from the Soviet journal *Vestnik AN SSSR*. The author expresses deep gratitude to Pamela Solomos for helping to put the translated manuscript into more literary English.

"Scientist, Thinker, Humanist" by Vitalii I. Goldanskii is reprinted from the August 1990 issue of *Physics Today*. Copyright 1990 by the American Institute of Physics. This article was excerpted with permission from the Soviet journal *Vestnik AN SSSR* and was translated from the Russian by David H. Parsons.

"An American's Glimpses of Sakharov" by Kip S. Thorne will appear in Russian in the May 1991 issue of *Priroda* magazine. It appears here in English for the first time.

"Sakharov: Man of Humility, Understanding, and Leadership" by John Archibald Wheeler will also appear in a volume of collected essays about Sakharov being edited by L. V. Keldysh and Boris L. Altshuler and scheduled for publication in May 1991 by Nauka Publishers.

"Tribute to Andrei Sakharov" by Sidney D. Drell was presented before

Andrei Sakharov in an address at the National Academy of Sciences, Washington, D.C., November 13, 1988. It is printed here for the first time.

"Sakharov in His Own Words" by Susan Eisenhower and Roald Z. Sagdeev first appeared in the August 1990 issue of *Physics Today*. Copyright 1990 by the American Institute of Physics.

"Physics, the Bomb, and Human Rights" by Sidney D. Drell and Lev B. Okun first appeared as "Andrei Dmitrievich Sakharov" in the August 1990 issue of *Physics Today*. Copyright 1990 by the American Institute of Physics.

"Sakharov's H-bomb" by Hans Bethe is reprinted with permission from the October 1990 issue of *Bulletin of the Atomic Scientists*.

"Sakharov and Induced Gravitation" by Stephen L. Adler appeared in a Russian translation in the August 1990 issue of *Priroda* magazine. It appears here in English for the first time. The work was supported by the U.S. Department of Energy under contract number DE-AC02-76ERO-2220.

"The Symmetry of the Universe" by Andrei D. Sakharov is translated from the August 1990 issue of *Priroda* magazine. It was excerpted from a 1968 article in the annual *The Future of Science*, published by Znanie, Moscow.

All other essays first appeared in the August 1990 issue of *Priroda* magazine, published by Nauka, the publishing house of the Soviet Academy of Sciences. Copyright of the original Russian essays is in each case in the name of the author. Copyright of the English translations is held by the American Institute of Physics. Essays were translated and reprinted with the permission and cooperation of Nauka Publishers.

Unless otherwise noted in figure captions, all photographs are courtesy of *Priroda* magazine and Nauka Publishers.

Index